THE NEW
PRIVATE PILOT

*Nearly 300,000 copies of this guide to the
FAA written exams and certificate have
been bought and used by student pilots
since it was first published in 1959.*

THE NEW

PRIVATE PILOT

A complete study guide to the Certificate, including
all required subjects, FAR's, and FAA written test guide

11TH REVISED EDITION

PAN AMERICAN NAVIGATION SERVICE
16934 SATICOY ST., VAN NUYS, CALIF. 91406

THE NEW PRIVATE PILOT

11th edition, 1980

Printed in the U.S.A.

LC Catalog Card Number 63-22008.

ISBN 0-87219-000-5.

*First published in 1959
Reprinted 1960
2nd revised edition 1960
3rd revised edition 1961
Reprinted 1961
4th revised edition 1962
Reprinted 1962
5th revised edition 1963
Reprinted 1964 (Aug.)
Reprinted 1964 (Dec.)
6th revised edition 1965
Reprinted 1966
7th revised edition 1967
Reprinted 1967
8th revised edition 1969
9th revised edition 1972
Reprinted 1973
10th revised edition 1976*

A NOTE
ABOUT THIS MANUAL

Learning to fly a light airplane is a relatively simple matter for anyone of average intelligence and physical coordination—not much more difficult than learning to drive a car. This can be misleading, though, because merely knowing how to handle the controls of an airplane is one thing, and being a capable pilot is something quite different.

One of the two aims of this manual is to help you become a capable pilot by providing the information you need in order to know and understand private flying. This information (you could equally well call it background or knowledge) is accessible enough, consisting of the basic rules and regulations of piloting, plus elementary weather, radio, navigation, theory of flight, and the safe and efficient operation of airplanes. No one expects you as a Private Pilot to be an authority on any of these subjects, but the more you understand of them the more satisfaction you will get out of flying.

The second aim is to prepare you for the Federal Aviation Administration's written exam, which you must pass before you can be certificated as a Private Pilot. To that end we include with this manual a copy of the FAA's *Private Pilot Written Test Guide* containing the hundreds of questions from which the actual tests are made up. You will be given a random combination of any 60 of these questions to answer, so obviously if your intent is to prepare for the test by memorizing the questions and the correct answers you'd have to memorize all 800 of them — a major feat. Moreover, as the FAA points out, it wouldn't help you much when new and different questions are introduced, as they are routinely. To answer correctly any questions you might conceivably get on the Private Pilot test you simply have to

7

know the subject matter covered in the test, which is also the subject matter covered in this manual.

The book is designed to be used either as a text in flight schools where classroom instruction is part of the program, or as a self-study guide for those who are taking flight training but who are on their own as far as ground school instruction is concerned. The subject matter follows the same logical sequence in which it is given in approved ground schools, and is based on the idea that what you study on the ground should provide you with a better grasp of what you learn in the air.

It is suggested therefore that you begin with a chapter-by-chapter study of the text before trying the exam in the FAA Written Test Guide—that is, unless you're curious enough to find out just what and how much you will have to know before you can pass the actual FAA written exam.

In preparing the book we have kept in mind the fact that the average student pilot is neither engineer nor scientist, and that flying an airplane is a new experience. For that reason, all technical explanations, when necessary, are presented in simple, non-technical terms. We have also tried to be quite specific in answering the hundred-and-one questions that usually occur to the beginning student pilot, questions such as "Where do I go for my physical exam?" "What makes an airplane stall?" "When do I solo?" "How do I go about getting a weather forecast?" and so on. The plan was to make it as practical a guide as possible without sacrificing any of the essential information.

All the study material needed for a complete Private Pilot course is contained in this package. This includes not only the subject matter of the tests as set forth by the FAA (navigation, meteorology, etc.) but the Federal Aviation Regulations as they apply to the Private Pilot, the test questions themselves (and correct answers), plus all necessary reference materials for the test.

Before you can take the actual FAA written exam you must show evidence that you have satisfactorily completed a home study course or ground instruction in the subjects required for the Private Pilot certificate. Because it thoroughly covers those subjects (and not incidentally also enables you to test yourself on them) this manual fully meets the FAA definition of a Private Pilot home study course. A certificate testifying to the fact that you have completed study of the manual is included on the first page. When signed by your ground or flight instructor it will qualify you to take the FAA written exam—your first official checkpoint on the route to your Private Pilot license.

For material contributions to this and previous editions of *The New Private Pilot* the publishers would like to thank the Federal Aviation Administration in general; the Los Angeles office of the National Weather Service; Grumman American Aviation Corp.; Cessna Aircraft Company; Piper Aircraft Corp.; Beech Aircraft Corp.; and Continental Teledyne Motors through its Director of Communications, Don Fairchilds.

9

CONTENTS

Accompanying the manual:

PRIVATE PILOT WRITTEN TEST GUIDE

FEDERAL AVIATION REGULATIONS

**THE NEW
PRIVATE PILOT**

1.

BECOMING A PRIVATE PILOT

Most airports have facilities for pilot training conducted by flying schools or individual flight instructors. Nearly always, the schools can provide a wider variety of training aids, special facilities, and greater flexibility than instructors working privately can. And, increasingly, colleges and universities are offering pilot training as part of their curricula.

You may encounter two different types of schools when you begin to look around. One is normally referred to as an FAA-approved school and the other non-approved. The basic difference is that the approved school has been granted an airman agency certificate by the FAA. Approved schools generally have an FAA-designated examiner on their staff who is qualified to administer flight tests. Enrollment in certificated pilot schools such as these usually guarantees that the quality of training is high since they must meet prescribed standards with respect to equipment, facilities, personnel, and curricula. But don't ignore the non-approved schools; many good pilot schools simply find it impractical to qualify for the FAA certificate. Your nearest FAA General Aviation District Office (the GADO) can be helpful in providing you with complete information on the location of all active pilot training facilities in your area. Each GADO maintains a current file on all schools and instructors operating within its district.

VETERANS' FLIGHT TRAINING

Under the Veterans Educational Assistance Act, an eligible military veteran may obtain financial assistance from the Veterans Administration for flight training "generally accepted as necessary to attain a recognized vocational objective in the field of aviation." To be eligible, a veteran must have at least 181 days of continuous active service after January 31, 1955. To qualify for financial assistance, an eligible veteran must hold a private pilot certificate and a second-class medical certificate, and must obtain his pilot training in an FAA-certificated school that also has the approval of the appropriate agencies.

Educational assistance allowance for flight training is computed at the rate of 90% of the established charges for tuition and fees which non-veterans in the same course and circumstances are required to pay. The allowance is paid monthly, and the veteran's entitlement is reduced one month for each $175 paid.

For information or assistance in applying for veterans' benefits, write, call, or visit the Veterans Administration Regional Office in your state.

YOUR FLIGHT INSTRUCTOR

The caliber of a pilot training program is directly dependent upon the quality of the ground and flight instruction received by the student pilot. A flight instructor certified by the FAA has had to demonstrate an understanding of the learning process, a knowledge of the fundamentals of teaching, and the ability to communicate effectively with the student. During the course of his licensing program the instructor has been tested on applying these skills to specific teaching situations. The knowledge and skills you acquire from your flight instructor will affect your entire flying career whether you plan to make a profession of it or simply a satisfying avocation.

STUDENT REQUIREMENTS

Since the FAA has no requirements to comply with before you begin flight training, you can start the moment you decide which school to attend. After you've made your decision to learn to fly, the flight school you select will be able to help you obtain the following items you'll need before your first solo:

(1) *Pilot log book:* You are required by the regulations to keep a detailed log of every flight from the time you receive your first airborne instruction. Properly filled out, your log is the official history of your flying career. You must be able to present it for inspection upon request of law enforcement personnel or the FAA, and while you're working toward your private pilot license you must carry it with you on all solo cross-country flights. It's important, therefore,

that before your first training flight you select an up-to-date log that provides space for all the flight data required by regulation (see Part 61.51 in the FAR booklet with this manual).

(2) *FAA Class III medical certificate.* Required of all student pilots, and issued after a physical exam by any FAA-authorized physician. Your flight school or instructor can provide a list of such physicians in the local area. The certificate is valid for two years (technically, 24 calendar months).

(3) *FCC restricted radiotelephone permit.* Required for operating aircraft radios. The application may be obtained from your flight school or the nearest field office of the Federal Communications Commission, which is usually listed in the telephone directory. A small fee is charged for this permit.

(4) *FAA student pilot certificate.* In some instances combined with the medical certificate, and valid for 24 calendar months. A certificate issued on 21 April 1980, for example, would expire at midnight on 30 April 1982. This would apply also to the medical certificate.

PREPARING FOR THE WRITTEN EXAM

It's important that when you begin to study for the written exam you set up a definite program and stick to it as closely as possible. If your study habits are careless or disorganized your score on your written test will probably reflect the disorganization. This text has been designed to present, as clearly and simply as possible, all the material you will need to know for the written test. If you establish realistic study goals for the time you allot to the effort and (equally important) a target date for completion, you will find the study enjoyable and rewarding.

Experience has shown that the written test is more meaningful to the applicant and more likely to result in a satisfactory grade if it's taken after the flight portion of the training has begun. The FAA has found that for optimum benefit the ideal time for the student to take his written exam is after completing his first solo cross-country. Reason: the operational experience acquired to this point can be used to advantage in the written exam.

Before taking the private pilot written exam you will be required either (1) to present the home-study-course certificate of completion on the first page of this manual and signed by either your flight or ground instructor, or (2) take the manual with you to the FAA GADO office in order that the inspector can satisfy himself through questioning that you have in fact studied the material. (It's simpler by far to have your instructor sign the home-study certificate, and in fact the FAA encourages you to do it that way.)

The current written test isn't an easy one to pass, but it's both fair and practical. It covers the entire area in which today's Private Pilot can operate in both personal and business flight under widely varying conditions. It assumes an understanding of traffic rules, weather, aircraft performance, radio navigation and principles of flight that can be achieved only through genuine study of these subjects.

For a general overview of the test and the instructions for taking it, be sure to read the introduction on pages 1-3 of the FAA Test Guide included in this package.

FINDING THE ANSWERS IN THE MANUAL

To locate information on the *general* subjects of the questions in the Private Pilot Test Guide (weather, powerplants, etc.) refer to the table of contents on page 11 of this manual. To locate information on *specific topics,* refer to the index in the final pages of the manual. *Example:* Question No. 638 in the FAA Test Guide asks you to define the change that occurs in the fuel/air mixture when carburetor heat is applied. If you don't know—or merely want verification—look in the index of this manual under either "fuel/air mixture" or "carburetor heat" to find the explicitly correct answer given on page 51: "Application of carburetor heat richens the mixture, resulting in some power loss."

2.

THE THEORY
OF FLIGHT

To be a good pilot—a skillful pilot—it is necessary to know more than how to move the controls in the cockpit. What, for example, are the physical forces that cause an airplane to climb smoothly from the runway on takeoff? Why does an airplane stall if its angle of attack is too steep? What is happening to an airplane when it is caused to bank, turn, descend, or go faster or slower?

The answers to these and many more questions are to be found in the subjects with which this chapter is concerned. If you learn the principles of flight (as discussed briefly here in simple, non-technical terms) you'll find that when at last you're on your own in the air you are a wiser and a safer pilot. And the practical advice that your flight instructor is capable of giving you will mean far more.

WING LIFT AND PRESSURE

The earth's atmosphere is the medium in which an aircraft moves and by which it is supported. The atmosphere is in actuality an envelope of air which entirely surrounds the earth and rests upon the earth's surface. Air differs from the solid earth and the liquid seas in that it is a gas, or more properly, a mixture of gases. It has mass and weight, but does not have shape. The mass and weight of air changes constantly with seasons of the year, geographic locations, temperature, altitude variations, etc. These changes have a positive effect on aircraft performance and engine power output. The air's mass and weight become less as altitude increases. This condition has a tendency to decrease aircraft performance at higher altitudes.

The force that makes flight possible is atmospheric pressure acting on the wings of the airplane. Air is one of the lightest substances known, but, because of its immense mass, air exerts a pressure at the earth's surface of approximately one ton per square foot, or 14.7 pounds per square inch. Normally this pressure is fairly well equalized, or in a state of balance. Consequently, it is scarcely noticeable.

A basic lesson in the understanding of weather applies here in the study of wing lift. Whenever the balance mentioned above is disturbed, air will attempt to move from areas of higher pressure toward areas of lower pressure and, in so doing, can exert tremendous force. Its power under such conditions becomes evident in windstorms, tornadoes, and hurricanes. The very same source of energy makes flight possible by exerting force upon the wings of the airplane.

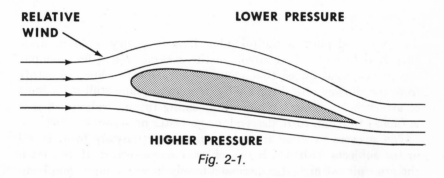

Fig. 2-1.

When the wing is stationary, the downward pressure of air upon its upper surface is equalized by the upward pressure on its under surface, and the forces are in balance. When the wing moves forward, it disturbs this balance by creating a low pressure area above the upper surface. The air below the wing, having a normal or slightly higher than normal pressure, tries to move upward into the low pressure area. The wing, however, lies between these two areas and consequently an upward pressure is exerted upon the wing. The force thus created is called *lift*. Moving the wing through the air, such as on takeoff, soon creates sufficient lift to overcome the weight (the pull of gravity) of the airplane, and the airplane is lifted from the runway.

The airplane wing is an *airfoil*—that is, any shaped device that obtains a useful reaction from air moving over its surface. In flying, an airfoil is usually considered to be a device capable of producing lift when it's moved through the air. The airplane's propeller and its horizontal and vertical tail surfaces are also examples of airfoils.

The primary source of lift is created by the reduction of pressure above the wing rather than by the increase in pressure below it. Of the total lifting force, approximately two-thirds is generated from the low pressure area above the wing, with the balance of the lifting force exerted by the positive pressure exerted on the bottom of the wing.

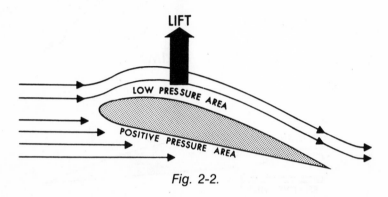

Fig. 2-2.

An airfoil produces lift because the streams of air passing above and beneath the wing reach the trailing edge at the same time. Due to the greater camber (curvature) of the upper wing surface, the air above the wing must travel farther and thus faster than the air under the wing. This results in a decreased pressure above the wing, with the higher pressure on the underside of the wing. This difference in pressure results in an upward or lifting force on the wing itself, thus providing the lifting force necessary for flight.

Relative wind
The relative wind is the direction of the air flow with respect to the wing. The relative wind is always parallel but in the opposite direction to the movement of the wing. It is important to understand that relative wind is not affected in any way by the speed and direction of the meteorological wind. Relative wind is produced by the movement of the aircraft through the air, like the wind you feel when putting your hand out the window of a moving car.

Angle of incidence
The angle of incidence is the very slight upward angle (about 2°) that the chord line of the wing is offset from the aircraft's longitudinal axis, which is an imaginary line extending from the nose to the tail of the aircraft. The purpose of the angle of incidence is to provide

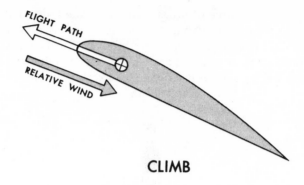

CLIMB

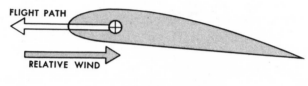

LEVEL FLIGHT

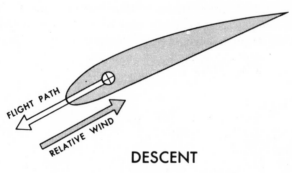

DESCENT

Fig. 2-3.

enough lift to support the aircraft during level cruise flight with a minimum amount of drag. It is a fixed value and can not be changed by the pilot.

Angle of attack

In flight, as the airplane moves along its flight path, the wing is inclined so that its chord (a hypothetical reference line running

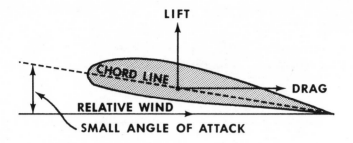

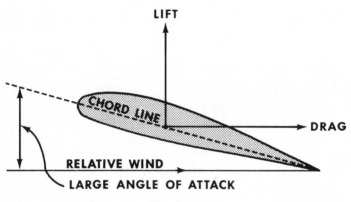

Fig. 2-4.

from the leading edge to the trailing edge of the wing) meets the relative wind at an angle called the angle of attack. At any given airspeed this angle of attack determines the amount of lift that the wing will develop. At small angles of attack the lift is at a minimum; as the angle of attack is increased, the lift is also increased, along with drag. Tests can show that lift and drag vary as the square of the velocity. The velocity of the air passing over the wing in flight is determined by the airspeed of the airplane. This means that if the airspeed of the aircraft is doubled, lift and drag will quadruple (assuming that the angle of attack remains the same).

There is, however, a limit beyond which an increase in angle ceases to produce an increase in lift. For most airplanes this maximum effective angle (called the stalling angle or burble point) occurs at approximately 16°–20° of angle of attack. At this critical angle of attack the boundary layer of air along the top surface breaks away from the wing's surface, producing a turbulent condition in the air above the upper wing surface. This turbulence results in the loss

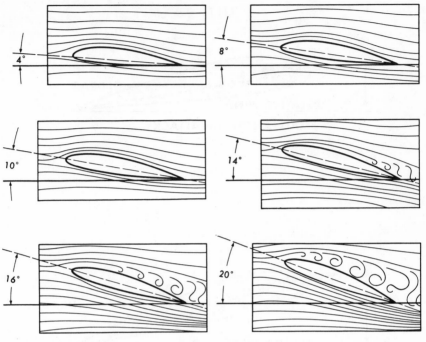

Fig. 2-5.

of the low pressure area above the wing and results in what is known as a *stall*. The stall is evidenced by a downward pitching of the nose as the lift is lost, and a momentary loss of control effectiveness. Recovery from a stall is effected by reducing the angle of attack so as to reestablish a smooth airflow over the wings, applying all available power, and rolling the wings to a level attitude. (Ailerons remain effective throughout the stall.)

STALLS

All stalls result from exceeding the critical angle of attack. Remember, the angle of attack is the angle between the relative wind and the chord of the wing. Thus an aircraft can be stalled from *any altitude* or at *any airspeed* by the application of abrupt or excessive back pressure on the elevators. Stalls that occur at high airspeeds (such as a too rapid pull-up from a dive) are referred to as accelerated or high-speed stalls. There are a number of other factors that affect stalls, so let's take a look at each of them.

1. Aircraft weight: As the weight of the aircraft is increased, stall speeds also increase. Particular attention should be paid to keeping the aircraft loaded within its maximum gross weight limitations because a greater angle of attack is necessary to support the increased weight. A heavily loaded aircraft will therefore stall at a higher airspeed than one that is lightly loaded.

2. Center of gravity: As the center of gravity of the aircraft shifts with different loading situations, stalling speeds also change. So long as you remain within the proper c.g. range, you will always be able to rely on the manufacturer's performance data as published in the owners' manual. When you exceed the limits of c.g. you create a condition in which you are wholly unable to predict or determine the speed at which the aircraft will stall. It is important that the center of gravity always be kept within the operating limits set forth in the owners' handbook; otherwise, serious stability problems can result. One such problem, which occurs when the aft c.g. limits are exceeded, is the inability of the aircraft to recover from stalls.

3. Flaps: The extension of flaps reduces the stalling speed of the aircraft. This can be confirmed by reference to the color coding of the aircraft's airspeed indicator, the lower airspeed limit of the white arc (power-off stalling speed with gear and flaps in the down position) is of a lower value than the low end of the green arc (power-off stalling speed with the gear and flaps up).

4. Frost, snow, or ice on wing surfaces: It's essential that you remove any frozen precipitation from the airplane before takeoff. Frost, snow, and ice disrupt the smooth flow of air over the wing, decreasing the lift produced by the wing. Loss of any amount of lift is dangerous: the runway may not be long enough for the airplane to attain the required speed to produce the additional lift necessary to compensate for the lift lost by the disruption of the air flowing over the wing's surface. Even if the aircraft became airborne, the angle of attack needed for flight might be so close to the critical stalling angle that it would be impossible to maintain flight once the aircraft climbed above the ground-effect zone. This is a shallow zone which exists between the lower surface of the wings and the surface of the runway. The ground effect here lowers the induced drag of the wings, requiring less lift than normally to support the aircraft weight. Because the zone is only about as thick as one wing-span, an attempt to climb out of it at a lower than recommended airspeed, or with insufficient lift, can lead to a stall condition.

5. Turbulence: Turbulence presents a hazard, especially to aircraft operating at low airspeeds. When an aircraft encounters an upward vertical gust, the gust causes an abrupt change in the direction of the relative wind, which in turn could cause the airplane to exceed the critical angle of attack and result in a stall. Bear this in mind when making landing approaches under turbulent conditions. A safe precaution in such cases is a higher than normal approach speed that provides a buffer against an inadvertent stall.

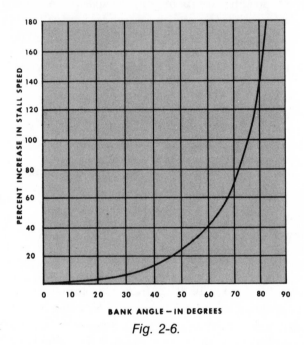

Fig. 2-6.

6. Angle of Bank: As the angle of bank increases in a constant altitude turn, the stalling speed increases proportionately. The reason is that part of the total lifting force in a turn is used to pull the aircraft around through the turn (inward lift component generated by the banked attitude). Consequently, additional lift must be generated to compensate for the lift devoted to pulling the aircraft through the turn. This is achieved by applying elevator pressure, which increases the effective angle of attack. Fig. 2-6 shows that the stalling speed of an airplane in a 60° angle of bank is 40% greater than when it's in straight and level flight.

7. Load Factor: The load factor is the ratio of the load supported by the wings of the aircraft to the actual weight of the aircraft and

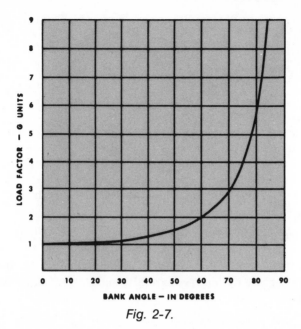

Fig. 2-7.

its contents. With a load factor of 2, the wings are supporting twice the weight of the aircraft; with a load factor of 4, they are supporting four times the weight of the aircraft. As the load factor increases, stalling speed also increases. Normal category aircraft with a maximum gross weight of less than 4,000 lbs. are required to have a minimum limit load factor of 3.8 (the maximum load factor without incurring structural damage). Referring to Figs. 2-6 and 2-7, note the relationship between load factor and angle of bank. The load factor chart (Fig. 2-7) shows that the minimum limit load factor of 3.8 is reached in a constant-altitude turn at a bank angle of approximately 75°. The stall speed chart (Fig. 2-6) reveals that the stalling speed at this angle of bank is twice as great as in straight and level flight. It is important that you be familiar with the situations in which the load factor may approach maximum (excessive bank angles, abrupt pull-ups from dives, steep descending spirals, etc.) and thereby avoid these situations.

OPERATING LIMITATIONS

Some aircraft are equipped with accelerometers which measure the load on the wings, but a pilot must normally use other means to determine if he is flying within proper limits. One indication is the feeling of body weight. When the load on the wings is increased, the effective weight of the pilot is also increased. The transition from level flight to a 60° bank doubles the weight of your body as well as the weight imposed on the wings, since in a 60° bank a load factor of 2 is imposed on the airplane structure. This added weight can easily be sensed and is a fairly reliable guide to indicated increases up to twice the normal load. As the load approaches three times normal you will notice a sensation of blood draining from your head and a tendency of your cheeks to sag. A considerably greater increase in load could cause you to black out, with temporary loss of vision.

Because of the sudden high loads that can be imposed at high speeds, maximum limits have been established to restrict each airplane to the speeds at which it is safe to execute maneuvers and to fly in rough air.

Never-exceed speed: the maximum speed at which the airplane can be operated safely in smooth air. If the plane should accidentally approach the never-exceed speed in violent aerobatic maneuvers it should at least be handled very carefully and the pull-out made slowly and gently.

Maximum structural cruising speed: the highest safe speed for gentle maneuvers in moderately rough air. It is also referred to as maximum cruising speed.

Maneuvering speed: the highest safe speed in abrupt maneuvers or very rough air. On encountering severe gusts the pilot should reduce airspeed to maneuvering speed in order to lessen the strain on the aircraft structure. For airplanes in which the maneuvering speed is not specified, it can safely be computed as 70% above normal stalling speed. To determine maneuvering speed, multiply the normal stalling speed of the particular aircraft by 1.7.

Flap speed: on airplanes equipped with flaps, the maximum speed for use of flaps as specified in the operating limitations. If flaps are used at speeds higher than specified, they may be subjected to severe strain with structural failure the possible result.

FORCES ON THE AIRPLANE

By definition, *lift* can be said to be the upward force exerted on the wing, which always acts perpendicular to the direction of the relative wind. Although lift is referred to as an upward force on the wing itself, it is not related to gravity. If the airplane is banked in a turn or is in a steep climb or dive, the lift exerted on the wing will not be upward with reference to the ground. As an example, in a loop the lift is constantly exerted toward the center of the circle.

At the start of the loop this force is upward from the ground. When the plane is flying straight up, the lift is parallel to the ground. Coming straight down, lift is again parallel to the ground. You will have little difficulty in understanding the direction of lift if you regard it as a force which always acts at right angles to the aircraft's flight path.

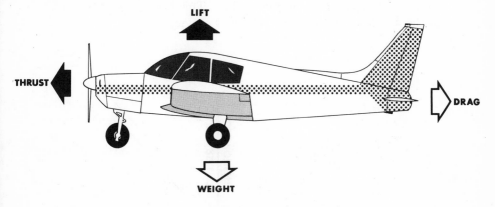

Fig. 2-8.

Drag may be considered as the total resistance of the air to the passage of the aircraft through it. Drag acts in a direction to the rear of the airplane and is parallel to the relative wind. Induced drag is a component of the resultant aerodynamic force. In more simple terms, induced drag is the drag created as a result of moving the wing through the air to create lift. Parasite drag is drag caused by the disruption of the streamline air flow over the aircraft. Examples of units that create parasite drag are the landing gear (if non-retractable), wing struts and radio antennas. Drag is also created by skin friction, a condition whereby the viscous air tends to be slowed down or stick to the outer surfaces of the airplane. Obviously, the cleaner and smoother the plane's outer surfaces, the less skin friction. A clean and well polished airplane will obtain added speed with the same relative power output. Total drag is the sum of all drag created on the airplane as described above.

Thrust is the forward pull created by the propeller and its resulting slipstream. In the case of jet aircraft, thrust is the reaction (forward) to the emission of gasses (rearward) through the tail pipe. In either case, the thrust depends upon the power output of the engine or engines under consideration. For all practical purposes, thrust acts parallel to the longitudinal axis of the aircraft (an imaginary line running through the center mass of the airplane from nose to tail).

Weight is the force of gravity acting on the airplane and its load. It consists of the flight crew, passengers, baggage, fuel, oil, cargo, etc. Its direction of force is always toward the center of the earth and does not change even though the aircraft changes attitude and flight path. The magnitude depends upon the mass of the aircraft and its load. The force of gravity may be changed in numerous ways such as the consumption of fuel and oil. This force acts from a point on the aircraft known as the center of gravity.

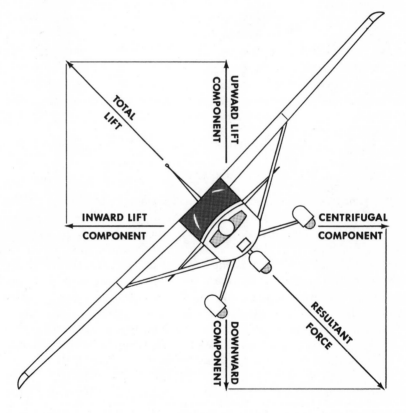

Fig. 2-9.

Relationship of the four forces

Lift, the upward force of the wing, acts perpendicular to the direction of the relative wind. In straight and level flight, lift exactly counteracts the airplane's weight. When the lifting force equals the aircraft weight, the airplane neither gains nor loses altitude. If lift becomes greater than weight, the airplane will climb; if the lifting force becomes less than the aircraft's weight, the airplane will descend.

Thrust and drag are equal in magnitude during straight and level flight at a constant airspeed. If the thrust output of the propeller is increased, thrust will momentarily exceed drag and the airspeed will increase (provided straight and level flight is maintained). As thrust is increased, drag also increases until at some new higher airspeed drag forces will again equalize and the speed will become constant. When thrust is decreased, the drag becomes the greater of the two forces and the airplane will decelerate to a slower airspeed (again, provided straight and level flight is maintained), until thrust and drag forces are once more equal in magnitude. Of course if the airspeed becomes too slow, the wings will not generate enough lift to support the aircraft weight and the airplane will stall. With any increase in airspeed, drag increases as the square of the airspeed. If we double the airspeed, drag will increase fourfold.

STRAIGHT AND LEVEL FLIGHT

In every condition of flight the forces acting on the airplane will have a definite relationship. Such is true of straight-and-level (steady) flight where weight acts downward toward the center of the earth; lift acts perpendicular to the relative wind and is equal and opposite to weight; drag acts parallel to the relative wind and to the rear, and thrust acts forward and parallel to the longitudinal axis and is equal and opposite to drag. Thrust in this case is considered as acting along the flight path. All these forces must balance for straight-and-level unaccelerated flight.

Aircraft attitude is the position of the aircraft's nose (the longitudinal axis) and wings (the lateral axis) relative to the earth. You will learn early in your flight training how the attitude of the aircraft plays a major part in determining the aircraft's flight performance.

Airspeed. At slow airspeeds, the angle of attack of the wing must be relatively great to produce the lift necessary to maintain level flight. As a result, the aircraft must be flown in a nose-high attitude. As power is increased and the aircraft is accelerated, the nose must be lowered. The angle of attack necessary to provide sufficient lift to maintain level flight at higher speeds will become smaller. Remember, any change in airspeed requires a change in attitude to maintain straight-and-level flight.

Air Density. The density of the air decreases with any increase of either altitude or air temperature. As air density decreases, aircraft performance also decreases; runway requirements increase, and take-off and climb performance decrease. A further explanation of aircraft performance related to air density is provided later in this text.

CONTROL SYSTEMS

While in flight, all movement of the aircraft is about one or more of three *axes.* You might think of these axes as imaginary axles around which the aircraft rotates. These three axes intersect at the center of gravity and each one is perpendicular to the other two.

Entering a bank, the aircraft rotates around the *longitudinal* axis.

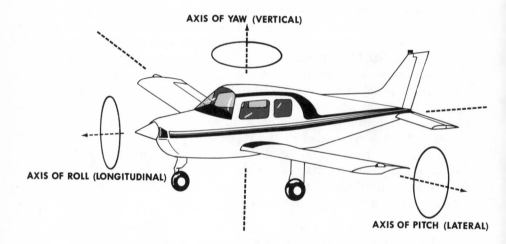

Fig. 2-10.

When a pitch change is desired, the aircraft is rotated about the *lateral* axis. The *vertical* axis is the imaginary line extending vertically through the center of gravity around which yaw action takes place. In normal flight attitudes the airplane may be moving about any one or more of these axes at any given time. In a climbing turn to the left, the raising of the nose creates movement about the lateral axis, rolling into the bank involves movement about the longitudinal axis, and the left turn involves some movement about the vertical axis. Since all axes converge at the center of gravity, it is obvious that all attitude movements of the aircraft are about the center of gravity.

The cockpit controls are connected to the appropriate control surfaces by cables or mechanical linkage. Control surfaces are similar in function to the wing in that they act as airfoils in obtaining the desired reaction from the air passing over them. Let's look at the control surfaces and how they work.

Elevators

The elevators control the movement of the aircraft about its lateral axis. This motion is called *pitch*. The elevators form the rear part of the horizontal tail assembly and are free to swing up or down. They are hinged to a fixed surface—the horizontal stabilizer. Together the horizontal stabilizer and the elevators form a single airfoil. A change in position of the elevators changes the camber of the airfoil, either increasing or decreasing lift. Forward application of pressure on the control wheel causes the elevators to move downward. This increases the lift produced by the horizontal tail surfaces, forcing the tail upward and causing the nose to move downward. Conversely, when back pressure is applied to the wheel, the elevators move upward, decreasing the lift over the horizontal tail surfaces, possibly even producing a downward force. The tail is then forced downward and the nose upward, increasing the wing's angle of attack.

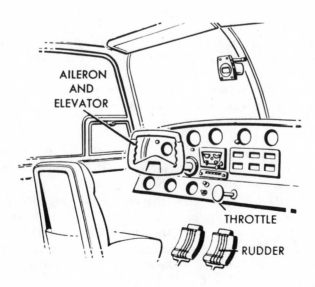

Fig. 2-11.

Rudder

The rudder controls the movement of the aircraft about its vertical axis. This motion is termed *yaw*. Like the other primary control surfaces (elevators and ailerons), the rudder is a movable surface hinged to a fixed surface which in this case is the vertical stabilizer. It functions much in the same way as the elevators except that it swings from side to side rather than up and down. The rudder pedals are connected to the rudder by cables. There is a fairly common misconception among non-flyers that the rudder is the primary means of turning the aircraft. Not so. It is actually used as a coordination tool when entering into a banked attitude to accomplish turns.

Ailerons

The two ailerons, one at the outer trailing edge of each wing, are movable surfaces that control movement about the longitudinal axis. This movement is called *roll*. It is utilized to roll or bank the airplane. When the wheel is turned to the right, the left aileron goes down (creating more camber, hence more lift) while the right aileron moves upward (somewhat spoiling that wing's lift), rolling the aircraft into a right bank. Once the desired bank angle is attained, the ailerons are returned to the neutral position and the aircraft continues turning at the desired angle of bank until opposite pressures are applied to return to level flight.

A rule to remember: Any time lift is increased, drag also increases. In the example above of the right bank, when the down aileron increases the lift of the left wing it also increases the drag, which unless counteracted by right rudder pressure will yaw the aircraft's nose left toward the raised wing. This is why the rudder is important to smooth turn entries. Your instructor will demonstrate this phenomenon, known as *adverse aileron drag.*

Flaps

Flaps, a secondary control, are a portion of an airfoil attached to the trailing edge of the wing inboard of the ailerons. In the retracted position the flaps streamline themselves with the wing and have no effect on the aircraft's performance. In the extended position the flaps increase the wing camber, with a resultant increase in both lift and drag. In landing with the flaps in the down position, a steeper angle of descent over obstacles can be made at a reduced airspeed. This enables the pilot to make an approach to obstructed runways that would be difficult or impossible without flaps; the reduced landing speed also results in a shorter landing roll. Flaps can also

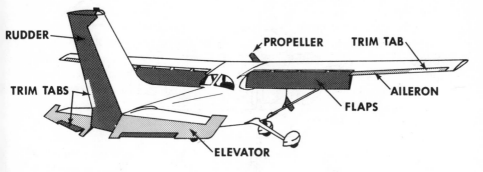

RUDDER

TRIM TABS

PROPELLER   TRIM TAB

AILERON

FLAPS

ELEVATOR

Fig. 2-12.

be used for short and soft field takeoffs since they greatly increase the lift of the wing, making for a shorter takeoff roll.

Caution: When the flaps are extended more than 25% of their total travel, they begin to create more drag than useful lift. This could result in the aircraft's inability to climb at all. Always consult the owners' manual for your particular aircraft before attempting to take off with the flaps extended.

Trim Tabs

Another secondary control is the trim tab, a small adjustable hinged surface on the trailing edge of the ailerons, rudder, or elevator control surfaces. These devices are designed to enable the pilot to remove any control pressures on the primary controls. As the control pressures change with different loading and power settings, the trim tabs relieve the pilot from having to exert unnecessary pressures on the controls to maintain any particular attitude. Some aircraft have trim tabs on all three control surfaces that are adjustable by a control in the cockpit, while others have trim tabs only for the elevator. You will rapidly learn during your flight training how much easier it is to maintain altitude and heading when control pressures have trimmed out, making for a much more enjoyable flight since the pilot workload is reduced.

PROPELLER TORQUE AND P FACTOR

As you sit in the cockpit you observe the propeller rotating to the right. And at the same time you might recall Newton's law, which states that for every action there is an equal and opposite reaction. It applies to the rotation of the propeller in the sense that, while rotating to the right the prop exerts a left turning force applied to the longitudinal axis of the aircraft. This turning force, or torque,

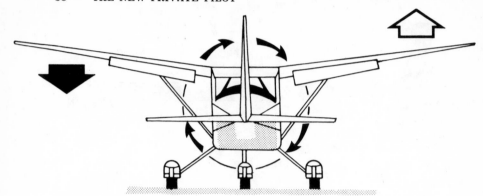

Fig. 2-13. Torque reaction to a counter-rotating propeller.

is usually compensated for by the aircraft manufacturer "building-in" a slightly higher angle of attack on the left wing (the incidence angle). At cruise airspeeds the left wing exerts just the right amount of additional lift to counteract engine torque.

When the aircraft is placed in a high angle of attack attitude, such as during a climb or slow flight, another turning force called the *P factor* is in effect. The P factor is simply the left-turning force exerted as a result of the descending blade of the propeller (the right side when viewed from the cockpit) creating more lift than the ascending blade. The reason for this is because the descending blade has a greater angle of attack with the relative wind. This force is present only while the airplane is in a nose-high attitude and thrust is being generated. When you find it necessary to hold right rudder pressure to keep the nose from turning to the left during climbs, that's the result of P factor force.

Another turning force worth mentioning is the corkscrew effect of the slipstream. As the slipstream spirals back around the fuselage from the propeller, it tends to create a left turning moment as a result of its impact on the left side of the vertical stabilizer. To counteract this force at cruise airspeeds, the vertical stabilizer is usually offset slightly from the center position.

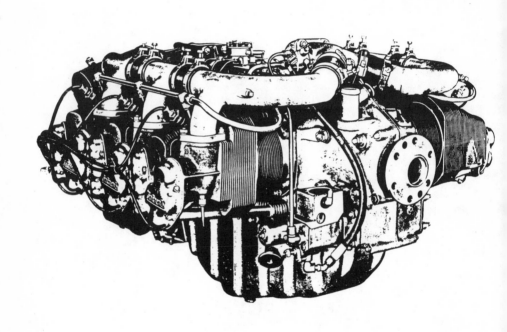

3.

AIRCRAFT POWERPLANTS

Although you are not expected (or required) to be an authority on engines and repairs, the overall performance of your aircraft depends to a large degree on your understanding of engine operating principles. The internal-combustion engine in your aircraft—like the one in your automobile—is a device through which heat energy is converted into mechanical energy. Gasoline is vaporized in the carburetor and mixed with air. The mixture is then drawn into a cylinder where it is compressed by a piston and ignited by a spark plug. The burning fuel-air mixture becomes heat energy, which is converted to mechanical energy within the cylinder and its components.

The process through which the internal combustion engine produces the mechanical energy or power necessary for flight is basically simple. This engine operates on the four-stroke cycle—the Otto cycle as it's also called. Four piston strokes are required to complete the series of events in each cylinder that provides power. These four piston strokes occur in very rapid succession, producing two complete 360° turns of the crankshaft. Refer to the accompanying diagram of the four-stroke cycle during the following discussion.

FOUR-STROKE CYCLE

1. Intake stroke. During the intake stroke the piston is pulled downward in the cylinder by the crankshaft rotation. This downward movement reduces the pressure within the cylinder and causes air under atmospheric pressure to flow through the carburetor, which meters the correct amount of fuel into the air flow. This fuel-air mixture passes through the intake pipes and open intake valves into the cylinders.

41

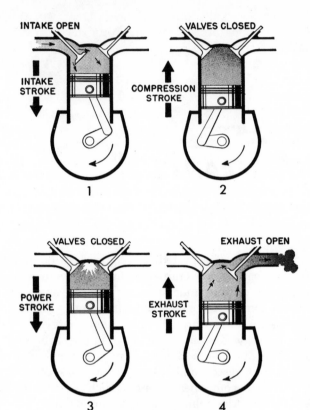

Fig. 3-1.

2. *Compression stroke*. After the piston has reached the bottom position in the cylinder during the intake stroke, the intake valve closes and the upward travel of the piston compresses the fuel-air mixture within the cylinder to obtain the desired burning and expansion characteristics.

3. *Power stroke*. Just prior to the piston reaching the topmost position in the cylinder during the compression stroke, an electrical discharge is fired from two spark plugs in the upper portion of the cylinder. The resultant expansion of the burning fuel-air mixture causes the piston to move inward (toward the center of the engine), creating the power stroke. This inward force on the piston can be greater than 15 tons (30,000 pounds) at the maximum power output of the engine. The temperature of these burning gases can approach 4,000°F.

4. Exhaust stroke. The timing of the exhaust valve opening is determined by (among other considerations) the desirability of (1) using as much of the expansive force as possible and (2) scavenging the cylinder of burned or exhaust gases as rapidly as possible. For these reasons, the exhaust valve is timed to open before the piston reaches the bottom position in the cylinder during the power stroke. This process starts to free the cylinder of burned gases through the exhaust port after the desired expansion and power have been obtained. During the upward travel of the piston, on the exhaust stroke, the piston continues to push the burned exhaust gases out the exhaust port. As the piston reaches the top position within the cylinder it is ready to start the next cycle. To increase power and achieve smooth operation as well as greater efficiency, the strokes of the other cylinders (most light aircraft have four- or six-cylinder engines) are such that the power strokes occur at successive intervals during the revolution of the crankshaft, thereby achieving smooth and balanced power.

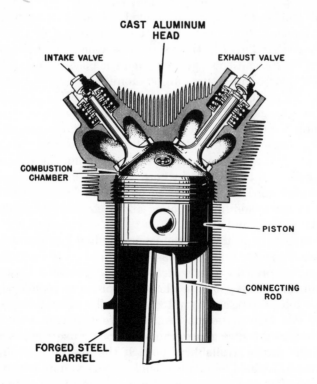

Fig. 3-2.

ENGINE COOLING AND LUBRICATION

To repeat, the burning of the fuel-air mixture creates a tremendous amount of heat. Although much of the heat is expelled through the exhaust system, a great amount still remains to be expelled in other ways. The automobile engine can use heavy liquid coolants and radiators but the added weight of a liquid-cooling system is generally considered too much of a penalty for most light aircraft. For this reason (and relative simplicity of design) aircraft engines are cooled by air. This is achieved by means of aluminum-alloy cooling fins which conduct heat from the cylinders and radiate it effectively into the surrounding air. The cowling of the aircraft is designed to create a good flow of air over and around the cylinders, dissipating much of the heat. Internal engine heat is also dissipated by the engine oil, which serves a dual purpose—lubrication of the moving parts of the engine plus the removal of heat through its circulation. It is important that only oil specified by the engine manufacturer be used, and that the oil be changed or replenished according to the manufacturer's recommendations for the particular engine.

During idle and engine run-up it is good operating procedure to head the airplane into the wind in order to maximize the air's cooling effects. Prolonged ground operations should be avoided if at all possible because of insufficient engine cooling and the possibility of fouled spark plugs. Engine temperature can be monitored either by means of a cylinder temperature gauge or by the pilot keeping an eye on the oil temperature gauge, which indicates accurate engine temperature. It is important to keep a close watch on engine temperature during ground operation and prolonged climbs at low airspeeds and high angles of attack—the amount of cooling air flowing over and around the cylinders is reduced in both situations. Many aircraft are equipped with cowl flaps which can be opened from the cockpit by the pilot to allow additional cooling air to circulate around the engine during takeoffs and climbs.

Oil pressure is as important to the engine as blood pressure is to humans. Always include all engine instruments in your scan of the panel. Loss of oil pressure will lead to engine damage if action is not taken immediately. If you note a loss of oil pressure, reduce power immediately while keeping a close watch on the oil temperature gauge. If the gauge remains on normal temperature you can suspect a malfunctioning oil pressure gauge, then cautiously use power while heading for the nearest available airport. If the loss of oil pressure is accompanied by high oil temperature indications, you must assume that you have in fact lost oil pressure; reduce power to the minimum and land as quickly as possible.

Overheating

An engine can overheat for any one of several reasons, and often (during climbs in hot weather, for example) any two or more of the following conditions may affect the engine adversely at the same time:

1. *Mixture too lean.* Harmful to the engine; it is far better to run it a bit rich than to over-lean.

2. *Using fuel of a lower octane than recommended.* Under all circumstances this should be avoided—engine damage can result.

3. *Too steep an angle of climb.* When you observe the oil temperature rising, either reduce climb or level off to get more air flowing over the cylinders.

4. *A power setting higher than recommended.*

Always keep these factors in mind during flight. When the engine operates at temperatures above those for which it was designed, the result can be loss of power, excessive oil consumption, detonation, and even structural damage to the engine. Treat your engine with respect, and it won't let you down before you are ready to come down.

AVIATION FUELS

Aviation fuels are classified according to octane rating or performance numbers. When the octane is below 100 the number is an *octane rating;* above 100 it is referred to as *performance number.* A dye is added to each grade of fuel so that the fuel grade can be identified easily by color. During preflight of the aircraft you should check the color of the fuel drained from the fuel sumps to verify the correct fuel grade and determine that no contaminants are present.

Grade of fuel	Fuel color
80	red
100	green
100LL (low lead)	blue
115	colorless

The octane or performance numbers signify the anti-knock quality of the fuel. Higher performance engines require higher grades of fuel to prevent detonation (the exploding of the fuel-air mixture within the cylinder rather than even-burning), high engine temperatures, power loss, and burned spark plugs. None of these conditions make for safe or efficient engine operation.

It is highly important that you use the proper grade of fuel to prevent damage to the engine. If you need fuel at an airport that is out of your recommended grade you can safely substitute the next higher grade. This won't improve engine performance, however, and may even be harmful in the long run. Never, under any circumstances, use a lower than recommended fuel grade or automotive fuel in your airplane since it can cause severe engine overheating and detonation and result in a power failure.

Vapor lock in fuel lines is caused by excessive heat near the lines. Liquid fuel is vaporized, creating vapor pressure that can stop fuel flow. Vapor lock is eliminated by "wrapping" fuel lines with heat-proof material and the installation of fuel boost pumps.

FUEL SYSTEMS

Because the fuel tanks of most aircraft are located in the wings, the fuel systems of high- and low-wing aircraft are different. High-wing aircraft can utilize a gravity-feed fuel system because the engine installation is relatively lower than the fuel tanks (see illustration). In low-wing aircraft the situation is reversed, with the engines generally located in a position above the tanks. For that reason the low-wing aircraft must incorporate an engine-driven pump to lift fuel from the tanks to the engine. In addition, an electric fuel boost pump is installed to provide fuel pressure during starting procedure and to serve as a safety back-up during takeoff and landing and while selecting fuel tanks in flight. Engine-driven pumps rarely fail, but the electric boost pump does offer a back-up system to the primary engine-driven pump. Because it's impractical here to discuss each aircraft model's individual operating procedures, the pilot should thoroughly study the owner's manual for the aircraft he flies.

Fuel strainers. Strainers are generally located on the bottom of each wing tank—at the lowest points in the fuel system—as well as at the fuel sediment bowl or gascolator near the carburetor. To check for the presence of contaminants or water during pre-flight inspection, with a quick-drain unit drain some fuel from each of the fuel strainers. At the same time, check for proper fuel color. If the fuel tanks have been left partially filled overnight, condensation can result in water collecting inside the tanks. It's best to prevent moisture from collecting by keeping the tanks filled, but the fuel strainer valves do provide a means of extracting any water that might be in the tanks. (Since water is heavier than gasoline it will slowly settle to the lowest portion of the fuel system.) Aircraft engines won't run on water, and therefore it's important that you always top off your tanks at the end

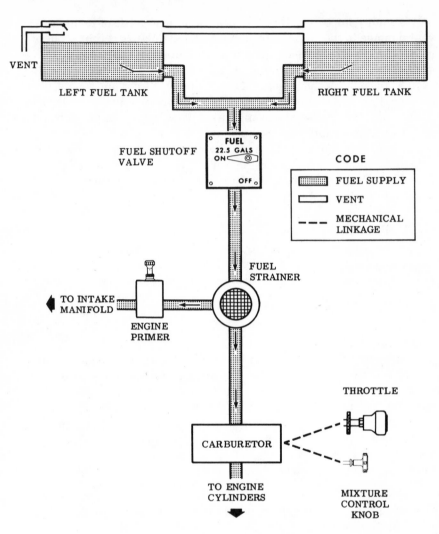

Fig. 3-3. Fuel system schematic.

of the day. Be certain during pre-flight to draw off enough fuel from the strainers to assure yourself there are no contaminants or water in the fuel system.

Fuel system management. Most light aircraft are equipped with a minimum of two fuel tanks; the more complex single- and twin-engine aircraft often have four or even six. For this reason you should become thoroughly familiar with the operation of the fuel system for the particular aircraft you fly. A large percentage of avoidable aircraft accidents are caused by mismanagement of the fuel system and poor planning on the part of the pilot. There has been more than one case of the pilot making an emergency landing because he thought his fuel was exhausted when actually more was readily available in an auxiliary tank. This is not only embarrassing but a needless risk to life and property.

CARBURETION SYSTEM

Gasoline and other liquid fuels will not burn at all unless they are mixed with air. The carburetor serves this mixing function by metering the fuel and air into the correct proportions prior to the

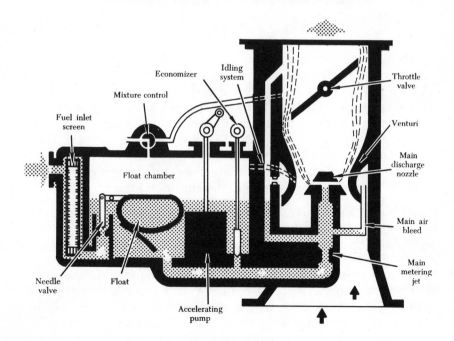

Fig. 3-4. Float-type carburetor.

mixture entering the intake manifold of the engine. The carburetor is mounted on the engine so that air to the cylinders passes through the barrel, the part of the carburetor which contains the venturi. Airflow through the venturi is accomplished by means of the pistons. As the piston moves downward on the intake stroke, the pressure within the cylinder is lowered. This low pressure causes air to rush through the carburetor and intake manifold to the cylinder because

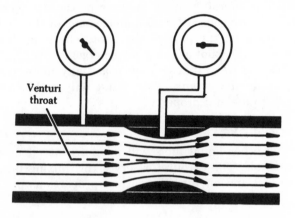

Venturi throat

Fig. 3-5. Simple venturi.

of the higher pressure at the carburetor intake.

The throttle valve is located between the venturi and the engine. The throttle is mechanically linked to the throttle control within the cockpit. It operates simply by the opening or closing of the main valve within the throat of the carburetor. When the throttle is fully opened the valve streamlines itself with the fuel-air mixture, thus permitting maximum flow. As the power is reduced the throttle closes until at the full *off* position the throat of the carburetor is completely blocked. A separate idle jet allows the engine to idle.

Carburetor icing. It is not necessary for the airplane to be operating in a cold environment for carburetor ice to form. It can form with an outside air temperature as high as 100°F. As air is cooled its capacity to hold moisture is reduced. Since there is a very large temperature drop within the throat of the carburetor (as much as 60°F), it is possible for water to condense and freeze in the fuel intake system. This temperature drop is attributed to two factors: (1) as the fuel-air mixture passes through the venturi there is a drop in pressure accompanied by a decrease in temperature; and (2) the vaporization of the fuel causes a further decrease in temperature.

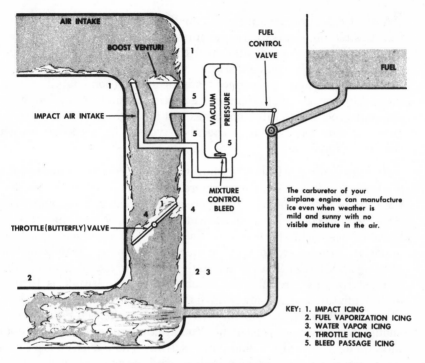

AIR INTAKE

BOOST VENTURI   1

FUEL
CONTROL
VALVE

FUEL

1

5

VACUUM
PRESSURE

IMPACT AIR INTAKE

5

5

MIXTURE
CONTROL
BLEED

The carburetor of your
airplane engine can manufacture
ice even when weather is
mild and sunny with no
visible moisture in the air.

4

THROTTLE (BUTTERFLY) VALVE

4

2

2 3

2

KEY: 1. IMPACT ICING
2. FUEL VAPORIZATION ICING
3. WATER VAPOR ICING
4. THROTTLE ICING
5. BLEED PASSAGE ICING

Fig. 3-6. Carburetor icing.

If sufficient moisture is present in the fuel-air mixture, the water vapor can condense and freeze in the intake system. On aircraft equipped with fixed pitch propellers the first indication will be a drop in RPM with no change of throttle setting. In aircraft with constant-speed propellers the first indication of carburetor ice is a drop in manifold pressure.

Carburetor heat. The heat produced by the exhaust manifold is used to heat the air passing through the induction system. This is accomplished by drawing heated air from an outer heat jacket installed around the exhaust manifold (this is generally also the source of your cabin heat). When carburetor heat is desired, the pilot simply pulls a knob on the panel, which closes off the direct outside air source and draws air from the heat jacket. Application of carburetor heat richens the mixture, resulting in some power loss. For this reason, carburetor heat should not be used when full power is required—during takeoff, for example. Use the heat sparingly when taxiing unless absolutely necessary—when carburetor heat is on, the air filter is bypassed and any blowing dust or sand is ingested directly into the induction system and engine.

Aircooled aircraft engines cool rapidly during power-off descents. For that reason, always leave carburetor heat full-on during closed-throttle descents. Periodically open the throttle smoothly for a few seconds to keep the engine warm; otherwise the carburetor heat still may not be adequate to keep ice from forming. Become familiar with the carburetor heating system in the particular aircraft you fly. Since different types of aircraft sometimes call for slightly different procedures, operate the system of the plane you fly in accordance with the owner's manual.

Mixture control. Airplane carburetors are normally calibrated for sea-level operation. As altitude increases, air density decreases and the ratio of fuel to air becomes increasingly greater. This causes the mixture to become richer as altitude is gained. When the mixture becomes over-rich, the engine loses power and runs roughly. It is important, therefore, to have a means of leaning the mixture as altitude is increased. The easiest method to use in leaning the mixture of most training aircraft after reaching cruising altitude is to pull out the mixture control slowly until the engine just begins to roughen, then move the mixture control forward toward the rich position just enough to smooth out the engine. You are then running at the proper mixture for your altitude and power setting. There may be occasions when you are flying out of a high altitude airport when it will be necessary to lean the mixture before takeoff in order to obtain full power from the engine. In this situation make a full-power run-up (be sure to pick a paved area to prevent rocks from being pulled into the prop), and lean the mixture until you have obtained maximum RPM. Then richen the mixture just slightly to prevent overheating of the engine. Among the aircraft instruments that can help you obtain the proper mixture is the cylinder head temperature gauge. Other instruments serve the same purpose. For correct use of these instruments check your airplane manual.

Fuel injection systems

The fuel injection systems generally used in higher performance engines have many advantages over the conventional carburetor system. One advantage is that there is much less chance of induction system icing since the drop in temperature caused by the vaporization process takes place either in or very near the cylinder. An additional advantage of fuel injection is that the fuel is distributed more efficiently, which means greater fuel economy. In standard carburetion systems the fuel-air mixture leaves the carburetor and must travel through curved induction pipes to the intake ports. The mixture, in other words, is not distributed as directly as it is in the fuel injection system, which mixes each individual cylinder's fuel and air just before the fuel and air enter the cylinder. The fuel-injected engine is equipped with a fuel pressure gauge, calibrated in percentage of power, which enables the pilot simply to lean the mixture until the fuel pressure is the correct reading for the power setting and altitude.

PROPELLERS

The propeller is an airfoil not unlike that of a wing. The primary difference of course is that the lift generated by the propeller is parallel to the longitudinal axis of the aircraft. The angle at which the relative wind strikes the chord of the propeller airfoil is the *angle of attack*—same as the angle of attack of the wing except that the wing operates in a horizontal plane and the propeller in a vertical plane. The area of decreased pressure, therefore, is in front of the propeller, and the dynamic pressure on the engine side of the propeller is greater than the atmospheric pressure. This results in a force or thrust in a forward direction. During your private pilot flight training you will most likely be flying aircraft equipped with simple non-adjustable fixed-pitch propellers, but you will probably also have occasion to fly higher performance aircraft with constant-speed propellers.

Fixed-pitch propellers. As the name implies, a fixed-pitch propeller's blade angle, or pitch, can not be changed. The manufacturer determines the most generally efficient pitch for (1) takeoff, (2) climb, and (3) cruise, and then builds the propeller with a pitch that represents the best compromise for all three situations. There is no special operating complications with this type of propeller: simply adjust your engine RPM to the most efficient setting for climb, cruise, or descent. Fixed-pitch propellers are generally used on engines of 150 hp or less.

Constant-speed propellers. The pitch of the constant-speed propeller is automatically controlled by a governor, which maintains a constant engine RPM. The governor allows the propeller pitch to change automatically in order to operate at best pitch efficiency in different attitude configurations. Thus, both engine and propeller efficiency are improved and fuel economy is increased.

The constant-speed propeller automatically changes the blade angle during attitude changes of the aircraft so that a constant engine speed is maintained. For example, when the aircraft is put into a nose-high climbing attitude at a constant power setting the load on the propeller increases as a result of the increased angle of attack of the propeller blades. The increased angle of attack puts an additional load on the engine and begins to slow it down. The propeller governor senses the change in RPM and automatically compensates for it by changing the propeller to a lower pitch, thus allowing the engine to maintain its original RPM. If the pilot lowers the nose without changing the power setting, the increasing airspeed tends to make the propeller windmill faster, with a corresponding increase in engine RPM. The governor senses the increase in RPM, and increases the pitch of the propeller enough to prevent overspeeding of the engine by increasing the drag of the propeller. In flight the pilot adjusts power with the throttle to the recommended manifold pressure while controlling engine RPM with the propeller control. For the exact procedures that apply to the aircraft you are flying, refer to your operating manual.

ELECTRICAL SYSTEM

The aircraft electrical system can be compared roughly to the one in your automobile except that the amount of electrical power required by the airplane with its many accessories is usually greater than that of the automobile. The electrical system utilizes two sources of power: the battery, for starting, and the alternator, which provides the needed electrical power after the engine is running. All electrical circuits in the airplane are protected by either fuses or circuit breakers which will disconnect the circuit before harmful over-load electrical charges can damage them. An additional protection against over-voltage is provided by the electrical bus which automatically shuts down the alternator in the event of over-voltage output within the alternator. Although delicate electronic circuits in the radio communications and navigation equipment are often further protected with their own bus, it is good operating practice to make sure all electrical equipment is turned off prior to engine start.

Ignition system. The engine ignition system is actually composed of two separate and complete systems independent of the rest of the aircraft electrical system. Each cylinder has two spark plugs, each of which is sparked by a separate engine-driven magneto. The two magnetos are basically high-voltage generators mechanically driven from the engine and providing the high-voltage spark needed to ignite the fuel mixture within the cylinders. Each engine is equipped with two magnetos, left and right, which provide spark for that engine. The ignition switch in the cockpit has four basic positions: *off, R, L,* and *both.* Sometimes the starter switch is also incorporated into this switch. During normal operation the switch is left on *both*

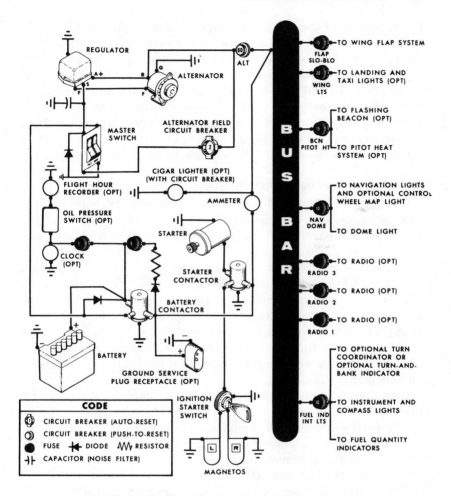

Fig. 3-7. Electrical system schematic.

but is capable of operating the engine on one magneto with a slight power loss. The *both* position operates both magnetos simultaneously, providing more efficient fuel burning. During engine run-up, check the operation of the magnetos by alternately switching to each one of the magnetos and noting the RPM drop (for the maximum allowable RPM drop on your type of aircraft see your owner's manual).

To reiterate, the ignition system is completely independent of the aircraft electrical system. Even with the electrical master switch in the *off* position the engine will continue to operate normally.

ENGINE STARTING PROCEDURES

Starting procedures differ slightly for different aircraft but the following steps apply in general. Again, check the owner's manual for your particular aircraft. Be absolutely sure there is nobody near the propeller during engine starting. Before engaging the starter—or even turning on the master switch—open your window and shout loud enough for everybody in the vicinity to hear: "Clear propeller!" The customary "Clear!" isn't quite explicit enough for any non-flyers who might be nearby; make it "Clear propeller!" and leave no doubt in anyone's mind about what you mean. Wait at least a few seconds after shouting so that anyone actually near the propeller has time to move out of the way. The emphasis—as it should be in all flying—is on maximum safety.

Here then, in sequence are the steps in the complete engine starting procedure:

(1) Preflight inspection complete and aircraft positioned to minimize blowing dirt over other aircraft.

(2) Seat belts fastened, doors secure and locked.

(3) Control locks removed, control movement free.

(4) Fuel selector *on,* and fuel selector set to appropriate tank.

(5) Fuel primer primed and locked.

(6) All non-essential electrical and radio equipment *off.*

(7) Mixture on *full-rich.*

(8) Carburetor heat *off.*

(9) Throttle open about ⅛ inch.

(10) Clear propeller.

(11) Brakes *on.*

(12) Magneto switch *on* as recommended by manufacturer.

(13) Master switch *on,* engage starter.

After engine start, observe the oil pressure gauge. If there is no oil pressure indication within 30 seconds, shut down the engine and investigate.

Cold weather starting. As the outside air temperature decreases, the ability of the battery to turn the engine over is diminished and the oil within the engine becomes increasing viscous. For easier starting, give the airplane five or six shots of primer before using the starter. Then make sure all switches are off and pull the propeller through several revolutions. This allows the oil to flow a bit more freely, draws fuel into the cylinders, and makes it easier for the battery to turn the engine over. Now follow the usual starting procedure. If the weather is extremely cold you might have to pre-heat the engine with a heater specially designed for this purpose. You might also need an external power source to cut down wear on the engine and electrical system.

When the outside air is very cold you might not have any indication of normal oil temperature by the time you are ready for takeoff. In this event, run the engine at least 3 to 5 minutes at 1000 RPM, then accelerate several times to the normal run-up RPM. If the engine accelerates smoothly and the oil pressure remains normal and does not fluctuate, the airplane is ready for takeoff.

EMERGENCY ENGINE PROCEDURES

Engine fire during starting. Over-priming or otherwise flooding the engine can cause fuel to accumulate in the intake duct. This fuel can ignite if the engine backfires. If it does, continue cranking over the engine. Once started, the engine will suck the flames and fuel into the engine without damage. If the engine doesn't start, continue cranking and have someone standing by with fire extinguishers ready. Turn master switch *off,* ignition switch *off,* fuel selector to *off* position, and put out fire with extinguishers.

Electrical fire. Electrical fires are becoming increasingly rare because of the reliable circuit-breakers and fuses that most aircraft are equipped with. The first indication of an electrical fire is the odor of wire insulation as it gets hot and melts. Your initial reaction should be to turn the master switch *off* (remember, the engine will continue to run even with the master switch *off).* Then follow this procedure:

(1) All other switches (except ignition switch) *off.*

(2) Check circuit breakers/fuses and identify faulty circuit.

(3) Master switch *on*.

(4) One by one, turn on each of the electrical switches; wait a couple of minutes between each one in order to be certain that the circuits are not burning.

(5) Leave faulty circuits *off* and open ventilators.

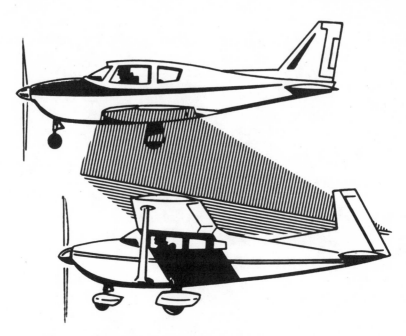

REMEMBER THE BLIND SPOTS

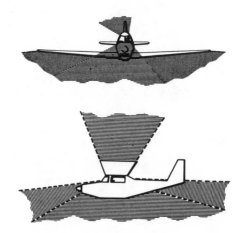

4. Flight and safety practices

YOUR FLIGHT INSTRUCTOR is (or will be) not only a pilot of wide experience but also a teacher and psychologist who has been trained thoroughly to teach you how to fly safely and enjoyably. But he will still need your full cooperation. To that end there are a number of techniques and practices you can develop on your own — techniques and practices which can't always be defined as precisely as, say, the Federal Aviation Regulations. This chapter, then, is intended as a guide to the more important of these practices.

PRE-FLIGHTING THE AIRPLANE

In the previous chapter we went through the run-up check of the engine, but the airplane itself also must be inspected before takeoff. This is sometimes called the line inspection, or walk-around, and the responsibility for it rests solely with the pilot of a light aircraft. The line check might not turn up *everything* that could possibly need repair or replacement, but unquestionably it prevents a good many potential accidents.

1. Walk slowly around the airplane, checking all external items.
    (a) Check the propeller for security on the engine shaft.
    (b) Check the propeller blade for nicks and scratches.
    (c) Check the engine cowling for evidence of oil leaks.
    (d) Check the tires for worn tread, ruptures, or spots. Also check them for proper inflation.
    (e) Closely check the wheel flanges for cracks.
    (f) Check the landing gear and struts. Make sure the struts are at the correct height. Look for loose bolts and nuts.
    (g) Inspect braces, wires, and cables for security.
    (h) Check outer fabric or metal covering for wrinkles

61

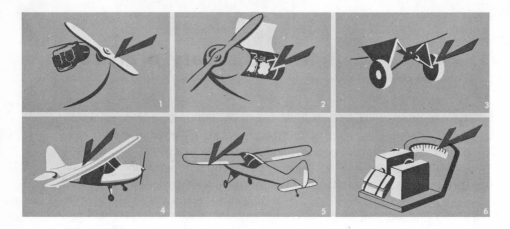

Pre-flight check should include (1) propeller, (2) engine, (3) landing gear, (4) wings and fuselage, (5) control surfaces and controls, and (6) weight of passengers and baggage.

or ruptures that would indicate defects.

    (i) Check the control surfaces for security of hinges and ease of movement.

    (j) Check all removable cowling, fairing, and inspection plates.

2. Open the engine cowling.

    (a) Check oil level, and refill if necessary.

    (b) Check the exhaust stacks for cracks.

    (c) Make sure spark plug terminals are clean and that all ignition harness and wiring is secure.

    (d) Drain a small amount of fuel from the bottom drain, and inspect for water, impurities, and shutoff operation.

    (e) Replace and fasten down the engine cowling.

3. Check fuel tanks and refuel as necessary.

    (a) Be sure the fuel-tank cap is locked securely in place.

4. Turn the propellers through two complete revolutions.

    (a) Check for proper compression. If the resistance to movement is about equal and fairly strong as each cylinder moves through the compression stroke, proper compression is indicated.

    (b) Turning the prop is also a check for an oil lock in one or more of the cylinders. Serious structural damage could result if the engine were started with an oil lock.

5. Enter the cockpit.
   (a) Check the safety belts.
   (b) Adjust your pilot seat for comfort and accessibility to controls.
   (c) Check the control surfaces for free and full movement.
6. Start the engine and proceed through warmup and takeoff procedures as outlined in the chapter on engines.

ENGINE FAILURE ON TAKEOFF

Engines rarely fail on takeoff, but of course there is always the possibility that one might, in which case the first rule is to keep calm. If the engine fails at low altitude, drop the nose to prevent a stall. While establishing a normal glide, you have a few seconds in which to decide on the next move. Your best bet is to continue straight ahead, landing into the wind or slightly crosswind. Do not make a 180° turn and a downwind landing unless you are *positive* that you have enough altitude.

Even though the terrain may be entirely unsuited for landing straight ahead, there is less probability of injury if you reach the ground in normal landing attitude than if you stall and spin into the ground while attempting to return to the field.

ANGLE OF CLIMB

Hold the airplane almost level, on leaving the ground at takeoff, to pick up additional speed before entering the climb. At times a pilot may take off at minimum flying speed and immediately point the nose of his airplane upward at a steep angle. He may believe he is obtaining maximum climb. Actually, such a procedure is dangerous because it places the airplane in a critical stalling attitude in case of engine failure or a sudden gust of air. Climbing steeply at slow speeds is an inefficient way to gain altitude.

The best rate of climb for airplanes with fixed-pitch propellers is attained when airspeed is about 50% greater than normal stalling speed. An efficient way to take off in an airplane with normal stalling speed of 50 mph is to leave the ground at 60 mph, level

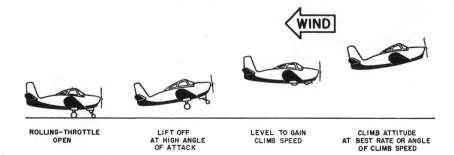

| ROLLING–THROTTLE OPEN | LIFT OFF AT HIGH ANGLE OF ATTACK | LEVEL TO GAIN CLIMB SPEED | CLIMB ATTITUDE AT BEST RATE OR ANGLE OF CLIMB SPEED |

Steps in a normal takeoff.

off until the speed reaches 75 mph, and then enter the climb, maintaining 75 mph. If you reduce power during the climb, lower the nose sufficiently to hold 75 mph. If you increase power, raise the nose accordingly. This is *best rate of climb*, and will enable you to reach the highest altitude in the least time at a given power setting.

CLEARING OBSTRUCTIONS

The *best angle of climb* is sometimes helpful in clearing an obstruction close to the airport. This enables you to gain the greatest altitude in the least *horizontal* distance. It is made at an airspeed about 25% above stalling. If prolonged, this type of climb is likely to cause overheating of the engine.

There is also a type of climb known as *zooming*. It is executed by attaining considerable airspeed, either in level flight or in a dive, and then pulling the nose up sharply into an excessive angle of climb, holding the airplane in this attitude until it has lost its upward momentum and is about to stall. The zoom merely translates airspeed into altitude, and it leaves the airplane at a critical angle of attack with insufficient flying speed. Recovery is made by nosing the plane down, thereby losing most of the altitude just gained.

Actually, a zoom does not attain as much altitude in a given distance as a steady climb at the best angle of climb. It is also an exceedingly dangerous maneuver because the slightest misjudgment may lead to disaster.

CRUISING

Normal operating or cruising speed is generally established by using enough power to provide relatively fast flight without undue wear on the engine or excessive fuel consumption. Most light planes with fixed-pitch propellers are operated at about 70 to 75% of the maximum horsepower. An easy way to determine this horsepower is to deduct 10% from the maximum cruising rpm as specified in the airplane operation manual. If the airplane is equipped with a high-pitch propeller which does not allow the engine to develop the maximum specified rpm, the 10% should be deducted from the rpm produced in level flight at full throttle.

Accordingly, an engine with maximum rpm of 2,000 would be operated at 2,000 minus 200 or 1,800 rpm. The advantages in using reduced power far outweigh the benefits of increased speed. For example, in a typical airplane with a 145-horsepower engine, the airspeed at 73% available power is 110 mph. At full throttle it is 121 mph, or a gain of only 11 mph. At full throttle the engine consumes 50% more fuel than at 73% power, and its range is reduced from 4 to $2\frac{2}{3}$ hours. Under no-wind conditions its range in miles is reduced from 440 to 320.

Familiarize yourself with the operating performance of all aircraft you are likely to fly. About 95% of the flying life of an airplane occurs under cruising conditions. It doesn't take a mathematician to figure out the overall savings that come from applying proper power settings for the best cruising performance.

LANDING

Of all the flight maneuvers in the pilot's repertory, the landing is the most important, and the one which usually causes the most concern among students.

It is advisable in an approach for landing to use a speed which gives a relatively slow rate of descent (a long glide) and at the same time one which provides a sufficient safety margin above stalling. The speed recommended for the approach is the same as for best climb, that is, 50% above stalling. If the airplane stalls at 50 mph, the approach should be made at 75 mph. In gusty air a slightly higher speed is desirable. A good pilot should be able to make at least three kinds of landings and select the one most suitable for the particular wind and terrain.

ACCURACY LANDINGS.   The power-off, full-stall landing is commonly used for light airplanes with tail wheels (conventional landing gears). Government flight tests require proficiency in accuracy landings.

In an accuracy landing the pilot must close the throttle on the downwind leg, turn onto base, and make final approach without power, touching down at a predetermined spot. This is an excellent maneuver for testing skill and judgment. It also has some value as practice for forced landings, and, in some ways it is the most difficult kind to do properly. Its success depends on accurate calculations of wind effect, holding a steady airspeed and rate of descent, and careful handling of the controls while the airplane is flying slowly near the ground

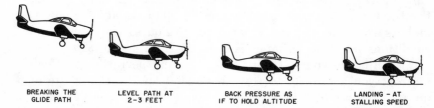

| BREAKING THE GLIDE PATH | LEVEL PATH AT 2–3 FEET | BACK PRESSURE AS IF TO HOLD ALTITUDE | LANDING – AT STALLING SPEED |

Steps in a normal landing.

at a critical angle of attack. Down-currents may cause the airplane to descend too rapidly and fall short of the field. Up-currents may carry it beyond the intended landing spot, and a gust may produce an unintentional stall. "Dropping in" imposes a severe strain on the landing gear, and bouncing or ballooning may cause loss of control.

POWER-OFF FULL-STALL LANDING.   A pilot should not try to touch down at the end of the runway when executing this landing. Select a spot several hundred feet from the boundary as a margin of safety in the event of unexpected downcurrents at the edge of the field. Keep one hand on the throttle, and don't hesitate to use power to correct for errors or to go around the field for another approach.

In general practice most pilots use a modification of the accuracy landing making the approach under reduced power, and closing the throttle for a full stall landing only after it becomes evident that the airplane will touch the runway at the desired spot.

POWER-ON FULL-STALL.   This landing is executed by using partial power during the descent, putting the plane into a stall just before it touches the ground, and reducing power still further or cutting it entirely after contact is made with the ground.

The power-on full-stall is useful for landing on snow, sand, or mud because the nose is slightly higher at the moment of contact and the forward speed is slightly less than in a power-off full-stall landing. Should the plane show any tendency to nose over, the throttle can be opened and the propeller blast on the tail will help to keep the plane in a three-point position.

WHEEL LANDING.   This is executed by using partial power during the descent, leveling off just before touching the ground, and making contact with the wheels while the tail is only slightly lower than in level-flight position. The throttle need not be fully closed until the wheels have settled on the runway. The control stick should be moved forward slightly as the wheels touch down in order to prevent the plane from bouncing and also to keep it firmly on the ground if the air is gusty. This landing is generally used for airplanes with tricycle landing gear and for heavy aircraft. The level attitude of the airplane on landing gives the pilot better vision over the nose than is possible with a full-stall landing.

THE AIRSPEED INDICATOR

Two flight instruments are constantly used in takeoff, climb, cruise, and landing. They are the airspeed indicator and the altimeter. Both are affected by changes in atmospheric pressure, and the pilot must know the corrections necessary to obtain correct readings.

The airspeed indicator registers the impact of air upon the airplane as it moves through the air. It translates this pressure into nautical miles per hour (knots) or statute miles per hour.

It is calibrated for a standard sea-level pressure of 29.92 inches of mercury ("Hg.) and a temperature of 59° Fahrenheit (F.). Under conditions other than standard sea level pressure and temperature, the readings will be inaccurate unless a correction is applied.

Airspeed indicator.

A general rule for making the correction is to add 2% of the indicated airspeed for each 1,000 feet of altitude above sea level. The result is the true airspeed of the plane. Thus for an indicated airspeed of 120 mph at 5,000 feet the correction would be 2 x 5, or 10% of 120, which is 12. Adding 12 to 120 gives 132 mph, the true airspeed. The problems in the written examinations, however, require *precise* correction, and for this purpose a navigation computer must be used. All computers include special scales for determining true airspeed on the basis of indicated airspeed, pressure altitude, and air temperature.

Although a correction is necessary to obtain true airspeed, the airspeed indicator itself without correction is a reliable guide to stalling speed. The changes in atmospheric pressure which affect flight characteristics of airplanes affect the airspeed indicator in much the same way. For example, an airplane which stalls at a true airspeed of 50 mph at sea level where the air is dense will probably stall at a true airspeed of 60 mph at 10,000 feet altitude where the air is thinner. However, the indicated airspeed in both instances would be 50 mph because the impact of the heavier air at a speed of 50 mph would be equivalent to the impact of the lighter air at a speed of 60 mph. Thus, a pilot who is familiar with the proper airspeeds for takeoff, climb, glide, cruising, and landing, need not convert indicated to true airspeeds as far as maneuvers are concerned, but may take his readings directly from the airspeed indicator.

THE ALTIMETER

The second of the two indispensable flight instruments is the altimeter, which is actually a kind of refined barometer. The altimeter measures atmospheric pressure at the aircraft's flight altitude, and then converts this value into terms of feet above sea level or above the terrain below. Virtually all altimeters can be set to the actual pressure at the ground stations over or near which they are flying. These are *sensitive* altimeters, and the altitude which they record (when set to local pressure) is the actual altitude above sea level.

Mechanically, however, the altimeter is constructed to record the altitude of an aircraft only under conditions of the arbitrary standard sea-level pressure of 29.92″ Hg. and the arbitrary sea-level temperature of 59° F. These standard conditions exist only rarely, and it is therefore necessary to build into the altimeter a device for setting it to the *actual* pressure at any given time. This device consists of a rotatable knob and a window in which pressure value in inches of mercury can be set. When the correct barometric pressure is set into the window with the knob, the

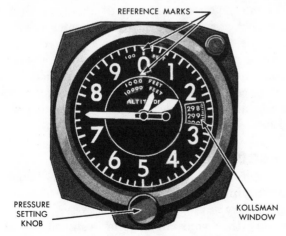

Sensitive altimeter.

Altimeter setting: 30.30. Altitude: 13,455 feet.

altimeter indicates the correct elevation of the aircraft above sea level.

Suppose, for example, your aircraft is parked on the ramp at Los Angeles International Airport, which has an elevation of 126 feet above sea level. The tower informs you that the current altimeter setting is 29.84″ Hg. You set your altimeter to this value, and if it's reading correctly it should indicate 126 feet.

The important thing to remember is that the altimeter, when set for the current and local barometric pressure, indicates the approximate height of the aircraft above *sea level*. The height of the aircraft above the terrain immediately below the aircraft is the difference between the altimeter reading and the elevation of the terrain as shown on the navigation chart.

To determine the *true* or exact altitude of an aircraft above sea level it is necessary to correct the altimeter reading for the actual outside air temperature and the *indicated* altitude. This correction can be made simply and quickly with a standard dead reckoning computer, such as the E-6B, which includes a special scale for such corrections. Most private flying, however, is done under Visual Flight Rules, which do not demand corrected true altitudes.

A WORD ABOUT ACROBATICS

Properly performed, acrobatics are no more dangerous than cross-country flying. Nevertheless, a certain amount of precaution is necessary:

(a) Be sure that your aircraft is designed for acrobatics, and be sure that it's in perfect operating condition.

(b) Observe all limitations of speed and weight — maneuvers which are safe within specified speed and weight limits become dangerous when limits are exceeded.

(c) Don't try new maneuvers without instruction from a qualified flight instructor.

(d) Keep a constant check for other traffic in the area before beginning *any* maneuvers.

(e) Wear a parachute, re-check your safety belt, and make sure the 'chute has been inspected within the allowable previous period.

(f) Be sure you've got plenty of altitude before beginning a maneuver, and allow for misjudging of altitude at the end of a maneuver by giving yourself a few thousand feet of extra altitude.

TURNS WHILE FLYING DOWNWIND

When making a turn, the lift of the wing is not as advantageous as in straight and level flight. Downwind turns can be treacherous, especially at low altitudes, since you do not have time (or space) to recover from a stall or spin. Any turn at low altitude has some element of danger, but a downwind turn carries additional hazards because air near the ground tends to be rough and gusty owing to obstructions such as trees and buildings. When the airplane is banked in a downwind turn, the wing nearer the ground may encounter a temporary lull at the same moment that the other wing receives the full force of the gust. This causes a sudden over-banking which could prove disastrous when the airplane is flying at slow speeds. Moreover, when flying downwind you may subconsciously interpret the increase in groundspeed as an increase in airspeed. For this reason you may allow the airspeed to approach stalling or try to climb at too steep an angle.

MANEUVERS AT LOW ALTITUDE

Perhaps your greatest deterrent to an accident is using extreme caution in flying at low altitude. Records bear out that most serious accidents are caused by maneuvers at low altitude.

CIRCLING AT LOW ALTITUDE. When an aircraft is circling at low altitudes a slight increase in bank may start a steep spiral, or unintentional back pressure on the controls may result in a stall. Neither condition is dangerous if you have enough altitude to recover, but without the altitude, and especially at slow speed, you may not be able to make the necessary correction before the airplane hits the ground.

A WORD ABOUT STUNTING. At some time in your flying career you will doubtless feel the urge to demonstrate your skill before your family or friends on the ground. When the urge comes — *think*. If friends know that you're a pilot and that you can take off and consistently return safely, that will be impressive enough. Even the non-flying layman is aware that stunting is dangerous, especially when it represents a hazard to people and property down below, as well as to yourself and the airplane.

Stunting generally consists of diving and zooming, often combined with a perverted kind of chandelle. All too often it ends in a stall, a half-spin, or even a nose-first crash into the ground. Apparently no amount of warning can serve to discourage a pilot who is determined to show off.

Here's a practical suggestion for your safety: If you feel the urge to stunt, you might ask your earth-bound friends to accompany you while you demonstrate your skill in such maneuvers at a safe altitude. If they refuse, you can dismiss them as being undeserving of a display of superb flying technique. You can express your disdain by remaining aloof and aloft.

HEDGE-HOPPING. This is another kind of low-altitude flying that invites trouble. Rough air near the ground, poor visibility, or lack of concentration on your part may cause misjudgment or momentary lack of control. This could result in a stall or even collision with trees, telephone wires, hills, or buildings. Briefly, that kind of flying is suicidal.

PRECAUTIONS ON FORCED LANDINGS. There are a number of circumstances under which forced landings can occur and it is difficult to give specific advice on how to cope with them all. It is best to understand the causes of forced landings, and then do everything in your power to avoid them. Early in your flight training, the instructor will teach you the procedures for forced landings: he can make them seem startlingly real.

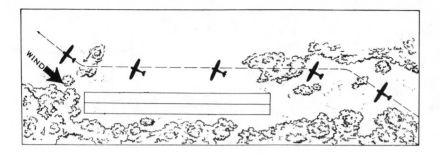

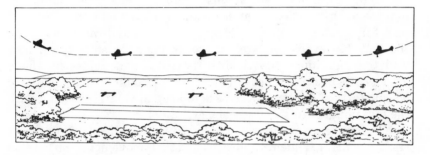

Selecting a suitable strip for an emergency landing.

Probably the best advice is to fly at an altitude that gives you a reasonable choice of landing area and enables you to establish a normal glide toward that area. Once you've decided where you'll land, stick by your decision and don't try to reach another area even though it may suddenly seem better.

Above all, keep the airplane under firm control in a forced landing. Don't stretch the glide more than necessary or maneuver too abruptly. In that direction lies the possibility of a stall.

The point is that a lot of pilots have made a lot of forced landings without the slightest injury to themselves or damage to the aircraft. In every case, common sense and good piloting techniques were responsible.

5. Air traffic control

AIR TRAFFIC control plays a vital part in safe and enjoyable flying. It is not proof against accidents, but rather an effort to prevent them. It is an intricate and (at least on paper) perfect plan for regulating air traffic by both visual and radio means. In the end, however, how well it works depends entirely on how well the individual pilot knows the rules and abides by them. These rules are based not only on logic or common sense but also on courtesy, and their objective is to keep air traffic moving with the maximum safety and efficiency.

There are primarily two kinds of traffic control: (1) airport traffic control, which applies to aircraft movements on and in the immediate vicinity of the airport, and (2) airway traffic control, which applies to traffic enroute between cities along the federal airways. To a lesser extent, traffic operating outside the airways and airport areas is also subject to some control.

Virtually all private flying (and a good deal of business or executive flying) is conducted under Visual Flight Rules, which, although not nearly as strict as the Instrument Flight Rules under which most airline operations are conducted, still require a basic understanding of what air traffic control is.

CONTROL TOWERS

Not all airports have control towers, but sooner or later as a private pilot you will operate from a field on which the traffic is controlled by the tower.

Tower operators are all licensed by the FAA, and the towers themselves are in most cases under the jurisdiction of the FAA, although some are independently run by the individual airports. Where traffic is heavy or is conducted often under Instrument Flight Rules, control is divided into three different operations: (1) local control, responsible for VFR traffic on and in the

74

vicinity of the airport; (2) approach control, which handles IFR traffic and acts as over-all supervisor; and (3) flight data, which supports the other two operations, assists with flight plans, and so on.

The tower directs all incoming and outgoing traffic by radio-telephone or light-gun signals, issues traffic clearances, and provides current weather data, altimeter setting, and any other information necessary to safe flight.

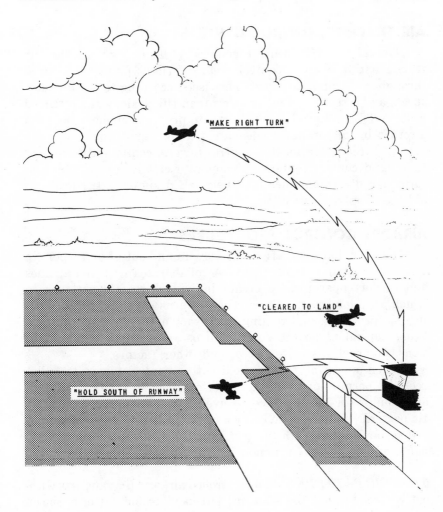

The tower issues clearances to prevent collisions and expedite air traffic.

FLIGHT SERVICE STATIONS (FSS)

One of the chief functions of the FAA Flight Service Station is to help the pilot with his problems of flight planning. These stations work in close cooperation with the control towers and air traffic control centers, broadcasting up-to-date weather reports at regular intervals, and supplying enroute weather information on request. They also play an important part in search and rescue operations.

AIR TRAFFIC CONTROL CENTERS

The air traffic control centers (ATC) regulate the air traffic within a given control area. All flight plans are cleared through ATC, and approved or revised according to the altitude, speed, and direction of other aircraft in flight along the intended route. ATC's main job is, of course, to prevent collisions between aircraft by maintaining adequate traffic separation.

All three operations — control towers, communications stations, and control centers — cooperate closely and combine to form a radio communications network designed specifically to aid the pilot — every pilot.

AIRPORT CONTROL PROCEDURES

In order that air traffic may flow in and out of an airport in a well-regulated manner, the FAA collaborates with the airlines and airport operators to create individual traffic patterns to which all pilots must adhere. The patterns cover takeoffs, landings, approaches, and taxiing, the exact nature of each pattern being dependent on the runway in use, prevailing wind conditions, obstructions in the area, and other factors.

When operating from a field with a control tower, the pilot requests permission from the tower operator to take off or land, and along with his clearance receives information about the traffic pattern. If there is no control tower, it is up to the pilot himself to be familiar with the traffic pattern, to follow the traffic rules, and to observe common courtesy toward other pilots.

TRAFFIC PATTERNS. At uncontrolled airports (i.e., airports without control towers) the standard left-hand traffic patterns shown in the diagram are recommended by the FAA when the patterns are not in conflict with other existing procedures at those airports.

1) Enter the pattern in level flight, abeam the midpoint of the runway, at pattern altitude.

2) Maintain pattern altitude until abeam approach end of the landing runway, on downwind leg.

3) Complete turn to final at least ¼ mile from runway.

4) Continue straight ahead until beyond departure end of runway.

5) If remaining in the traffic pattern, commence turn to crosswind leg beyond the departure end of the runway, within 300 feet of pattern altitude.

6) If departing the traffic pattern, continue straight out until reaching pattern altitude, then make a 45° turn (either left or right, depending on which pattern is in use), or continue straight out.

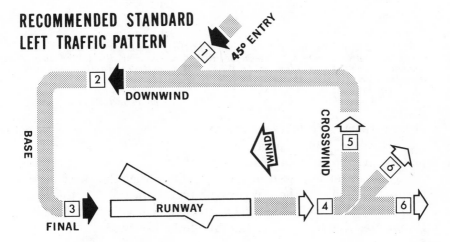

RECOMMENDED STANDARD LEFT TRAFFIC PATTERN

45° ENTRY

DOWNWIND

BASE

WIND

CROSSWIND

RUNWAY

FINAL

When departing a *controlled* airport (i.e., one with an FAA tower) departures using other than the standard 45° turn out should be requested and approved through the tower. It's also good operating practice to verify local pattern procedures since variations from the standard for noise abatement and terrain clearance purposes are in effect at many airports, for both arrival and departure.

L-SHAPED TRAFFIC MARKERS. These are standard visual markers that indicate the direction of turns in the traffic pattern

TRAFFIC PATTERN INDICATED BY SEGMENTED CIRCLE

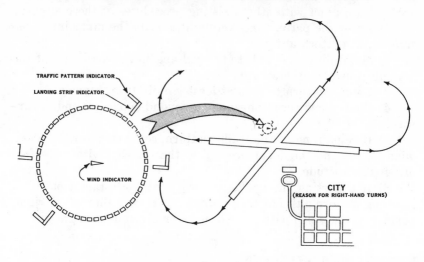

Safe flying requires that a pilot know the traffic pattern for the airport when landing or taking off. The segmented circle marker, illustrated above, furnishes the pilot this information. When traffic pattern indicators are used with the circle marker, they tell the pilot to make his turn in the direction in which the indicators point. If the traffic pattern indicators are not used, the pilot will know that the normal left-hand pattern must be followed.

of an airport. The markers are placed on the outside of a segmented circle telling pilots whether the turns in the traffic pattern are to the right or left.

The marker is placed in such a position that the short member of the L shows the direction of traffic in the air, the long member of the L points out the runway to be used, and the entire L indicates the direction of the turn to be executed.

THE TETRAHEDRON. This is a wind or runway indicator which may or may not be controllable from the tower. At fields where there is no tower the tetrahedron is moved by hand. Its purpose is to inform pilots of the surface wind direction or the runway-in-use at a given airport.

THE WIND TEE OR WIND SOCK. At airports where traffic is not radio controlled, the wind tee may be utilized. Two arms, one shorter than the other, are assembled in the shape of the letter "T." The wind tee is used for the same purpose as the tetra-hedron, with the top of the tee indicating the wind direction or runway-in-use. The top of the tee, in this case, indicates the direction the wind is moving *from,* or the landing direction.

The wind sock has been used as a wind indicator from the earliest days of flying. Consisting of an open-end cloth enclosure, it is placed on a tower or standard in a conspicuous area of the airport. As the wind enters the open end of the sock, the sock moves into somewhat of a horizontal attitude. You need only observe the direction in which the sock is extended from its standard to determine the wind direction and, to a certain extent, the wind velocity.

LIGHT SIGNALS

These light procedures apply only where an airport is equipped with a control tower and an aircraft using the particular airport is not equipped with two-way radio. Traffic controllers may use this means of communications if radio contact can not be made or continued. Pilots must understand, however, that they may proceed in a conventional manner if no signals are displayed as they approach or depart an airport.

Color and type of signal	Aircraft on the ground	Aircraft in flight
Steady green_____	Cleared for take-off_____	Cleared to land.
Flashing green_____	Cleared to taxi_____	Return for landing (to be followed by steady green at proper time).
Steady red_____	Stop_____	Give way to other aircraft and continue circling.
Flashing red_____	Taxi clear of landing area (runway) in use.	Airport unsafe—do not land.
Flashing white_____	Return to starting point on airport.	
Alternating red and green.	General warning signal—exercise extreme caution.	

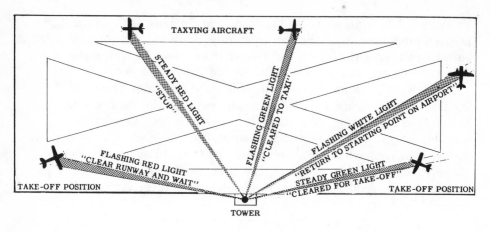

Visual signals.

Airport tower controllers use a directive traffic signal which emits an intense narrow beam of a selected color, either aviation red, white, or green. The signal light has many advantages and at least two disadvantages: (1) you may not be looking at the tower at the time the signal is directed toward you, (2) the directions transmitted by the signal are limited, since only approval or disapproval of your anticipated actions may be transmitted.

AIRCRAFT IN-BOUND. At night a pilot wishing to land should turn on a landing light as he approaches the airport unless he has already been given a green light. A series of flashes of a landing light by a pilot intending to land will mean: (1) if the floodlight is on, the pilot wants it turned off, and (2) if the floodlight is off, the pilot wants it turned on. Pilots should acknowledge light signals by rocking their wings during hours of daylight, or by blinking their landing or navigation lights during hours of darkness.

AIRCRAFT ON THE AIRPORT. Between sunset and sunrise, a pilot wishing to attract the attention of the control tower should turn on a landing light and taxi the aircraft in position so that the light is visible to the tower operator. The landing light should remain on until appropriate signals are received from the tower.

Pilots should acknowledge light signals by moving the ailerons or rudder during the hours of daylight, or by blinking the landing or navigation lights during the hours of darkness.

Rotating beacon.

LOW CEILING AND VISIBILITY. During daylight hours the lighting of the rotating beacon at an airport means that ground visibility is less than three miles and/or ceiling is less than 1,000 feet. After dark the same information is posted by means of flashing lights which outline the traffic direction indicator (tetrahedron, wind sock, or wind tee). Both of these signals indicate that a clearance from Air Traffic Control is required for landing, takeoff, or flight in the traffic pattern when the airport is within a control zone.

Flashing lights outlining tetrahedron.

NOTE: VFR flying may be continued under the conditions above, but each pilot must request a clearance from the tower, and not continue the ground or flight activity unless clearance is granted. Each pilot must follow specific instructions and report back to the tower as requested. This is known as controlled VFR flight.

CLOCKWISE FLOW OF TRAFFIC.   During flight in the United States, all turns when departing or arriving at an airport must be made to the left (counter-clockwise) *unless otherwise instructed by the tower.* If there is no tower in operation, use other means to determine the direction of traffic, such as noting the segmented circle and L-shaped traffic markers and other traffic, in the pattern.

Flashing amber light: clockwise flow of traffic.

A clockwise flow of traffic may also be indicated by the L-shaped traffic pattern markers of the segmented circle marker system. The vertical member of the L, which points to the runway or strip-in-use, indicates the direction of turn in an approach and landing. The horizontal member or base indicates the direction of the turn on takeoff.

VISUAL FLIGHT RULE (VFR) PROCEDURES

Except when authorized by Air Traffic Control (ATC) to fly according to a special VFR clearance within a control zone, in order to fly under visual flight rules, you must have weather conditions which are equal to or better than the *basic* VFR weather minimums *(see FAR 91.105 in the FAR booklet).* Study this rule — read it over and over and try to visualize each situation described. Look up the definition of controlled airspace in FAR Part 1, and then see the definition of each of the types of controlled airspace in FAR Part 71. Know also the difference between *ground* and *flight* visibility *(see FAR 1 again).*

Often, with the ceiling below 1,000 feet or the visibility less than 3 miles, pilots without Instrument ratings may find it necessary to fly out of, or into, airports within a control zone. Unless the airport is one of the major terminals mentioned in FAR 93.113, ATC will usually issue the VFR pilot a Special VFR clearance. The Special VFR weather minimums are given in FAR 91.107 in the FAR booklet.

Aircraft may be operated VFR above a well-defined cloud or an obscuration, provided climb to and descent from such on-top flight can be made in accordance with VFR weather minimums.

When an aircraft is operated VFR in level cruising flight at 3,000 feet or more above the surface (not MSL), specified flight altitudes or flight levels (if above 18,000 feet MSL) must be maintained. The specific altitude or level depends on the *magnetic course* being flown. The rule is stated in FAR 91.109 in the FAR booklet; study it thoroughly.

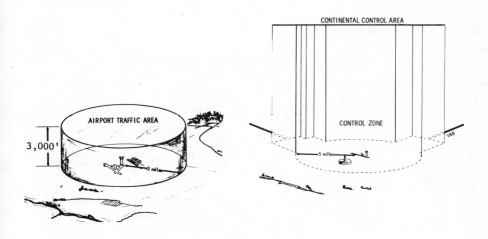

MINIMUM VISIBILITY AND DISTANCE FROM CLOUDS—VFR

ALTITUDE	UNCONTROLLED AIRSPACE		CONTROLLED AIRSPACE	
	Flight Visibility	Distance From Clouds	** Flight Visibility	** Distance From Clouds
1200' or less above the surface, regardless of MSL Altitude	*1 statute mile	Clear of clouds	3 statute miles	500' below 1000' above 2000' horizontal
More than 1200' above the surface, but less than 10,000' MSL	1 statute mile	500' below 1000' above 2000' horizontal	3 statute miles	500' below 1000' above 2000' horizontal
More than 1200' above the surface and at or above 10,000' MSL	5 statute miles	1000' below 1000' above 1 statute mile horizontal	5 statute miles	1000' below 1000' above 1 statute mile horizontal

* Helicopters may operate with less than 1 mile visibility, outside controlled airspace at 1200 feet or less above the surface, provided they are operated at a speed that allows the pilot adequate opportunity to see any air traffic or obstructions in time to avoid collisions.

** In addition, when operating within a control zone beneath a ceiling, the ceiling must not be less than 1000'. If the pilot intends to land or takeoff or enter a traffic pattern within a control zone, the ground visibility must be at least 3 miles at that airport. If ground visibility is not reported at the airport, 3 miles flight visibility is required. (FAR 91.105)

ALTITUDES AND FLIGHT LEVELS

CONTROLLED AND UNCONTROLLED AIRSPACE VFR ALTITUDES AND FLIGHT LEVELS			
If your magnetic course (ground track) is	More than 3000' above the surface but below 18,000' MSL fly	Above 18,000' MSL to FL 290 (except within Positive Control Area, FAR 71.193) fly	Above FL 290 (except within Positive Control Area, FAR 71.193) fly 4000' intervals
0° to 179°	Odd thousands, MSL, plus 500' (3500, 5500, 7500, etc)	Odd Flight Levels plus 500' (FL 195, 215, 235, etc)	Beginning at FL 300 (FL 300, 340, 380, etc)
180° to 359°	Even thousands, MSL, plus 500' (4500, 6500, 8500, etc)	Even Flight Levels plus 500' (FL 185, FL 205, 225, etc)	Beginning at FL 320 (FL 320, 360, 400, etc)

UNCONTROLLED AIRSPACE – IFR ALTITUDES AND FLIGHT LEVELS			
If your magnetic course (ground track) is	Below 18,000' MSL, fly	At or above 18,000' MSL but below FL 290, fly	At or above FL 290, fly 4000' intervals
0° to 179°	Odd thousands, MSL, (3000, 5000, 7000, etc)	Odd Flight Levels, FL 190, 210, 230, etc)	Beginning at FL 290, (FL 290, 330, 370, etc)
180° to 359°	Even thousands, MSL, (2000, 4000, 6000, etc)	Even Flight Levels (FL 180, 200, 220, etc)	Beginning at FL 310, (FL 310, 350, 390, etc)

The responsibility for avoiding collision with other VFR flights in the pattern, under the above conditions, rests solely upon the pilots.

Requests for authorization of departure from or entry into a control zone will be handled individually. In each case, standard separation will be effected by air traffic control between such operations and all IFR traffic, as well as other operations of the same nature.

AIR TRAFFIC AND PILOT TECHNIQUE

It is assumed that most private flying is done from airports not equipped with control towers. Under these conditions, the entire responsibility for avoiding accidents rests upon you the pilot. Know the rules and abide by them.

Taxi slowly, and unless your visibility is unimpeded by the forward section of the airplane, use a zig-zag pattern to be sure your path is clear at all times. Before crossing any runway, be certain that no planes are approaching for takeoff or landing. Immediately before takeoff make sure that the runway is clear, and check incoming traffic.

Aircraft approaching have the *right-of-way*. A plane on the ground should face incoming traffic and delay takeoff until there is absolutely no danger of collision.

After takeoff, continue straight flight until you have reached the airport boundary and have gained at least 500 feet of altitude. After checking for other aircraft, you may make a turn 90° to the left (unless otherwise instructed), followed by a turn of 45° to the right, in order to leave the traffic pattern. All turns in the vicinity of the airport must be to the left unless otherwise specified.

Before landing, circle the field to observe traffic. This gives you a chance to determine the wind direction and velocity, general traffic conditions, and runway in use. Use caution on the final landing approach, making certain that the runway is clear and that no other plane is approaching from a different angle or altitude.

Above all, don't insist on your right-of-way. The pilot in the other plane may not see you in time to avoid an accident. His visibility may be restricted or his attention momentarily diverted.

Where control towers are in operation, the operators are able to help pilots in avoiding accidents both on the ground and in the air. Under these conditions *all* pilots are required to follow directions from the tower by radio or by light signals. The fact that a tower is in operation, however, does not relieve pilots of the need for exercising care and judgment in carrying out instructions.

RADIO AND AIR TRAFFIC CONTROL

Without a doubt, radio communication between airplane and ground station is the most effective means of traffic control. Other methods, such as light signals, are limited and even inadequate.

All private pilots should know the basic radio procedures. At some point in your flying career your airplane will be radio-equipped and you will operate from a radio-controlled field. Use the radio as you would your telephone at home. Be sure the radio is turned on and tuned to the correct frequency of the station you are calling. When the station answers, make your request brief and to the point. Listen carefully to the reply, and then if you fully understand the instructions, acknowledge them and hang up your mike. There may be other aircraft in the vicinity trying to call the same tower or station.

When flying near a controlled airport, keep the volume up and listen. The tower may want to issue instructions even though you haven't requested any. Remember, the tower operators are in a vantage position on the airport and have a 360° view of all traffic.

Federal Regulations require that pilots follow instructions given by either radio or lights from the control tower. When ready to taxi, the pilot calls the control tower by radio for taxi instructions. He follows the tower operator's instructions before and during takeoff, keeping his radio tuned to the tower frequency until he is out of the airport traffic area.

Approaching the airport under VFR conditions, the pilot calls the tower when he is several miles from the field. He remains in radio contact thereafter with the tower and follows the approach and landing instructions until he is on the runway and has taxied to the parking area. Control by the tower continues until the plane is parked.

6. Radio operation and services

MANY BEGINNING private pilots harbor the notion that two-way radio and the federal airways are strictly for instrument flying. Actually, these facilities can and should be used also under VFR conditions in good weather, both for safer and more pleasant flying. Radio contact with the ground stations along the airways is as simple as a telephone conversation, and usually a good deal more informative. Radio enables you to keep pace with changes in the weather, to determine the location of other traffic enroute, and most important of all to have access to instructions and help in the event of an in-flight emergency.

Chances are the airplane in which you learn to fly (or later, the one you rent) will be equipped with at least one 360-channel two-way VHF transmitter/receiver, the minimum needed to take advantage of the many FAA communications facilities available to pilots. If eventually you buy your own plane—new or used—you may be in the market for a new VHF transceiver. The basic equipment with 360 channels is available from well-known manufacturers at prices around $1,000. Sets with 720 channels, doubling the communications capability, are more expensive of course.

The advantages of two-way radio are most evident in cross-country flying. You can automatically receive weather reports in flight every 30 minutes, or you can request special reports any time you wish. These reports enable you to keep informed about the weather ahead on your course and terminal conditions at the airport where you intend to land. Ground control can keep you posted on other traffic in the vicinity. And when you enter the airport control area at your destination you will be given precise landing instructions.

USING YOUR RADIO

Learning to use an aircraft radio is easy. The actual procedures for tuning to the proper frequency, adjusting the volume, and handling the microphone will be outlined by your instructor at an early stage in your training program. The secret of using good radio techniques (if it can be called a secret) is to remain relaxed and deliver your message or question in a normal conversational way.

There are no mysteries in the language of aircraft radio communications. Standard procedures, words and phrases have been developed only to speed up transmission and reduce the chances of misunderstanding. Eventually, you will have to learn the vocabulary, but it's not really necessary to ignore the radio until that time. Plain, uncomplicated English is quite adequate to express any message you are likely to communicate. Before pressing the button to open the microphone, give a little thought to what you want to say, and then say it. This will prevent stammering and searching for the right words.

Aircraft radio is literally fun to operate. It takes only a few short hours experience to become as proficient at it as you need to be. And the best time to start is at the very beginning of flight training.

Compact radio transmitter and receivers in a Cessna 172 installation.

HOW TO OBTAIN RADIO LICENSES

When you own your own airplane, two radio licenses are required, one for the airplane (which is a mobile radio station) and one for yourself as operator of the equipment. When taking flight training from a local flight school, the airplane will be licensed by the school but you will need the operator's license if airport traffic is controlled by a tower. Your airport may not be a controlled field, and if it isn't, then radio licenses are not required. However, it's still a good idea to have one.

The transmitter in the airplane requires a radio station license which must be posted in the aircraft at all times. The Federal Communications Commission makes it easy to obtain this license. After the transmitter is installed you fill out an application for the station license, get it properly signed and notarized, and forward it to the FCC. The FCC will mail you the license. If the radio is factory installed in the airplane, the dealer can issue a temporary station certificate good for 30 days.

Your operator's license is even easier to get and can be used in operating any aircraft radiotelephone. The application may be obtained from your local airport or the nearest FCC office, or you may write to the FCC in Washington, D. C., for the application. Complete the application by answering *all* questions, and then sign it. This may be mailed to the FCC office indicated on the application. The Restricted Radiotelephone Permit then will be issued or mailed to you. It is good indefinitely. You do not have to know the Morse code or understand radio circuits.

PHRASEOLOGY

Assuming that your airplane is properly radio-equipped, let's look at the standard radiotelephone phraseology. It should be used where practicable in radiotelephone communications.

Word or Phrase	*Meaning*
ACKNOWLEDGE	"Let me know that you have received and understood this message."
AFFIRMATIVE	"Yes."
CORRECTION	"An error has been made in this transmission. The correct version is . . . ."
GO AHEAD	"Proceed with your message."

HOW DO YOU HEAR ME? ..... Self-explanatory.

I SAY AGAIN .... Self-explanatory.

NEGATIVE .... "That is not correct."

OUT .... "This conversation is ended and no response is expected."

OVER .... "My transmission is ended and I expect a response from you."

READ BACK .... "Repeat all of this message back to me."

ROGER .... "I have received all of your last transmission." (To acknowledge receipt; shall not be used for other purposes.)

SAY AGAIN .... Self-explanatory.

SPEAK SLOWER .... Self-explanatory.

STAND BY .... If used by itself means "I must pause for a few seconds." If the pause is longer than a few seconds, or if "STAND BY" is used to prevent another station from transmitting, it must be followed by the ending "OUT."

THAT IS CORRECT .... Self-explanatory.

VERIFY .... "Check with originator."

WORDS TWICE .... (a) As a request: "Communication is difficult. Please say every phrase twice."
(b) As information: "Since communication is difficult, every phrase in this message will be spoken twice."

PHONETIC ALPHABETS. Phonetic letter equivalents are communications safety tools that should only be used when receiving conditions are such that the information cannot be readily received without their use. Under such adverse communications conditions, phonetic equivalents are employed for single letters, or to spell out groups of letters or difficult words.

STATEMENT OF FIGURES. Figures indicating hundreds and thousands in round numbers, as for ceiling heights, flight altitudes and upper wind levels up to 9000, shall be spoken in accordance with the following examples:

500 .... FIVE HUNDRED
1300 .... ONE THOUSAND THREE HUNDRED
4500 .... FOUR THOUSAND FIVE HUNDRED
9000 .... NINE THOUSAND

Numbers above 9000 shall be spoken by separating the digits preceding the word "thousand." Examples:

10000 .... ONE ZERO THOUSAND
13000 .... ONE THREE THOUSAND
18500 .... ONE EIGHT THOUSAND FIVE HUNDRED
27000 .... TWO SEVEN THOUSAND

All other numbers shall be transmitted by pronouncing each digit. Examples:

10 .... ONE ZERO
75 .... SEVEN FIVE
583 .... FIVE EIGHT THREE
1850 .... ONE EIGHT FIVE ZERO
18143 .... ONE EIGHT ONE FOUR THREE
26075 .... TWO SIX ZERO SEVEN FIVE

The digit "O" shall be spoken "ZERO" when it occurs alone or in a group of figures other than those described herein. For numbers containing a decimal point, the number shall be spoken by separating the digits, the decimal point being spoken as "POINT." Examples:

122.1 .... ONE TWO TWO POINT ONE
126.7 .... ONE TWO SIX POINT SEVEN

STATEMENT OF TIME. The 24-hour-clock system shall be used in radiotelephone transmissions. The hour is indicated by the first two figures and the minutes by the last two figures. Examples:

0000 .... ZERO ZERO ZERO ZERO
0920 .... ZERO NINE TWO ZERO

Time may be stated in minutes only (two figures) in radio-telephone communications when no misunderstanding is likely to occur. Current time in use at a station shall be stated in the nearest quarter minute in order that pilots may use this information for time checks. Fractions of a quarter minute less than eight seconds shall be stated as the preceding quarter minute; fractions of a quarter minute of eight seconds or more shall be stated as the succeeding quarter minute. Examples:

Time
9 :29 :05 a.m. .... TIME, ZERO NINE TWO NINE
9 :29 :10 a.m. .... TIME, ZERO NINE TWO NINE AND ONE-QUARTER
9 :29 :28 a.m. .... TIME, ZERO NINE TWO NINE AND ONE-HALF

The time zone designator shall not be stated. If the time zone designator in forecasts, individual weather reports, upper winds reports or NOTAMS differs from that used by the transmitting facility, the time shall be converted to the zone in use at that facility.

STATEMENT OF FIELD ELEVATIONS. Field elevations shall be stated in feet in accordance with the following examples:

10 ft. .... FIELD ELEVATION ONE ZERO
75 ft. .... FIELD ELEVATION SEVEN FIVE
583 ft. .... FIELD ELEVATION FIVE EIGHT THREE
600 ft. .... FIELD ELEVATION SIX ZERO ZERO
1,850 ft. .... FIELD ELEVATION ONE EIGHT FIVE ZERO
2,500 ft. .... FIELD ELEVATION TWO FIVE ZERO ZERO

PREFLIGHT BRIEFING
Before the start of a flight, a telephone call or visit to the nearest FAA flight service station and weather office is in order. The purpose of the visit is to obtain preflight assistance in planning your flight. Among the questions you'll want to ask here are: (1) What's the weather like along the route and at destination? (2) What is the current condition of the runways or landing strip at destination? (3) Are all radio aids enroute operating and reliable? (4) Are fuel and servicing available at the proposed stops?

Complete details on all services available to pilots—on the ground and in the air—are contained in two indispensable government publications: (1) *Airman's Information Manual,* for basic flight data and air traffic control procedures, issued twice a year; and (2) the *Airport/Facility Directory* (airport locations, runway lengths, navigation aids, communications frequencies, lighting, fuel, servicing, etc.), which is issued periodically on a regional basis. No pilot should depart cross-country without a current copy of each publication in the cockpit. A third source, *Notices to Airmen,* with safety data of a temporary nature, should at least be checked on the ground before takeoff.

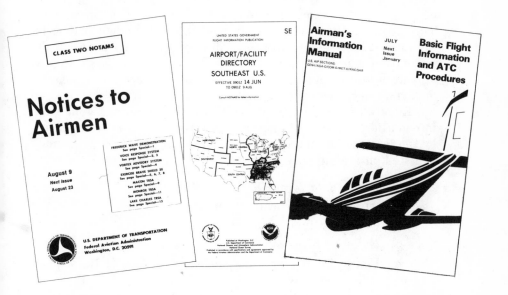

The preflight briefing is tailored specifically to the needs of general aviation, a term which includes just about all flight activity except airline and military operations. The personnel who staff the weather and briefing stations are nearly always genuinely interested in helping you. They realize that you're not a 20,000-hour veteran of the airlines, and there's no reason whatsoever to be embarrassed by asking obvious questions.

Briefings can be obtained also by telephone or radio, but a personal visit to the station, where you can check the weather maps, teletype sequences, pilot reports, etc., is much more satisfactory.

FILING A FLIGHT PLAN

Flight plans are not required for VFR flying, but the FAA heartily recommends that you file one anyway, for your own convenience and security. Flight plans *are* required for all instrument flights. They must be filed with the FAA prior to departure from within, or prior to entering, a control area or control zone. In addition, while flying IFR pilots must request and receive air traffic clearances before proceeding beyond the last cleared fix or position.

There are a number of obvious advantages in filing a flight plan, even if you're going VFR. The FAA keeps a running record of your flight as you progress from checkpoint to checkpoint. This provides them with a clear picture of all known traffic in the area. The flight plan also enables you to keep an accurate navigation log. Most important of all, however, it assures you of search and rescue assistance if for some reason you have to make an emergency landing.

Regardless of how you file the flight plan, the following information is required and may be entered on forms furnished by the FAA. If the standard form is not available, the items may be listed on a plain sheet of paper.

Flight plan data for VFR flight:
1. Aircraft identification number.
2. Color and type of aircraft.
3. Name of pilot.
4. Point of departure, or position of aircraft if flight plan is filed enroute.
5. Cruising altitude/s and route to be followed.
6. Intermediate stops and destination.
7. Proposed time of departure.
8. Actual time of departure (to be forwarded to FAA by yourself or control tower at actual takeoff time).
9. Estimated elapsed time until arrival over point of first intended landing.
10. Fuel on board expressed in hours and minutes.
11. Any other information which the pilot in command of the aircraft, or Air Traffic Control, deems necessary for traffic control purposes.

Form Approved: OMB No. 04-R0072

DEPARTMENT OF TRANSPORTATION FEDERAL AVIATION ADMINISTRATION **FLIGHT PLAN**	CIVIL AIRCRAFT PILOTS. FAR Part 91 requires you file an IFR flight plan to operate under instrument flight rules in controlled airspace. Failure to file could result in a civil penalty not to exceed $1,000 for each violation (Section 901 of the Federal Aviation Act of 1958, as amended). Filing of a VFR flight plan is recommended as a good operating practice. See also Part 99 for requirements concerning DVFR flight plans.						

1. TYPE	2. AIRCRAFT IDENTIFICATION	3. AIRCRAFT TYPE/ SPECIAL EQUIPMENT	4. TRUE AIRSPEED	5. DEPARTURE POINT	6. DEPARTURE TIME		7. CRUISING ALTITUDE
☑ VFR ☐ IFR ☐ DVFR	*N1174C*	*CESSNA 172*	*131* KTS	*OMAHA*	PROPOSED (Z) *1700*	ACTUAL (Z) *1720*	*5500*

8. ROUTE OF FLIGHT
VIA DES MOINES

9. DESTINATION (Name of airport and city)	10. EST. TIME ENROUTE		11. REMARKS
QUAD CITY MOLINE	HOURS *1*	MINUTES *46*	*MOLINE CAVU*

12. FUEL ON BOARD		13. ALTERNATE AIRPORT(S)	14. PILOT'S NAME, ADDRESS & TELEPHONE NUMBER & AIRCRAFT HOME BASE	15. NUMBER ABOARD
HOURS *3*	MINUTES *55*		*E. BROOKS* *VAN NUYS, CALIF.*	*3*

16. COLOR OF AIRCRAFT	
BLUE/WHITE	CLOSE VFR FLIGHT PLAN WITH *CEDAR RAPIDS* FSS ON ARRIVAL

FAA Form 7233-1

Flight plan data for IFR flight:

1. All information required above for VFR flight, plus:
2. Pilot's or flight commander's full address and number of certificate held by him.
3. Proposed true airspeed at cruising altitude/s.
4. Alternate airport or airports as required.
5. Frequency or frequencies of radio transmitter and receiver in the particular aircraft.

FILING A FLIGHT PLAN BY RADIO. After preflighting your airplane, briefing yourself on the weather, and entering your flight plan data, call the nearest FAA station by radio just prior to or after actual takeoff and submit the flight plan data. You may decide to take off first and file by radio as soon as possible thereafter. It is not a standard procedure, but you may also file your flight plan through the local or neighboring control tower. This is generally discouraged by the FAA but there may be instances where it is the best procedure to use. Control towers have direct telephone lines to other traffic facilities.

FILING A FLIGHT PLAN BY TELEPHONE. This procedure takes a minimum of time all around. Your airport should have the telephone number of the nearest FAA station prominently posted. If not, refer to your local telephone directory or a current

Airman's Information Manual. When your call gets through to the FSS, just say: "I'd like to file a flight plan." Be ready with all necessary data and make the conversation brief. FAA personnel have many duties, and other pilots may be in need of the telephone line.

FILING A FLIGHT PLAN IN PERSON. Have your flight plan data all set when you arrive. Filing it in person gives you an opportunity to check weather reports enroute and study other flight data that is always available at the station.

FILING A NOTICE OF ARRIVAL. When you arrive at destination or the point of closing your flight plan, be sure to file a notice of arrival. This requires nothing more than calling the nearest FSS or ATC facility, telling them you have completed your flight, and will they please close your flight plan. This can be done by radio, telephone, or in person. Neglecting to close the flight plan may start an unnecessary search for you, with the consequent hazards to search pilots. Because of this, Federal Aviation Regulations provide penalties for wilful neglect on the part of the pilot.

RADIO ASSISTANCE IN FLIGHT

Keep in mind that the same information available to you in preflight briefing is also available on request by radio from each FSS along the proposed route of flight. Because of the large volume of traffic on the relatively few radio frequencies available for air-to-ground communications, the information is communicated in abbreviated form as compared to the preflight briefing.

An important part of in-flight radio assistance is the scheduled broadcast of weather reports at 15 minutes past each hour. The broadcasts emanate from each FSS having voice facilities on VORs or non-directional beacons. The weather is for all reporting points within about 150 miles of the broadcast stations.

Here are the kinds of radio assistance which can be requested by pilots or volunteered by the ground stations:

1. Weather. The services of the Weather Bureau are fully used by FAA personnel for information concerning weather analysis and forecasts.
2. Advice concerning the operating status of radio aids.

3. Advice concerning any change in airport conditions at destination or any hazard existing along the route or at destination.
4. Assistance in obtaining air traffic control clearances.
5. Assistance in establishing the aircraft's position by furnishing VOR radials, direction finding services, etc., when lost.
6. Unscheduled broadcasts of notices to airmen and special weather reports as necessary.
7. Answers to any reasonable requests for aid or information desired.

EMERGENCY ASSISTANCE IN FLIGHT

Authentic emergencies in flight don't happen very often, but as long as they *can* happen it's good to know that assistance is no farther away than your radio microphone. The emergency may not be of your own making. In the air, however, this is an academic problem. The point is to act firmly and quickly, not wait to see if the situation is going to improve. If you are unsure of what to do next, call the nearest communication station immediately. Specialists are there at all times to offer you advice and suggestions. You're not alone with your problem.

The FAA personnel on the ground also can help you locate your position if you should ever become lost in flight. They may be able to pinpoint you by radar, by visual reference to the terrain, or by orienting you in relation to a radio facility. In any case, the first thing to do is to call and advise them of your situation. They will probably ask you for some of the following information:

1. The last known position of the aircraft.
2. Heading since the last known position.
3. Time of last known position.
4. Destination and departure points.
5. Airspeed and altitude.
6. Minutes of fuel remaining.
7. The signal being received from the range or radial of the omnirange (VOR).
8. Terrain, lights, or prominent landmarks visible to you.

The FAA station will drop all other duties and devote full attention to helping you in every way possible. The specific course of action will be determined by the answers to the above questions.

Visual emergency signals.

You will be kept informed as to just what steps are being taken to solve your problem.

SEARCH AND RESCUE

When a pilot who has filed a flight plan is reported missing or overdue at his destination, the FAA sets up a communications search. This search is based on the information contained in the flight plan and the pilot's enroute position reports. All stations and airports along the route are provided with the aircraft's registration number, its make, color, and markings. If the plane has not been located and identified within one hour after transmission of the alert notice, a full-scale search gets underway.

The actual search is conducted by any or all of the agencies which cooperate in this program — the Coast Guard, Air Force, state highway patrols, local police, Civil Air Patrol, and civilian pilots flying their own aircraft. The search is thorough, expensive, and sometimes hazardous. For this reason a false alarm — which can result when a pilot fails to close his flight plan after landing at destination — is a serious matter.

The search and rescue facilities, however, are available to all pilots, and the chances of being found and rescued in case of an emergency landing are very good indeed if a flight plan has been filed.

(ICAO) INTERNATIONAL PHONETIC ALPHABET

Letter	Code	Word	Pronunciation		Letter	Code	Word	Pronunciation
A	. —	Alfa	(Al-fah)		N	— .	November	(No-vem-ber)
B	— . . .	Bravo	(Brah-voh)		O	— — —	Oscar	(Oss-cah)
C	— . — .	Charlie	(Char-lee)		P	. — — .	Papa	(Pah-pah)
D	— . .	Delta	(Dell-tah)		Q	— — . —	Quebec	(Keh-beck)
E	.	Echo	(Eck-oh)		R	. — .	Romeo	(Row-me-oh)
F	. . — .	Foxtrot	(Foks-trot)		S	. . .	Sierra	(See-air-rah)
G	— — .	Golf	(Golf)		T	—	Tango	(Tang-go)
H	. . . .	Hotel	(Hoh-tell)		U	. . —	Uniform	(You-nee-form)
I	. .	India	(In-dee-aH)		V	. . . —	Victor	(Vik-tah)
J	. — — —	Juliett	(Jew-lee-ett)		W	. — —	Whiskey	(Wiss-key)
K	— . —	Kilo	(Key-loh)		X	— . . —	Xray	(Ecks-ray)
L	. — . .	Lima	(Lee-mah)		Y	— . — —	Yankee	(Yang-key)
M	— —	Mike	(Mike)		Z	— — . .	Zulu	(Zoo-loo)

1	. — — — —	Wun		6	—	Six
2	. . — — —	Too		7	— — . . .	Sev-en
3	. . . — —	Tree		8	— — — . .	Ait
4	. . . . —	Fow-er		9	— — — — .	Nin-er
5	. . . . .	Fife		0	— — — — —	Zero

For further emergency information see page 225.

7. Radio aids to navigation

WITHIN THE UNITED STATES and most of the other nations where there is aeronautical activity, radio aids are the primary means of setting an aircraft's course and establishing its position. Until fairly recent years, however, private pilots relied more on visual identification of landmarks for getting from one place to another than they did on radio. But now with the enormously increased volume of air traffic and tightened-up regulations, the private pilot depends more and more on radio navigation. This may have been a necessity at first, but the private pilot has since discovered that radio is also a convenience, that it really makes navigation simpler and flying safer.

This chapter is concerned with the radio aids which the private pilot commonly uses, and the equipment which he is most likely to find in the light planes he flies. Because these planes are limited in the amount of radio gear they can carry, the equipment will probably consist of one or a combination or possibly all of the following units:

(1) VHF (very high frequency) voice transmitter and receiver.
(2) VHF omnirange navigation receiver.
(3) LF/MF (low-medium frequency) voice transmitter and receiver.
(4) LF/MF direction-finder, either automatic or manual.
(5) Marker beacon receiver.

The aids described are all installed, operated, and maintained by the Federal Aviation Agency, and are frequently checked (in flight) for accuracy.

FLYING THE OMNIRANGE

The VHF omnidirectional radio range (abbreviated VOR) transmits radio waves in all directions to produce a theoretically infinite number of courses. For practical purposes, the number of courses transmitted is 360 — one for each whole degree of the compass. The omnirange has many advantages over other radio aids — not the least of which are its simplicity and accuracy — but to fully appreciate these advantages it's necessary first to discuss briefly a few of the basic principles of omni operation.

VHF RADIO WAVES. Low-frequency radio waves (such as those which your standard radio receives) travel over relatively long distances because they are reflected back and forth between the earth and a heavily charged layer of ions (called the ionosphere) high above the earth. Very high frequency waves, on the other hand, ordinarily do not bounce. They continue straight out into space, and therefore can be received only slightly below a line-of-

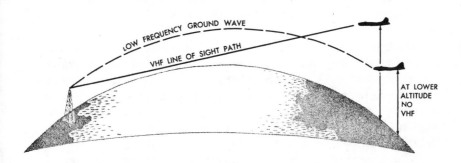

sight course from the transmitter. This fact is responsible for one of the few disadvantages of VHF radio, that is, a certain limitation of range. However, in the United States the VHF omni transmitters are spaced closely enough along the airways so that even an aircraft flying at low altitudes is hardly ever out of range of at least one of them. Moreover, because of the line-of-sight characteristic, VHF stations below the horizon and several hundred miles apart can not interfere with each other, even when transmitting at or near the same frequency.

Here is the approximate range for VHF transmission over flat terrain:

Aircraft Altitude	Range
1,000 feet	40-45 miles
1,500 feet	65 miles
2,000 feet	75 miles
2,500 feet	85 miles
5,000 feet	110 miles
10,000 feet	150 miles
15,000 feet	185 miles
20,000 feet	210 miles
30,000 feet	255 miles
40,000 feet	290 miles
50,000 feet	320 miles

TRANSMITTER OPERATION. The omnirange transmitter sends out radio waves in all directions of the compass, producing courses which radiate out like spokes from the hub of a wheel. These courses are called radials. Directional information is thus generated at the station and transmitted to the aircraft continuously. Airborne omnirange equipment intercepts this signal and converts it into a visual directional indication for use by the pilot.

Omniranges (VOR and VORTAC) operate within the 108-118 mHz frequency band with a power output of about 200 watts. The equipment is VHF, and therefore subject to line-of-sight restriction. Its range varies proportionally to the altitude of the receiving equipment. There is some spillover, however, and reception at an altitude of 1,000 feet is about 40 to 45 miles. This distance increases with altitude (see table above).

The accuracy of course alignment of the omnirange is excellent, being generally ±1°. On some omniranges minor course roughness may be observed, as evidenced by course-needle or brief flag-alarm activity. Some receivers are more subject to these irregularities than others. At a few stations, usually in mountainous terrain, the pilot may occasionally observe a brief course-needle oscillation similar to the indication of "approaching station." Be on the alert for these vagaries when flying over unfamiliar routes. Use the "to-from" indicator to determine positive station passage.

Certain propeller rpm settings can cause the VOR course deviation indicator (CDI, or left-right needle) to fluctuate as much as 6°. Slight changes in the rpm setting will normally smooth out this roughness. Check for propeller modulation before reporting a VOR station or aircraft equipment as operating unsatisfactorily.

The only positive method of identifying an omnirange is by its Morse code identification or by the recorded automatic voice identification which consists of the spoken word "VOR" following the range's name. Reliance on determining the identification of an omnirange should never be placed on the voice transmissions from the FSS or approach control facility involved. Many Flight Service Stations remotely operate several omniranges all of which have names different from each other; in some cases none of them have the name of the "parent" FSS. (During periods of maintenance, incidentally, the coded indentification is removed.)

Voice identification is a feature of most omniranges. The transmission consists of a voice announcement, "AIRVILLE VOR" (or "VORTAC") alternating with the usual Morse Code identification. If no air/ground communications facility is associated with the VOR, "AIRVILLE UNATTENDED VOR" (or "VORTAC") will be heard.

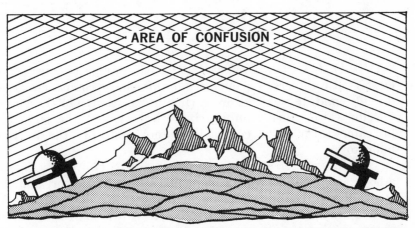

Insofar as possible, VOR stations operating on the same frequency are separated by a distance which will guard against co-channel interference. However, with the increased installation of VOR stations, it is possible at certain locations and altitudes to receive both stations with approximately equal signal strength. Note that in the illustration the *area of confusion* is generally located equidistant between stations and at higher altitudes. You can recognize this area by the oscillation of the visual indicators and an aural whistle. This situation can be eliminated by selecting another VOR station nearer to your position along your route of flight.

Omni bearing selector (OBS)

To-from indicator

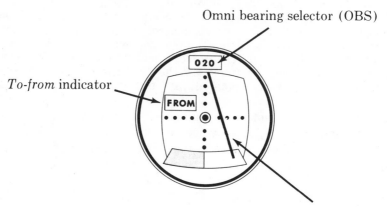

Course deviation indicator (CDI)

THE NAVIGATION COMPONENTS. The navigation circuits of most VOR receivers are connected to three basic components that provide omnirange course or bearing information: (1) the course selector (also called omni-bearing selector), (2) the left-right indicator (also called course indicator), and (3) the to-from indicator.

The *course selector* may be either one of two types. One is a 360° azimuth dial with a manually rotatable pointer, and the other is a three-digit mechanical counter on which any value from 0° to 360° may be set. In either case, it is used to establish the magnetic bearing or course of an aircraft to or from a VOR station.

The *to-from indicator* may be either a small needle that points to the words "to" or "from" printed on the dial or it may be a simple indication of either word as it appears in a small window in the dial.

The *left-right indicator* is a vertical needle pivoted at the top of a dial — the same needle used to indicate left or right deviation from the ILS localizer during an approach and letdown on the Instrument Landing System. In omnirange flying, the

Deviation from omni course is indicated by left or right displacement of the vertical needle. The horizontal needle is used only for glide path indication in the Instrument Landing System.

left-right indicator tells the pilot when he is left or right of a selected course to or from the VOR station. When the needle is centered, the magnetic course the aircraft is making good is the value set on the course selector.

These are the three basic navigation components of the airborne omnirange receiving system — the course selector, to-from indicator, and left-right indicator. Some receivers combine the indications of all three on one dial, and still others combine two of the indications on a single dial.

DETERMINING A BEARING. To determine the bearing of an aircraft from an omnirange station:

(1) Tune in the station, and identify it aurally by means of

Course selector, to-from indicator, and left-right needle combined in one omni instrument. (Lear, Inc.)

its three-letter code transmission. When the station is too far from the aircraft or is otherwise receiving a weak signal, the to-from needle points to a red warning sector rather than "to" or "from." Some instruments provide an "OFF" alarm for the same purpose.

(2)   If the station's signal is being received properly, rotate the course selector until the left-right indicator is centered.

(3)   The magnetic bearing of the aircraft to or from the station is then indicated on the course selector, regardless of the aircraft's heading.

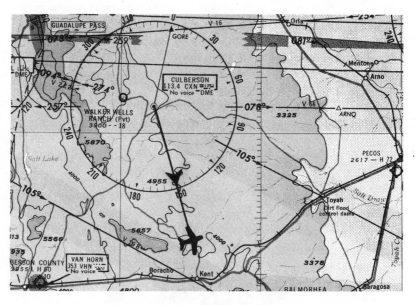

Omni bearing: 152° FROM the station.

Suppose, for example, that a pilot flying in a general west-to-east direction is passing somewhere to the south of a VOR station, and decides to take a bearing on it. He tunes in the station and receives a strong signal. The left-right indicator is at the extreme left side of the dial. The pilot slowly rotates the course selector, and the needle begins to move toward the center. When it is finally centered vertically, the pilot notes the course selector is set at 152° and the to-from needle points to "from." This means that at that moment the aircraft bears 152° from the VOR station.

The heading of the aircraft does not in any way enter into the determination of this bearing. The bearing is as rigidly fixed in space as a highway is on the earth's surface: regardless of the aircraft's heading, the aircraft bears 152° magnetic from the station.

FLYING A VOR COURSE. Flying a course directly toward or away from a VOR station is even simpler than taking bearings, since no plotting or chart work is involved. Suppose a pilot wants to fly directly toward a station. He tunes in the station and rotates the course selector until the left-right needle is centered. If the to-from indicator points to "to," the value on the course selector is the magnetic course to fly to the station. If it points to "from," the pilot can either fly a course reciprocal to the one indicated on the course selector or else rotate the course selector approximately half way around the dial until the left-right needle is centered again and the to-from indicator points to "to."

If the pilot wants to fly a course away from a station, the procedure is reversed. That is, the course selector is rotated until the left-right needle is centered and the to-from indicator points to "from."

In either case, whether he wants to fly a course toward or away from a station, he takes up a magnetic heading approximately the same as the value set on the course selector when the left-right needle is centered. As long as he keeps the needle centered he is making good a course that will bring him directly over the station, assuming of course that the to-from needle indicates "to."

In effect, the omnirange automatically compensates for drift. A crosswind can cause the aircraft to drift from a selected VOR course, but not if the pilot keeps the left-right indicator centered. In the process he may have to alter the compass heading to left or right, but the point is that he will automatically find the heading necessary to hold the course as long as he keeps the left-right indicator centered.

In cases where the plane does drift off course, the left-right indicator can be recentered and a new course flown to the station. When an aircraft drifts off course while flying away from a station, however, the aircraft should be returned to the original course by altering the heading, as usual, in the direction toward which the left-right needle points.

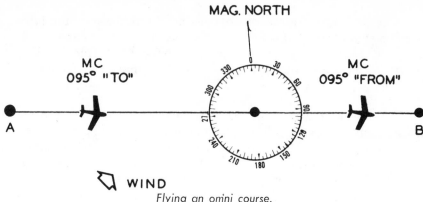

Flying an omni course.

In most cases the pilot will preselect a course that he wants to make good to a VOR station. Suppose, for example, he wants to fly from A to B, as in the illustration. This course leads directly across an omnirange station. The true course from A to B (090°) he measures with a plotter on the chart, and then applies the average variation (5° westerly) to determine the magnetic course (095°). He turns his aircraft to a magnetic heading of 095°, and rotates the course selector also to 095°. The left-right indicator is centered and the to-from needle points to "to."

Eventually, the left-right indicator begins to move to the right of center, although the pilot is still holding a magnetic heading of 095°. This means that the aircraft is drifting to the left of course. The indicator, as usual, points the way back to course. The pilot increases the magnetic heading to 105°, and slowly the left-right needle returns to center. Further on along the course, however, the needle moves slightly to the left of center. The pilot has corrected heading too much to the right, and the aircraft has now drifted a small distance to the right of course.

This time the pilot corrects the magnetic heading back to 100° — a correction of 5° left. The left-right indicator will swing back toward center again (at a rate depending on the distance of the aircraft from the station), but just before it reaches center the pilot corrects heading about 2° *right* — to 102°. This heading is calculated to hold the aircraft on the 095° radial to the omni station. In effect, the omni has determined for the pilot the amount of crab angle necessary to make good the course. All the pilot is concerned with, however, is keeping the left-right indicator centered.

As the pilot approaches the station the left-right needle begins to oscillate slightly. Finally, as the aircraft crosses the station, the to-from indicator changes abruptly from "to" to "from." The course selector and the magnetic heading remain the same — 095° — as the aircraft proceeds away from the station. The left-right needle indication is also the same. If the aircraft drifts off to the right, the needle still points to the left and the pilot corrects the heading to the left.

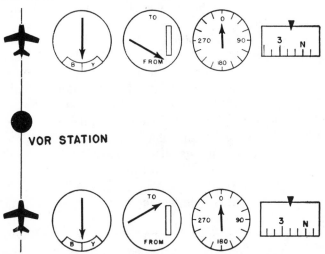

Left-right needle remains centered but to-from indicator changes from TO to FROM after crossing station.

In other words, regardless of whether the aircraft is heading toward or away from the station, the left-right needle points to the omnirange course set on the course selector. If there is any convenient rule about omnirange flying, it is this:

Always fly into the needle. When the needle points to the left, the aircraft must be turned to the left in order to return to course. When it points to the right, a correction to the right is required. Like most rules this one involves a minor exception. It was seen in the foregoing example how the to-from indicator changed from "to" to "from" as the aircraft passed over the VOR station but the pilot continued on the same heading and the left-right needle maintained the same sense indication. However, if the pilot after passing over the station had made a 180° procedure turn without changing the course selector, the to-from indicator would still indicate "from" but the left-right needle would now point from the 095° course rather than toward it. The simplest procedure in this case would be for the pilot to rotate the course selector to the reciprocal bearing of 275° while making the procedure turn. The to-from indicator would then indicate "to" and the 275° course would be flown by making corrections toward the left-right needle as usual.

Remember that the heading of the aircraft has nothing to do with the indications of the omni receiver. The omni simply tells you your magnetic direction to or from the station. You could be on a compass heading of 005°, 110°, 240°, 320°, or any of 356 other headings and still bear (for example) 165° magnetic from a given omni station. When the left-right needle is centered, the course selector is set to 165°, and the to-from indicator reads "FROM," the aircraft is located on a line bearing 165° magnetic from the station regardless of heading. You could make a complete 360° turn without any change in the indications on the omni receiver except that the left-right needle would show you at all times your position relative to the 165° "FROM" radial. And moreover, if you were more than just a few miles away from the station, the left-right needle wouldn't even move off center in a tight turn.

Unlike the pointer of an automatic direction-finding compass, the left-right needle of the omni does not tell you where to go to reach the station or to a selected course. It merely tells you where you are in relation to a course that you have set up on your course selector . . . in effect, the needle says you are right of this selected course or you are left of it. If the needle is to the left of center you will have to turn to the left to reach that course. How much you will have to turn and how long you will have to fly before reaching the course (or radial) depends upon how far away from it you are.

OFF-COURSE VOR FLYING. In aircraft equipped with a single VOR receiver but not equipped with distance measuring equipment or a course-line computer, the simplest method of flying the omnirange is to fly a course from station to station. However, it is also possible to fly VOR between any two points not equipped with omnirange facilities but which are within signal-reception range of a VOR transmitter.

For example, a pilot plans to fly from St. Clair to Laurel-

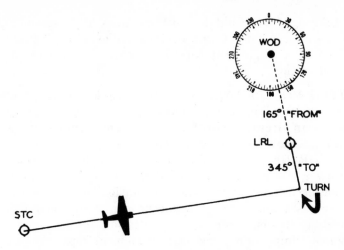

Off-course flying on a single VOR station.

grove. Laurelgrove has no omnirange facility, but is located 25 miles south of Woodbridge, which does have. On his chart the pilot draws a course line from St. Clair to a point intersecting the bearing line from the Woodbridge VOR to Laurelgrove. This course is set definitely to one side or the other of the destination in order to prevent any uncertainty about which way to turn once the Woodbridge VOR bearing is intercepted. In the example the course is set to the right of Laurelgrove simply because it represents the shorter distance between St. Clair and Laurelgrove.

The pilot sets 165° on his course selector, the value of the bearing from Woodbridge to Laurelgrove, and then maintains by dead reckoning a heading calculated to make good the course between St. Clair and the turning point to Laurelgrove. When he starts out from St. Clair the left-right needle is at the side of the dial. As he approaches the 165° radial from Woodbridge, however, the needle moves toward center.

When the needle is finally centered and the to-from indicator points to "from," the pilot knows he has reached the bearing line extending from the Woodbridge VOR through and beyond Laurelgrove. He resets the course selector to 345°, the reciprocal of the 165° bearing, and the to-from indicator changes to "to." The pilot turns the aircraft to a magnetic heading of 345° and keeps the left-right needle centered until he arrives over Laurelgrove, his destination.

If Laurelgrove should be within range of a second VOR station the pilot could obtain a definite fix over his destination, even if he were on instruments, by taking a cross-bearing on the second station.

PLOTTING VOR BEARINGS AND FIXES. Flying an omnirange course or taking a single bearing on an omnirange station does not fix an aircraft's position — it provides only a single line of position somewhere along which the aircraft is located. A definite VOR fix is obtainable only (1) when the aircraft is directly over the station, (2) when a VOR bearing is crossed with another bearing from a second station, or (3) when the aircraft crosses an airway marker beacon while on an omnirange course. In fast aircraft this limitation of the single VOR bearing is not important, since VOR stations are spaced along the airways about every 100 miles, providing a fix nearly every 20 or 30 minutes. Fixes for off-airway flying in slower aircraft, however, require the plotting of two or more bearings on a chart.

All aeronautical charts used in civil flying in the U.S. show the location, frequency, and identification of VOR stations. In addition, a 360° compass rose is printed around each station. These compass roses are oriented to magnetic north, which means that they are offset from true north by the amount of magnetic variation at the omnirange site. The compass rose around each

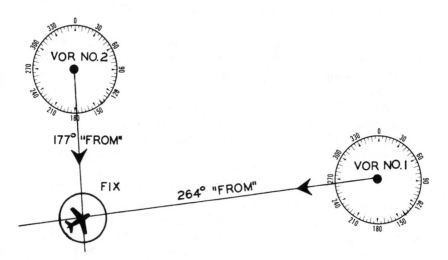

Plotting a fix from two VOR stations.

station thus represents the exact magnetic bearing of each radial from the station.

To plot a VOR bearing on a chart:

(1) Tune in the station, rotate the course selector until the left-right needle is centered, and note whether the bearing is "to" the station or "from" it.

(2) If the bearing is from the station, place the straight-edge of a plotter along the VOR site and through the value on the compass rose corresponding to the value on the course selector. Draw a light pencil mark along the straight-edge in the approximate vicinity of the aircraft's estimated position. This is a single line of position.

(3) If the bearing is to the station, either (a) add or subtract 180° from the value on the course selector, or else (b) rotate the course selector about 180° until the left-right needle is again centered and the to-from indicator reads "from." Plot the bearing on the chart exactly as above.

To plot a position fix, select a second VOR station and plot the bearing from it in the same way as outlined in (2) and (3) above. The point where the two bearings intersect is the aircraft's position.

ADF FOR VFR NAVIGATION

The discussion here is concerned only with the basic and more common methods of automatic direction finding (ADF) suitable for flights in which pinpoint accuracy is not a vital factor. These methods include (1) how to fly to the station, (2) how to determine your position from the station, and (3) how to determine the ADF indication that signifies arrival at a desired direction from the station.

What type of radio stations can be used for ADF? Most ADF receivers receive signals in the frequency spectrum of 190 kHz to 1,750 kHz, which includes low frequency and medium frequency navigation facilities as well as the AM (amplitude modulation) commercial broadcast stations. Primarily for air navigation, the LF/MF stations consist of nondirectional radio beacons (Rbn), ILS compass locators (LOM), and four-course radio ranges (MRA). Marine radio beacons *can* be used for ADF but their utility is limited inasmuch as they transmit only for brief scheduled periods and are arranged in groups of three or more along the coast, with each in the group transmitting on the same frequency. Standard broadcast stations are useful for air navigation; but remember that they can be identified only when the broadcast is interrupted for station identification. Some operate only during daylight hours, and many of the low-powered stations transmit on identical frequencies, causing erratic ADF indications.

How does an ADF instrument indicate direction to the station? As implied by its nickname "bird dog," the ADF has automatic directional qualities which result in the indicator always pointing toward the station to which it is tuned. This action is presented to the pilot on the face of the instrument. When the pointer is straight up (nose position), the station is ahead of the aircraft; when the pointer is straight down (tail position), the station is behind the aircraft; and when pointing 90° to either side (wingtip position), the station is off the respective wing tip.

What does the ADF indication mean in terms of bearings to the station? The more commonly used ADF instrument (sometimes called radio compass), to which the Private Pilot written examination relates, has a stationary azimuth dial graduated up to 360° (with N or 0 at the top of the instrument representing the aircraft nose). The bearing pointer shows only the *relative* bearing, or angle from the nose of the aircraft to the station; e.g., the relative bearing in Fig. 1 is 060°.

How can ADF be used to fly to the station? The easiest and perhaps most common method is to "home" to the station. Since the ADF pointer always points to the station, you simply head the aircraft so that the pointer is on the 0° or nose position. The station, then, will be directly ahead of the aircraft. With a crosswind, however, the aircraft would continually drift to one side of the course; unless a change in heading were made, the aircraft would no longer be headed straight toward the station. This would

Fig. 1

be indicated by the pointer moving to the windward side of the nose position. By turning into the wind (toward the pointer), so as to continually return the pointer to the 0° position, the aircraft will fly to the station but in a curving flight path, as shown in Fig. 2 inbound. Because this curving flight path deviates from the direct course, you must use caution to avoid drifting into unanticipated obstructions or terrain. The lighter the crosswind and the shorter the distance to the station, the less the flight path curves. As the aircraft arrives at and passes over the station, the pointer will swing from a nose position to a tail position.

Is it possible to home away from the station? For all practical purposes — no. Homing away from the station can be accomplished only if there is no crosswind. Attempting to keep the station directly behind the aircraft in a crosswind by turning in order to hold the pointer on the tail or 180° position requires that the aircraft be turned more and more to the downwind heading. This, of course, results in the aircraft getting farther and farther away from the desired course (Fig. 2 outbound).

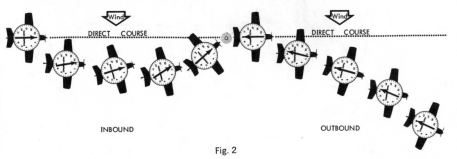

Fig. 2

Of what importance is the magnetic heading of the aircraft when using ADF? The ADF should be considered as a moving, "fluid thing." The number to which the indicator points on the fixed azimuth dial does not mean anything directionally until it is related to the aircraft's heading. Because of this relationship the heading also must be observed carefully when reading the relative bearing to the station. Whenever the heading is changed, the relative bearing will change an equal number of degrees.

How can the magnetic bearing to a station be determined on a fixed ADF azimuth dial? Looking at the ADF instrument, imagine yourself being in the center of the fixed azimuth, with the nose of the aircraft at the 0° position, the tail at the 180° position, and the left and right wing tips at the 270° and 090° positions respectively. When the pointer is on the nose position you are heading to the station and the magnetic bearing can be read directly from your compass (plus or minus deviation). If the pointer is left or right of the nose, note the direction and number of degrees of turn that would (if you were to head to the station)

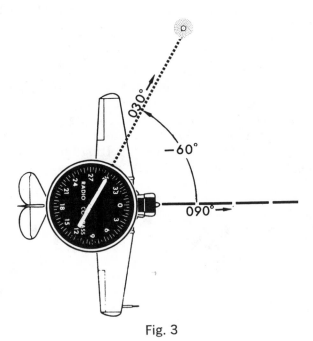

Fig. 3

move the pointer to the nose position, and mentally apply this to your heading. For example, in Fig. 3, a turn 60° left would place the pointer on the nose position; 60° left of 090° magnetic heading is a magnetic bearing of 030° to the station. Your location, then, is southwest of the station, and if you were to head toward the station your heading would be 030°.

How can the magnetic bearing from the station be determined? Since the direction *from* the station is the opposite of the direction *to* the station, it can be determined by following the steps discussed in the preceding paragraph and adding or subtracting 180°, as appropriate, to the aircraft-to-station bearing. In other words, find the reciprocal of that bearing. If the ADF pointer happens to be behind the wing-tip position (when you are flying away from the station), the procedure is to note the number of degrees and the direction of turn that would move the pointer to the tail position, and apply it to the heading. For example, in Fig. 4 a turn 45° to the right would move the pointer to the tail posi-

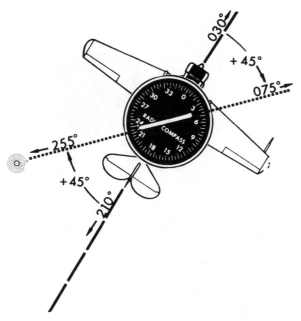

Fig. 4

tion; 45° to the right of the 030° magnetic heading is a magnetic bearing of 075° from the station (east-northeast of the station). Just as radials always extend outward from a VOR station in a magnetic direction, the magnetic bearings from an ADF station should be thought of as radials of that ADF station. It is important to determine the radial (the bearing from the station) because in order to locate your position, the line of position must be plotted from the known station location, just as in VOR orientation.

Can the ADF indication which signifies arrival at a specific bearing to the station be predetermined? Yes. From the aeronautical chart, first ascertain whether the station is left or right of the course being flown. Then, after selecting the magnetic bearing to the station that you desire to intercept, determine the angular difference between that bearing and your magnetic heading (angle of intercept). With the aircraft headed to the 0° position

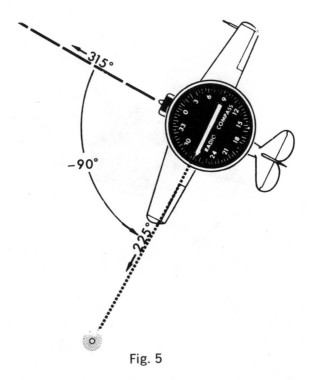

Fig. 5

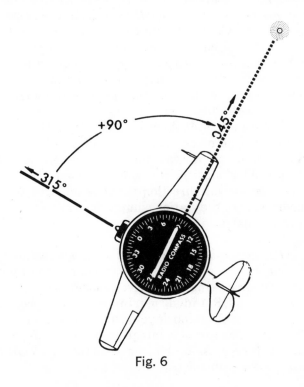

Fig. 6

of the ADF azimuth, the bearing indicator, in pointing to the station, will show the relative angle between the aircraft's nose and the station. As you continue on course this angle will gradually change since the position of the aircraft relative to the station is changing. Arrival at the preselected bearing to the station will be indicated when the pointer shows the difference between the heading and that bearing (angle of intercept). For example, as shown in Fig. 5, if your magnetic heading is to be 315° and the selected bearing to the station is 225°, the angular difference is 90° left. Arrival on this bearing, then, will be indicated when the pointer is 90° left of the nose position. If the station is to the right of the course on a bearing of 045°, the 90° angle between the heading and the bearing would be shown to the right of the nose position, as in Fig. 6.

How can magnetic bearings to or from an LF/MF station be determined on aeronautical charts? Since a compass rose or azimuth is not shown at LF/MF or commercial broadcast stations on WAC or Sectional charts, the most accurate way to obtain a magnetic bearing is to measure the direction with a plotter, taking into account the local magnetic variation. However, the charts do show many VOR azimuths and airway courses already oriented to magnetic direction, and these can be used satisfactorily for approximation of ADF bearings on VFR flights. This approximation can be made on the basis of the direction of the nearest VOR radial or airway that most closely parallels the bearing of the ADF station. Remember, though, that the VOR radial or printed airway direction is outbound *from* the station. To find the bearing *to* the station, simply determine the reciprocal of the parallel radial or airway.

How can ADF be used to supplement VOR navigation? One of the most valuable uses of ADF is the determination of your position along the course being flown. Even though you are following a course along a VOR radial, obtaining an ADF bearing that crosses the course will establish your "fix" or position along that course. This is particularly advantageous when an off-course VOR is not available for a cross-bearing or when the only VOR receiver must be used as the primary tracking system.

What can cause an erroneous ADF indication? As mentioned earlier, two or more standard broadcast stations may transmit on the same (or close to the same) frequency and interfere with each other's signal. This causes the ADF pointer to oscillate as it attempts to discriminate between stations. Whenever possible, choose stations of higher power and lower frequencies or wait until you are closer to the station before using it. Another source of erroneous bearings is improper tuning, or tuning in the fringes of a signal. Always tune to the center of the signal, which may be a few kHz (kiloHertz) or mHz (megaHertz) on either side of the published frequency. And, of course, always make an absolute identification of the station before using it for navigation purposes. In the vicinity of electrical storms, the ADF pointer tends to swing from the radio station to the center of the storm at every flash of lightning. This makes it difficult to obtain reliable bearings. Erroneous or fluctuating bearings may also result from the deflection of radio waves from the surface of mountains. Use caution when taking bearings over mountainous terrain.

STANDARD BROADCAST STATIONS

Standard broadcast stations are not of course, government radio aids, but they can sometimes be useful in air navigation. Most LF/MF aircraft receivers incorporate the 550-1500 kc. band on which these stations transmit. In an emergency the broadcast stations can be used for approximate bearings or for homing, but interference with the transmitters' ground waves by sky waves from distant stations may result in grossly inaccurate bearings.

Some stations offer periodic weather broadcasts of value to fliers.

The locations of major broadcasting station transmitters are shown on most navigation charts. At night the transmitting towers are marked by flashing red obstruction lights.

MARKER BEACONS

Marker beacons serve to identify a particular location in space along an airway or on the approach to an instrument runway. This is accomplished by means of a 75 MHz transmitter which sends out a directional signal to be received by aircraft flying overhead. These markers are generally used in conjunction with enroute navaids and the Instrument Landing System as point designators.

The class FM fan marker produces an elliptical-shaped pattern, which at an elevation of 1,000 feet above the station is about 4 nautical miles wide and 12 long. At 10,000 feet the pattern enlarges to about 12 nautical miles wide and 35 long.

Ordinarily there are two marker beacons associated with an ILS: an outer marker (OM) and an inner marker (IM). The OM, identified by continuous dashes sent out at the rate of two per second, normally

MARKER BEACONS FAN	DUNGENESS

indicates a position at which an aircraft at the appropriate altitude on the localizer course will intercept the ILS glide path. The MM, identified by alternate dots and dashes keyed at the rate of 95 dot/dash combinations per minute, indicates a position at which an aircraft is about 3,500 feet out from the landing threshold and about 200 feet above the elevation of the touchdown zone.

DISTANCE MEASURING EQUIPMENT (DME)

In the operation of DME, paired pulses at a specific spacing are sent out from the aircraft (this is the interrogation) and are received at the ground station. The ground station (transponder) then transmits paired pulses back to the aircraft at the same pulse spacing but on a different frequency. The time required for the round trip of this signal exchange is measured in the airborne DME unit and is translated into distance (nautical miles) from the aircraft to the ground station.

Operating on the line-of-sight principle, DME furnishes distance information with a very high degree of accuracy. Reliable signals may be received at distances up to 199 NM at line-of-sight altitude with an accuracy of better than ½ mile or 3% of the distance, whichever is greater. Distance information received from DME equipment is *slant range* distance, not actual horizontal distance.

DME operates on frequencies in the UHF spectrum between 962 MHz and 1213 MHz. Aircraft equipped with TACAN equipment will receive distance information from a VORTAC automatically, while aircraft equipped with VOR must have a separate DME airborne unit.

VOR/DME, VORTAC, ILS/DME, and LOC/DME navigation facilities established by the FAA provide course and distance information from colocated components under a frequency pairing plan. Aircraft receiving equipment which provides for automatic DME selection assures reception of azimuth and distance information from a common source whenever designated VOR/DME, VORTAC, ILS/DME, and LOC/DME are selected.

VOR/DME, VORTAC, ILS/DME, and LOC/DME facilities are identified by synchronized identifications transmitted on a time-share basis. The VOR or localizer portion of the facility is identified by a coded tone modulated at 1020 Hz or by a combination of code and voice. The TACAN or DME is identified by a coded tone modulated at 1350 Hz. The DME or TACAN coded identification is transmitted once for each three or four times that the VOR or localizer coded identification is transmitted. When either the VOR or the DME is inoperative, it is important to recognize which identifier is retained for the operative facility. A single coded identification with a repetition interval of approximately 30 seconds indicates that the DME is operative.

Aircraft receivers which provide for automatic DME selection assure the pilot of reception of both azimuth and distance information from one source when he tunes in a VOR/DME, VORTAC, or ILS/DME facility.

NON-DIRECTIONAL RADIO BEACONS

Low-powered non-directional radio beacons operate in the 200-400 kc. band, and are installed at some fan marker sites or at other locations near airports. These facilities, serve as radio fixes generally used in connection with instrument approaches, and to help the pilot follow a more precise holding pattern when holding is required.

Radio beacons are low-powered transmitting stations which can be identified on charts by a purplish-red dot enclosed by a small circle of the same color. Around the circle will be found a purplish-red shading forming a larger circular pattern about three miles in diameter. They are rarely useful at distances of over 15 or 20 miles.

Beacons are identified on charts by three-letter designators and code, together with transmitting frequency.

8. Meteorology
and weather recognition

DURING THE EARLY stages of your training to become a private
pilot, weather and its effect on flying will become very
evident. You may arrive at the airport one day and simply be
told "no training flights today, weather is below minimums."
This means, in effect, that the visibility is less than three miles
(horizontally), or the ceiling is less than 1,000 feet (vertically),
or there is a combination of both.

Training flights for the person working toward the private
pilot certificate must be conducted under Visual Flight Rules.
The one exception: when an airport is under the radio control
of a tower, flights may be continued if the weather is below
minimums. This is described as "controlled VFR operations."
Its continuance is entirely at the discretion of the traffic controllers on duty. Basically, controlled VFR operations limit the
frequency of takeoffs and landings. Pilots must obtain clearances
from the tower prior to takeoff and prior to letting down into
the traffic pattern. In general, traffic controllers must know the
exact location of each aircraft in the control zone surrounding
the particular airport. Thus, the flight trainee may come into
contact with weather problems even before he becomes a private
pilot.

Private pilots are usually not trained or qualified to fly
through bad weather, nor are the small aircraft they usually
operate equipped with the expensive instruments required for
instrument flying. It is therefore important that the private pilot
know how to avoid hazardous weather — when to fly and when
not to fly — and in order to recognize hazardous weather it is
necessary to understand the nature of the atmosphere and the
behavior of weather.

124

It really isn't enough to take only the forecaster's word for it that it may be good flying weather today. His forecasts are based on the movements of large air masses and on local conditions at the specific points where weather stations are located. Air masses do not always perform as predicted, and weather stations are sometimes spaced far apart. It is thus necessary for the pilot to know what can happen to the weather between stations. He must also understand conditions he encounters which are different from those indicated in the weather reports he has received.

The meteorologist can only predict the weather *likely* to occur. It is up to you to decide whether your particular flight may be hazardous. You must consider your type of aircraft, the equipment installed, and your own flying ability, experience, and physical limitations.

Here are some of the weather subjects you should know and which are covered in this chapter and the next: (1) weather aids provided by the Weather Bureau and FAA to furnish you with information; (2) sources of weather data available; (3) weather terms and reports commonly used; (4) interpretation of weather maps, teletype sequence reports, winds aloft reports, and flying-weather forecasts; (5) cloud conditions, winds, and weather which is merely inconvenient and not dangerous to normal flight activities; (6) weather conditions that can be used to advantage;

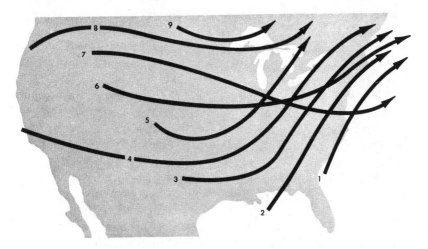

Average tracks of storms across the U.S.

(7) how to avoid dangerous weather conditions; (8) significance of cloud formations and precipitation which you encounter in flight; (9) procedures advisable in the interest of safety in flight.

Throughout the United States there are more than 500 stations maintained by the U.S. Weather Bureau. These stations are a means of determining current weather and predicting future weather. In most cases, trained personnel are on duty 24 hours a day making observations, sending out hourly reports to central stations, forecasting weather, and in general amassing a wealth of information which is free for the asking.

Weather near the surface of the earth is the result of atmospheric conditions at high altitudes. For this reason, about 150 stations release and track weather balloons every six hours to determine the wind direction and velocity at the upper levels. There are approximately 50 radiosonde stations. From each of these a balloon ascends every 12 hours with a radio transmitter attached. The balloon reaches altitudes in excess of 10 miles, providing a complete record of temperature, pressure, and humidity at the higher levels.

At each six-hour interval, this information is assembled and plotted on weather maps, together with other data collected by radio, telephone, and teletypewriter. These maps provide specific information concerning the weather in all parts of the country and furnish the meteorologists with material from which they are able to make forecasts. Four times daily, each flight advisory center issues forecasts especiallly designed to indicate flying conditions anticipated for the following 12 hours. Area forecasts are made for the 24 areas into which the United States is divided for forecast purposes, and terminal forecasts are completed for more than 300 airports.

These services are available to pilots at airports and weather stations, as well as by radio. Also, meteorologists are on duty, day and hight, at approximately 200 air terminals to chart and analyze weather reports and to discuss weather conditions *with pilots*.

Especially for private pilots is another weather service known as the trip forecast, available on request in person, by telephone, or by telegraph. This is issued for an individual flight, and predicts the weather likely to be encountered along a given route. To take full advantage of this special service, you must specify

(1) your type of plane; (2) cruising speed; (3) type of flight (whether contact VFR or instrument IFR; (4) place and estimated time of departure; (5) route to be taken; (6) intermediate stops planned and their duration; and (7) destination and estimated time of arrival.

NATURE OF THE ATMOSPHERE

The large mass of air that surrounds the earth is called the *atmosphere*. The atmosphere is an odorless, tasteless, transparent, mobile, gaseous mixture. No definite upper limit can be given to the atmosphere since its density decreases with height and it is capable of indefinite expansion.

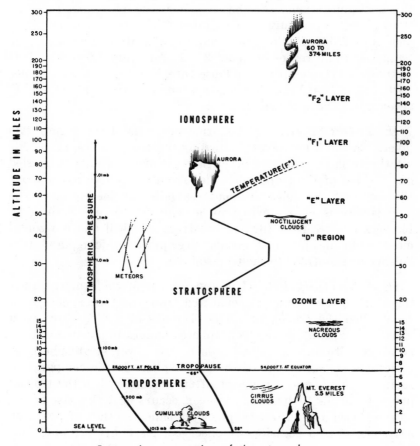

Schematic cross-section of the atmosphere.

Some elements or activities of the atmosphere, such as turbulence, clouds, fog, haze, rain, and snow, can be seen directly or felt. Others, such as pressure, temperature, wind direction and speed, and relative humidity can be best measured by instruments. Any or all of these elements are called *weather*. Some of the components of the atmosphere have a direct bearing on weather, while the others furnish us only background information. Because of this, it is important to know the atmosphere, its composition, and its properties.

Near the earth's surface the air is relatively warm because of its contact with the earth. Heat reaches the earth in the form of short waves from the sun. These waves pass through the air without warming it appreciably. The surface of the earth absorbs this heat and returns it to the air principally by contact (conduction). The temperature in the United States (at sea level) averages about 59° F. the year round. As altitude increases, the temperature decreases by about $3\frac{1}{2}$° F. for every 1,000 feet. This is known as the temperature lapse rate. The lapse rate continues with altitude until the air reaches a temperature of about –69° F. seven miles above the earth.

THE TROPOSPHERE. The atmosphere is divided into two layers. In the lower layer, known as the *troposphere,* all of our weather occurs, and here practically all of our flying is carried on. The top of the troposphere lies from about five miles above the earth at the poles to about ten miles at the equator. The troposphere is characterized by a relatively rapid decrease in temperature with height, and by strong vertical and horizontal movements of air. Most clouds, precipitation, icing, and turbulence are confined to the troposphere.

THE STRATOSPHERE. The upper layer of the atmosphere is the *stratosphere,* which is separated from the troposphere by a zone called the *tropopause.* The decrease of temperature with increasing altitude in the troposphere changes to a constant temperature with increasing altitude in the lower stratosphere. A noticeable characteristic of the stratosphere is the comparative rarity of clouds and turbulence often encountered in the troposphere. Clear air turbulence, however, occurs near the base of the stratosphere, and a cirrus-type cloud, called mother of pearl, or nacreous, is also occasionally observed. As a private pilot you will have no occasion to go as high as the stratosphere, so your interest will naturally center in the troposphere.

COMPOSITION OF THE AIR. Although extremely light, air has weight and is highly elastic and compressible. It is a mixture of gases in which a volume of pure dry air contains about 78% nitrogen, 21% oxygen, and a 1% mixture of about 10 other gases. These proportions are, for all practical purposes, about the same at all elevations up to at least 12 miles above the earth. Air contains water vapor which varies in amount from 0 to 5% by volume. Water vapor (for ordinary considerations) acts as an independent gas mixed with air. The atmosphere, even when clear, contains an enormous number of impurities, including dust. When they become excessive they appear as haze, and visibility is reduced.

TEMPERATURE

Temperature is probably the single most significant of all the elements that go to make up the phenomenon we call weather, and certainly it is the one most responsible for changes in the weather.

Thermometers are calibrated on the basis of two reference points or standards. Melting ice provides the point for the so-called freezing temperature, and boiling water at sea level pressure provides the reference for boiling point temperature. In the Fahrenheit scale, the freezing temperature of water is 32° and the boiling point is 212°. In the Centigrade scale the freezing point is 0° and the boiling point is 100°. The Fahrenheit and Centigrade scales are illustrated; 180 Fahrenheit divisions are equal to 100 Centigrade divisions. Thus, to convert degrees Fahrenheit to degrees Centigrade, first subtract 32 degrees from the Fahrenheit temperature to compute the number of divisions between the freezing point and the indicated temperature. Then, since 9 Fahrenheit degrees equal 5 Centigrade degrees, five-ninths of the Fahrenheit degrees will give the number of Centigrade degrees.

Thus, Temperature $°C. = 5/9 \; (°F. - 32°)$

or, $\qquad\qquad °F. = 9/5 °C. + 32°$

Many air navigation computers are marked for direct conversion between Fahrenheit and Centigrade temperatures.

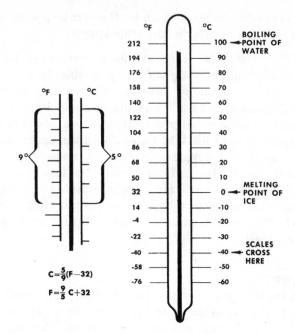

Fahrenheit-Centigrade temperature scales.

The temperatures that are considered in aviation weather are those of the free air — that is, the temperature - measuring elements are exposed in such a way that they are not in direct sunlight and so that other effects which might cause inaccuracies in the readings are minimized.

All meteorological upper-air measurements are made in Centigrade degrees, but Fahrenheit degrees are used on the sea-level weather map.

TEMPERATURE LAPSE RATE. An aircraft taking off and beginning to gain altitude will encounter a change in air temperature. This change in temperature with altitude is termed "temperature lapse rate." Thus, if the surface temperature was 60° F. and at 10,000 feet the temperature was 23° F., this portion of the air would have a lapse rate of 37° per 10,000 feet. Usually the lapse rate is given in degrees per 1,000 feet. The average temperature lapse rate is 2° C. (3½° F.) per 1,000 feet. This has been determined from hundreds of observations. However, individual situations may differ greatly.

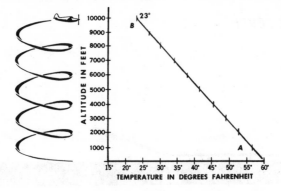

Change of temperature with height.

TEMPERATURE INVERSION. Many times, especially at night, there is an increase of temperature with height in the lower levels; this is called an inversion of temperature, or just an inversion. It indicates that the normal decrease in temperature with height is inverted. An example of how an inversion may form is evident on a clear, relatively still night when the ground loses heat rapidly and cools the layer of air next to it. The air somewhat higher up is not affected, thus the lower layer of air may become colder than the air just above it. The upper layer of air forms a lid through which air pollutants (smoke, dust, etc.) can not escape. This weather phenomena is generally known as smog, and creates adverse conditions, especially in areas of oil refineries and heavy manufacturing.

ATMOSPHERIC PRESSURE

The second major weather element is pressure. Changes in barometric pressure not only affect the flight characteristics of the aircraft but also create errors in the pilot's pressure instruments (instruments which operate on the basis of measuring outside air pressure) such as the altimeter, airspeed indicator, rate of climb, etc. It is essential that the pilot understand the effects of constantly changing pressure in order to correct and properly intepret the pressure-type instruments. He must also understand the pressure reactions on his aircraft, especially during changes in altitude and while taking off and landing at airports of different sea level elevations.

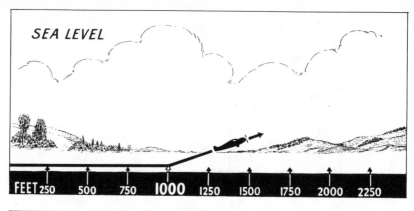

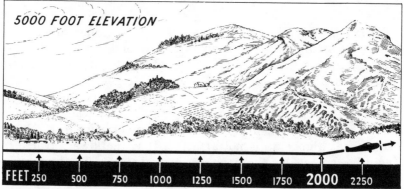

Distance required for takeoff increases with altitude of field.

An airplane, for example, will need more runway for take-off from an airport 5,000 feet above sea level as compared to its take-off from a sea level airport. This is due to the lighter air at 5,000 feet, which lessens the lift value of the wing. To obtain sufficient lift for take-off at the higher airport, it becomes necessary to propel the wing at a higher relative speed, thus the need for more runway to achieve this higher speed.

Accurate data concerning the barometric pressure is of great importance to the forecaster in the preparation of his weather maps and forecasts. *The barometric pressure at any given level is the force which the vertical column of air above that level exerts on a unit area at the level by reason of the weight of the air in the vertical column.* For example, suppose the area of the inside of a barometer tube to be just one square inch. Then a

DENSITY ALTITUDE CHART

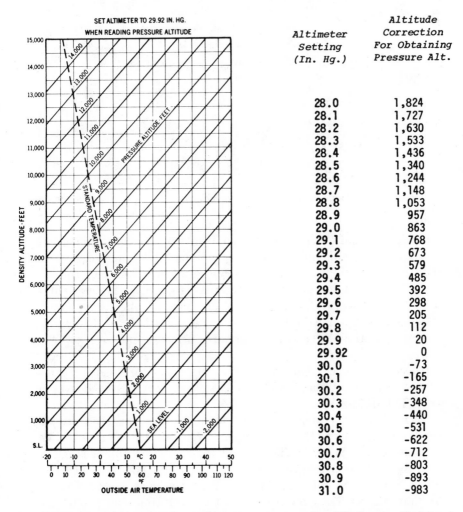

Altimeter Setting (In. Hg.)	Altitude Correction For Obtaining Pressure Alt.
28.0	1,824
28.1	1,727
28.2	1,630
28.3	1,533
28.4	1,436
28.5	1,340
28.6	1,244
28.7	1,148
28.8	1,053
28.9	957
29.0	863
29.1	768
29.2	673
29.3	579
29.4	485
29.5	392
29.6	298
29.7	205
29.8	112
29.9	20
29.92	0
30.0	-73
30.1	-165
30.2	-257
30.3	-348
30.4	-440
30.5	-531
30.6	-622
30.7	-712
30.8	-803
30.9	-893
31.0	-983

The density of the air is determined by pressure, temperature, and humidity. Density altitude is not an actual height reference but rather an index to aircraft performance. Low density altitude *increases* performance. High density altitude *decreases* performance in three ways: (1) it reduces power because the engine takes in less air to support combustion, (2) it reduces thrust because the propeller gets less grip on the light air, and (3) it reduces lift because the light air exerts less force on the airfoils.

Sample problem: airport elevation = 3,165 ft; OAT = 93°F; altimeter setting = 30.10"Hg. What is the density altitude?

Solution: from the right of the chart find a correction of −165" for altimeter setting of 30.10"Hg. PA = 3,165 ft − 165 or 3,000 ft. Enter chart with 93°F, proceed straight upward to intersection with PA line at 3,000 ft, then straight across to left edge of scale for density altitude of 5,800 ft.

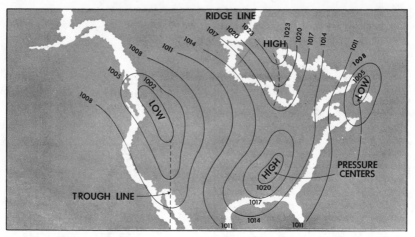

Lines connecting points of equal pressure indicate "highs" and "lows" on the weather map.

30-inch barometric column will contain just 30 cubic inches of mercury. One cubic inch of mercury weighs 0.4906 pounds, which, multiplied by 30, gives the ordinary sea-level pressure of the air to be 14.718 pounds per square inch. This quantity is frequently used by engineers and is called a pressure of one atmosphere. In the main, it is nothing more than the weight of an air column having a sectional area of one square inch and extending vertically to the upper limits of the atmosphere. For meteorological purposes, the force exerted by this weight is expressed in terms of *millibars,* a millibar being a measure of force exerted over a specified unit area.

The extreme variation in barometric pressure recorded in the United States ranges from about 27.40 inches to 31.50 inches of mercury at sea level. The normal variation, of course, is much less. Barometric pressure is now reported and shown on weather maps in terms of millibars, one inch of mercury being equal to 33.86 millibars. Thus the pressure at a given time and place may be expressed either as 29.92 inches of mercury or as 1013.2 millibars.

STATION PRESSURE AND SEA LEVEL PRESSURE. The pilot must understand that when he is given a station pressure in a weather report, the pressure given is reduced to its sea level value. He thus has a pressure reading that indicates a relative value, i.e., whether the pressure is standard, or above standard.

He can then cope with corrections or adjustments to his pressure instruments and conclude what effect, if any, the reported pressure may have on the flight characteristics of his aircraft.

INCHES OF MERCURY ("HG.) AND MILLIBARS (MBS.). Atmospheric pressure, as already indicated, is measured in terms of inches of mercury and/or millibars. The following conversion table (approximate) may be used for all practical purposes:

Sea level standard pressure at 59° F. is 29.92 inches of mercury or 1013.2 millibars.

    30" Hg. = 1,000 mbs.

     1" Hg. = 1,000 feet change in altitude

     1" Hg. =   34 mbs.

     1 mb. =   30 feet

ALTIMETER SETTINGS. Though altimeter settings are available at controlled airports and enroute to destination, a knowledge of correcting altimeters by the above conversion is very valuable when altimeter settings are not available. A typical problem follows:

A pilot departs from an airport (elevation 4,500 feet) which has an altimeter setting of 29.70. The altimeter reads 4,500 feet. He flies to and lands at a sea level airport that is broadcasting an altimeter setting of 30.20. The pilot, however, fails to reset his altimeter prior to landing. After "rolling out" on the runway he glances at his altimeter and finds it to read approximately: (1) 500 feet below zero (2) zero (3) 500 feet (4) 1,000 feet. The answer of course, is (1) 500 feet below zero. He arrives at his answer by the following solution:

The pilot has descended from the departure airport (4,500

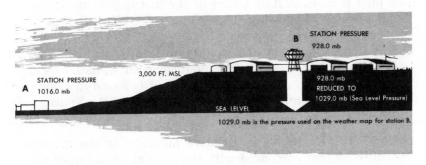

Reducing station pressure to mean sea level pressure.

29.7   4500'

30.2 = 0

x .5 = 5000

-500

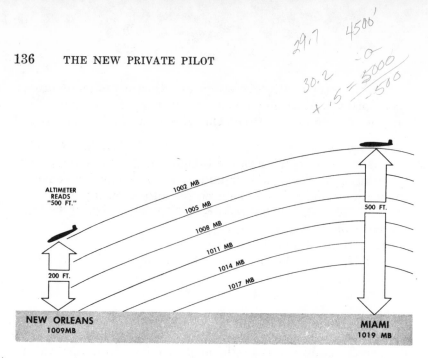

Altimeter error due to change in surface pressure.

feet) to destination airport (0 feet or sea level). The altimeter settings (pressure reduced to sea level) vary from 29.70″ Hg. at departure to 30.20″ Hg. at arrival, a difference of plus (+) .5″ Hg. Higher atmospheric pressure indicates a lower altimeter reading (.5″ Hg. equals 500 feet). Thus, his altimeter at destination airport will read 500 feet lower than he actually is.

MOISTURE

Moisture is the third major element having an important part in the creation of weather condtions. To a certain extent, the pilot is more acutely aware of the moisture element than of temperature and pressure. This is due to the effect that moisture has on ground and flight visibility.

Water exists in the atmosphere in three states: solid, liquid, and gaseous. As a solid it takes the form of snow, hail, ice-crystal clouds, and ice-crystal fogs. As a liquid it is found in clouds and fog, which are composed of minute water droplets, and as rain. In the gaseous state it is known as vapor.

RELATIVE HUMIDITY. Relative humidity is the amount of moisture content compared with the amount of moisture the air could contain if saturated at that temperature, and is expressed as a percentage.

DEW POINT. Knowledge of the moisture content of the air is of extreme importance to forecasters, pilots, and others in anticipating the formation of fog, thunderstorms, cloudiness, etc. In airway weather reports such information is contained in an element known as *dew point*. The dew point is that temperature to which a given mixed volume of air and vapor must be reduced before saturation occurs, resulting, after further reduction of temperature, in the condensation of some of the moisture in the form of dew, fog, frost, clouds or precipitation. If the dew point and temperature readings as given to the pilot show a gradual coming together, he may expect fog or precipitation in some form. If the readings show a temperature of 34° F. and the dew point 33° F., the pilot could expect fog or precipitation, in some form, and *icing conditions*.

CLOUDS

Clouds are a direct expression of the physical processes taking place in the atmosphere. An accurate description of both type and amount plays an important part in analysis of the weather and in forecasting. If the pilot can properly interpret the meaning of clouds he will be able to avoid the types which are dangerous to the flight of aircraft.

The ability to identify clouds and familiarity with weather associated with various types of cloud formations cannot be overemphasized as this is the pilot's most direct method of "knowing the weather" that lies in his flight path.

Clouds are classified in two basic families: layer type or stratus (stratiform) and vertical type or cumulus (cumuliform). These are divided into four groups depending upon their mean altitude. The four groups are:
1. *Low Clouds*   (mean upper level 6,500 feet
                   mean lower level close to surface)
    a. Stratus: Low uniform sheet cloud (St)
    b. Stratocumulus: Globular masses or rolls (Sc)
2. *Middle Clouds*   (mean upper level 20,000 feet
                   mean lower level 6,500 feet)
    a. Altostratus: Medium high uniform sheet cloud (As)

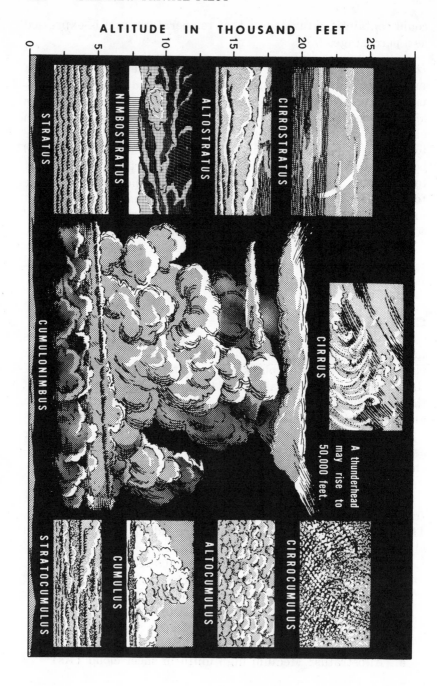

ALTITUDE IN THOUSAND FEET

   b. Nimbostratus: Amorphous and rainy layer (Ns)

   c. Altocumulus: Sheep-back-like cloud (Ac)

3. *High Clouds*   (mean lower level 20,000 feet)

   a. Cirrus: Thin feather-like clouds (Ci)

   b. Cirrostratus: Very thin high sheet cloud (Cs)

   c. Cirrocumulus: Thin clouds, cotton or flake - like (Cc)

4. *Clouds of Vertical Development* (mean upper level that of cirrus, mean lower level to the surface)

   a. Cumulus: Dense dome-shaped puffy looking cloud (Cu)

   b. Towering or Swelling Cumulus: cumulus of vertical development (Cu)

   c. Cumulonimbus (Thunderstorm, Thunderhead): Cauliflower towering clouds with cirrus veil on top (anvil-top) (Cb)

WINDS AND GENERAL CIRCULATION

Wind is the flow of air. The movement may be vertical, horizontal, or both. Vertical and horizontal motions of air affect the flight of aircraft. In addition, these air motions bring about changes in flying weather because they affect the distribution of pressure, temperature, moisture, and other factors.

For purposes of identification, wind is the horizontal, or nearly horizontal, natural movement of air; that is, air naturally in horizontal motion with any degree of velocity. Vertical move-

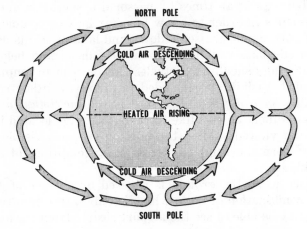

Paths which air currents would follow if the earth did not rotate.

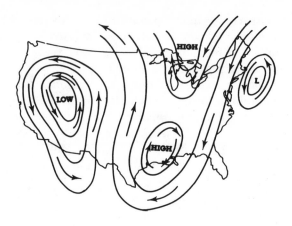

Wind flow around high and low pressure areas.

ments of air are not considered wind, but as air currents convective in nature. They are better known to pilots as updrafts and downdrafts.

VISIBILITY

Prevailing visibility is extremely important to a pilot at all times during operation on the ground or in the air. It is a factor he must live with at all times by personal observation and from weather reports in order to know how far he will be able to see during takeoff, climb, cruise, letdown and landing at his destination. With adequate visibility, landmarks ahead and below can be easily distinguished and obstacles can be seen in ample time to be avoided. Visibility is included in airway weather reports.

Visibility *in a definite direction* is the *maximum distance* to which prominent objects like trees, houses, etc., located in that direction and viewed against the horizon sky, are visible to an observer of normal eyesight under existing conditions of atmosphere, light, etc.

At times when the ground is covered by a layer of fog or haze, or a combination of both, which is only a few hundred feet deep, you may be able to see the airport clearly from the aircraft as it passes over the field. However, the observer on the ground may only be able to see objects at a distance of a few hundred feet, and reports low visibility. You may, on occasion, feel that a safe landing can be effected. Caution under these conditions must be observed because upon entering the fog or haze layer on the approach glide your visibility may be reduced to the danger point. The visibility during the final glide will be the same as that reported by the ground observer and a landing should not be attempted when the visibility is below safe limits.

VFR AND IFR VISIBILITY. Pilots must be aware at all times of visibility restrictions, as this condition in itself may determine whether a flight can be made under VFR or IFR. When determined under which rules the flight must be made the flight plan is completed and strict adherence must be made. If prevailing conditions change, the pilot may request, and be given, permission to deviate from the original flight plan. Flights made under conditions of IFR require that the pilots in command possess a valid Instrument Rating.

OBSTRUCTIONS TO VISIBILITY. The chief offenders in reducing visibility are fog, haze, smoke, blowing dust, blowing sand and most types of precipitation. Pilots flying in and around large industrial centers are hampered by reduced visibility, generally created by a combination of haze, fog and industrial smoke.

AIR MASSES

An *air mass* is defined as a widespread body of air which is approximately homogeneous in its horizontal extent. Air masses are classified or named in three different manners; first by the latitude of origination as "A" Arctic, "P" Polar, "T" Tropical, and "E" Equatorial; second by the type of surface over which they form as "c" Continental, or "m" Maritime; and third by the relative temperature of the air mass as compared to the surface over which it is passing, as "w" warmer than the surface, "k" colder than the surface. The complete designation of an air mass, then, will contain three classifications; i.e., a Maritime Polar air mass warmer than the surface over which it is passing would be designated by the following abbreviation: "mPw". Arctic and Equatorial air masses seldom reach the United States and the majority of the weather is concerned with the Tropical or Polar air masses.

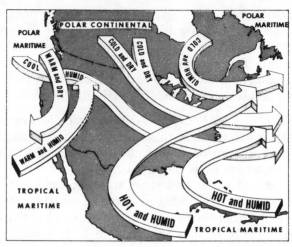

Paths of typical air masses crossing the U.S.

Polar continental air masses in winter are cold and dry, because having moved over land they have little moisture and low temperature. Polar maritime masses naturally take in moisture from the water. Tropical continental is the warm mass, drier because of land sources, while the tropical maritime takes on a greater amount of water vapor from the water over which it passes.

The region where the air mass attains its original characteristics is known as its source region. There are two general source regions, tropical and polar; and two types of surfaces from which the air may take its properties, continental and maritime.

FRONTS

When two air masses of different properties of temperature, dewpoint, etc., are brought into juxtaposition, a rather sharp boundary or discontinuity surface is formed between them. There is very little tendency for the two air masses to mix. This discontinuity surface is called a "front" and although it may be given different names, depending upon its direction of movement, it will always form with the colder, denser air underlying the warmer, less dense air. Because the atmosphere is continually in motion, this front will not be a horizontal one but will slope upward from the surface in such a manner that the colder air will underly the warmer air in the form of a long flat wedge.

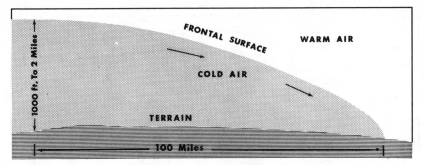

Cross-section of a front.

A front separating two air masses is named by the relative temperature of the air moving in behind the frontal surface. Thus, if the front is traveling in such a direction that the warmer of the two air masses is moving in behind the front, it is called a "warm" front. Likewise, if the colder of the two air masses is moving in behind the front, it is called a "cold" front. In either case, the frontal surface will be found to slope upward and over the cold air mass from the point where it intersects the surface of the earth. (The front as shown on a weather map is the intersection of the frontal surface and the surface of the earth.)

WARM FRONTS. These are fronts along which warmer air is displacing cold air. Since warm air will have a tendency to overrun the colder and more dense air near the surface, the slope of the warm front will be approximately one mile in height to 50 miles in breadth (1:50). The slope will vary to one mile in height to over 200 miles in breadth (1:200 plus). The gradual slope of the warm front may be taken advantage of by pilots seeking the best tail winds. The winds above and below the warm frontal surface usually vary considerably.

As the warm air moves gradually up the slope of the frontal surface, a broad prefrontal cloud system is formed. This prefrontal cloud system (usually of stratiform clouds when the warm air is stable) may extend as much as 1,000 miles ahead of the surface front in the form of high cirrus clouds. The progression of cloud forms will be in the following order. First in appearance will be the cirrus or cirroform clouds, then, as the frontal surface approaches the ground, alto-stratus, then stratus, and finally nimbo-stratus. With the arrival of the nimbo-stratus clouds the

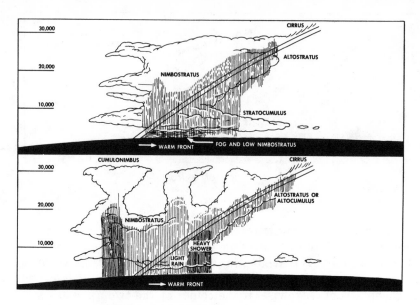

Cross-section of clouds in a warm front.

rain area reaches the ground, and precipitation is the steady, drizzly kind that would be expected to fall from stratiform clouds.

With the passage of the front, the clouds generally disappear, a wind shift is noticed, and there is an appreciable temperature rise.

In cases where the warm air is unstable, thunderstorm activity may be experienced over a wide area ahead of the front with scattered showers continuing after the passage of the front.

COLD FRONTS. In the case of a cold front where the colder air is displacing warm air, the coldest air will tend to underrun the warmer air, resulting in a more or less pronounced uplifting of the warm air. This comparatively rapid ascent of the warm air forms a deep, narrow cloud system generally of cumuliform clouds extending from the surface front up to possibly 300 miles to the rear. The cold front slope ranges from 1:50 to 1:150, being steeper than the warm slope.

In the case of a rapidly moving cold front, ground friction has a tendency to retard the surface air, thereby allowing the air at higher levels to become farther advanced. Under such conditions, a certain amount of the warm air is trapped near the

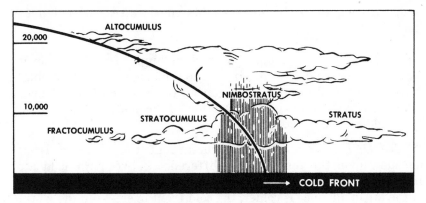

Cross-section of clouds in a cold front.

surface until it breaks through the wedge of cold air above it. Such a case of extreme instability will result in towering cumulonimbus clouds and widespread thunderstorm activity concentrated in a narrow band along the front.

STATIONARY FRONTS. Sometimes the opposing forces exerted by adjacent air masses of different densities are such that the frontal surfaces between them shows little or no movement. In such cases it is usually found that the surface winds tend to blow parallel to the front rather than against or away from it, as is the case with the cold and warm fronts. Since neither air mass is replacing the other, the front is referred to as a "stationary front." The weather conditions occurring in a stationary front are similar to those found within a warm front but are usually less intense. An annoying feature of the stationary front and its weather pattern is that it persists in one area for several days,

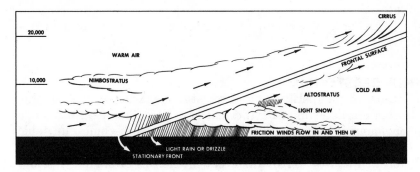

Cross-section of clouds in a stationary front.

and, in some cases, hampers flights in the area for extended periods at a time.

FRONTS ALOFT. A front is termed an "upper front" whenever there is a very cold layer of air next to the ground and the frontal activity takes place above the top of the very cold air. Upper fronts occur when the eastern portion of the continent is covered by a cold cP air mass.

OCCLUDED FRONTS. The structure of the occluded front depends upon the temperature difference between the cold air in advance of the system and cold air to the rear of the system. If the air in advance is colder, the cold front overtaking the warm front will move up over the colder air in the form of an upper cold front. In this case, most of the weather is in advance of the surface front. The surface front is called a warm-front occlusion.

When the air behind the system is the colder it will push in under the cool air in advance of the system and produce a cold-front occlusion. In this case most of the weather will occur near or behind the surface front.

FLYING THROUGH A FRONT. Following are some of the weather conditions the pilot may expect to encounter when flying through a front from the warm air to the cold air:

1.   Wind will shift in a distance of 25 to 50 miles.

2.   In a cold front, turbulence will be encountered in the frontal zone.

3.   Temperature will fall.

4.   Clouds will lower and a lower altitude will probably have to be flown to maintain visual reference.

5.   Precipitation, and possibly thunderstorms, will be encountered.

6.   Icing may occur in clouds or precipitation if the temperature is below freezing.

THUNDERSTORMS

Certain temperature and moisture characteristics of the atmosphere determine its thermal stability. Thunderstorms are phenomena which occur when an air mass becomes unstable to the point of violent overturning. They are formed in two different ways — (1) by different intensities of surface heating in adjacent regions (thermal type), or (2) by the overrunning

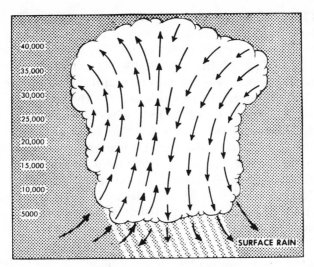

Circulation within a thunderstorm
in the mature stage.

and underrunning of warm, moist air by much colder air (mechanical type). A cold air mass, as previously explained, is retarded at the base due to surface friction, and much farther advanced above the surface. It is this condition that causes the forced ascent of air currents.

The thermal type thunderstorm is the most common and usually occurs on hot, sultry, calm days in summer. Local heating causes ascending air currents to rise into temperature areas favorable for the formation of cumulus clouds. These finally merge into a large black cloud, in some cases with a relatively flat or anvil cloud marking a warm layer through which the rising air cannot penetrate.

The mechanical type thunderstorm results from the interaction of a low and a high pressure area, i.e., the underrunning of warm, moist air by cold air. When cool, dry, and relatively heavy air brought by northwesterly winds replaces the warm, moist, and relatively light air, the lighter air is forced up to a level where condensation occurs. This type has characteristics similar to the thunderstorm or heat type but is much more dangerous to airmen. Instead of being isolated, it often forms along a line or series of storms with a definite line squall extending several hundred miles.

FLIGHT RULES IN THUNDERSTORM AREAS. To the pilot, regardless of the type and size of his aircraft, a thunderstorm presents a flying problem that cannot be disregarded or taken lightly. In view of the availability of weather observations and reports, a pilot should never permit his flight to become involved in thunderstorm conditions with the excuse that he did not know of its occurrence. In light aircraft the best policy is to fly entirely around the storm (if this is feasible), or land at a suitable airport until the disturbance has passed the area. In larger aircraft, the procedure presents a problem, the solution of which is entirely dependent on the particular conditions at hand. General rules which apply here: (1) fly around the disturbance, (2) fly below the disturbance, providing at least 3,000 feet above the highest terrain can be maintained, (3) fly "over the top" providing the service ceiling of the aircraft is considerably higher than the actual known top of the disturbance, or (4) land at a suitable airport until the disturbance has passed.

WINDS IN MOUNTAINOUS AREAS

Wind in blowing over a mountain ridge is forced aloft. On the leeward side of the ridge the air becomes turbulent with eddy currents which may cause the unwary pilot to lose several thousand feet in a very short time. Pilots flying upwind are in the greatest danger and thus should allow the greatest possible clearance. Pilots flying downwind will be carried upward with the wind as it is forced up the side of the mountain. This will have a tendency to carry them out of the danger area on the leeward side of the ridge.

Wind flow over a mountain.

FOG

Fog is composed of a multitude of minute water droplets suspended in the atmosphere. In a fog, these minute droplets are sufficiently numerous to scatter the light rays, and thus visibility is reduced.

Fog is formed at or near the surface when the air is cooled below its dew point (the temperature at which a given air becomes saturated with moisture). A general rule that all pilots should know and remember is: *When the temperature and dew point of a given air are within two degrees, fog may be expected within the hour.* Temperature and dew point relationship is noted on weather maps, teletype reports, and may be obtained by the pilot on the ground and in the air (via radio). Though a general rule, it serves the pilot well to be cautious when these two weather elements are in close proximity to each other.

Fog may be formed when the air travels over a surface that is colder than the air itself. This type of fog is called advection fog and is prominent at sea in the spring and summer, when warm air from the continents streams over the cold water. In winter, advection fog is most frequent inland when moist and warm air from the ocean invades cold continents.

Fog may also form in stagnant air after clear weather when the ground is cooled by outgoing radiation to such an extent that it cools the air below its dew point. This type of fog, which is called radiation fog, is most frequent in winter over level country and reaches its maximum about sunrise. Radiation fog, which forms overnight in calm air, is usually very shallow. Advection

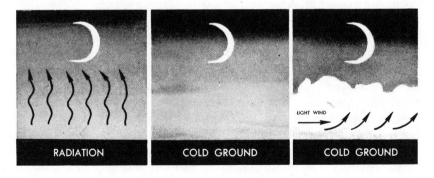

The development of radiation fog.

fog, which occurs in moderate or strong winds, is usually very deep and may persist for many hours.

Both kinds of fog have a tendency to lift or burn off during the day because of the diurnal heating and mixing of air. Radiation fog burns off shortly after sunrise.

ICE FORMATION ON AIRCRAFT

Icing is a major problem in aviation. It is difficult to forecast, because under apparently identical situations the icing intensity on the aircraft can vary considerably. The ice accretion rate may vary from less than one-half inch per hour to as high as one inch in a minute for brief periods. Experiments have shown that an ice deposit of one-half inch on the leading edge of some types of airfoil presently in use will reduce their lift by about 50%, increase the drag by an equal percentage, and greatly increase the stalling speed. Obviously, the consequences of ice accumulations can be very serious.

There are only two fundamental requisites for ice formation on an aircraft. First, the aircraft must be flying through visible water in the form of rain or cloud droplets, and second, when the liquid water droplets strike, their temperature, or the temperature of the airfoil surface, must be 32° F. or below. Water droplets cooled below 32° F. without freezing are called supercooled water droplets. They often exist in clouds when the temperature within the clouds is below 32° F.

CLEAR ICE (GLAZE). A transparent or translucent coating of ice which has a glassy surface appearance. When transparent, it looks like ordinary ice, and is identical with the "glaze" which forms on trees and other objects when freezing rain falls to the earth. It can be smooth or stippled. However, when mixed with snow, sleet, hail, etc., it may be rough, irregular, and whitish. It has an appearance different from that of rime, due to its different mode of formation and structure. It adheres very firmly to the surfaces upon which it forms, and is very difficult to remove. Glaze usually forms on the leading edges of wings, antennas, etc., more or less in the shape of a blunt nose, and spreads back tapering along the wings. When deposited as a result of freezing of super-cooled raindrops or large cloud droplets unmixed with solid precipitation, it can be quite smooth and approximately of a streamline form, although when mixed with solid

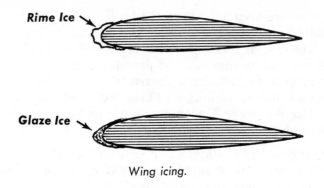

Wing icing.

precipitation, the deposit can become especially blunt-nosed and rough with heavy protuberances which build out across the normal streamlines of airflow.

RIME ICE. A white or milky, opaque, granular deposit of ice which accumulates on the leading edges of wings, antennas, etc., of an aircraft. Its surface is ordinarily rough. It has a granulated, crystalline or splintery structure. Rime usually accumulates on the leading edges of exposed parts and projects forward into the air stream. It usually builds outward from the leading edge into a sharp-nosed shape. Wherever the particles of supercooled water impinge on surface projections of the aircraft, like rivet heads, the deposit acquires the form of a bulge, which may cling rather firmly to the projecting parts.

THE EFFECTS OF ICE. When ice forms on an aircraft it can affect the flying characteristics in several ways:

1. Lift is decreased. This is caused by a change in airfoil

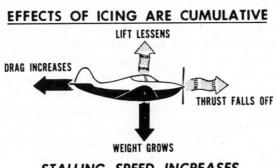

shape when ice accumulates on the leading edges. (The aircraft will stall at air speeds well above the normal stalling point.)

2. The drag is increased. This results when rough ice forms back of the leading edges and on protuberances.

3. Propeller efficiency is decreased. Uneven ice deposits on the blades cause vibration and blade distortion and consequent loss of effective power. Under icing conditions all available power may be needed.

GOOD OPERATING PRACTICES. 1. When flying in regions of possible icing condition, plan your flight so as to be in the region for the shortest possible time.

2. Caution should be exercised when flying through rain or wet snow with the temperature at flight levels near freezing.

3. When flying into clouds above the crest of ridges or mountains, maintain a clearance of 4,000 or 5,000 feet above the ridges if the temperature within the cloud is below freezing. Icing is more probable over the crest of ridges than over the adjacent valleys.

4. Watch for ice when flying through cumulus clouds with the temperature at flight level near freezing.

5. When ice has formed on the aircraft, avoid maneuvers that will increase the wing loading.

6. Remember that fuel consumption is greater when flying under icing conditions, due to increased drag and the additional power required.

7. Consult the latest forecasts for expected icing conditions.

CARBURETOR ICING. Carburetor icing is a possible cause of engine failure. The vaporization of fuel, combined with the expansion of air as it passes through the carburetor, causes a sudden cooling of the mixture. The temperature of air passing through the carburetor may drop as much as 60° F. within only a very few seconds. Water vapor is condensed out by this cooling and, if the temperature in the carburetor reaches 32° F. or below, the moisture will be deposited as frost or ice inside the carburetor passage. Even a slight accumulation of this deposit will reduce power and may lead to complete engine failure, particularly when the throttle is partly or fully closed.

On dry days, or when the temperature is well below freezing, the moisture in the air is not sufficient to cause trouble, but if

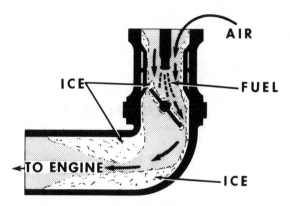

Carburetor icing.

the temperature is between approximately 20° and 70° F. with visible moisture or high humidity, carburetor ice should be expected. The carburetor heater is an anti-icing device which preheats the air before it reaches the carburetor, thus melting any ice or snow entering the intake and keeping the fuel mixture above the freezing point. The heater is usually adequate to prevent icing, but it will not always clear out ice which has already formed.

During prolonged glides with closed throttle the carburetor heater may not provide sufficient heat to prevent icing unless the throttle is opened periodically to keep the engine warm. Preheating of the air tends to reduce the power output of the engine and to increase the operating temperature. Therefore, it is considered good practice *not* to use the carburetor heater on warm, dry days (when the engine may overheat), nor on takeoff (when full power is required) unless weather conditions are such as to make the use of preheating desirable.

9. Weather maps, reports, and forecasts

WEATHER MAPS

THE DAILY weather maps used in aviation contain a tremendous amount of up-to-date information, mostly in the form of code numbers and pictorial symbols which the average private pilot can learn to read without much trouble at all. A brief study of these maps before takeoff on a cross-country flight is highly recommended. They provide both an overall picture of the weather in the United States and a detailed closeup of current and expected conditions along any given route. The meteorologist on duty is there to answer questions about the weather and to provide a forecast for anyone who wants one, but the pilot himself should also be able to interpret the weather maps if for no other reason than that the weather in its own way is as much a part of flying as the airport is. And there's a second very practical reason: the written examinations for all pilot ratings include questions based on weather map analysis.

Included as an insert with this manual is a typical daily surface map issued by the National Weather Service. The following discussion is based on the weather shown on this map.

Weather maps are issued four times daily, at 1:30 A.M. and P.M. and 7:30 A.M. and P.M., Eastern Standard Time. The data on the maps is collected by weather stations from all over the U.S. and sent to the central forecasting center in Washington, D.C., where a master map is compiled on the basis of the information received. Facsimile copies are then transmitted to local weather offices throughout the country.

To save space and simplify, the weather data from the reporting stations is coded in symbols and numbers and entered

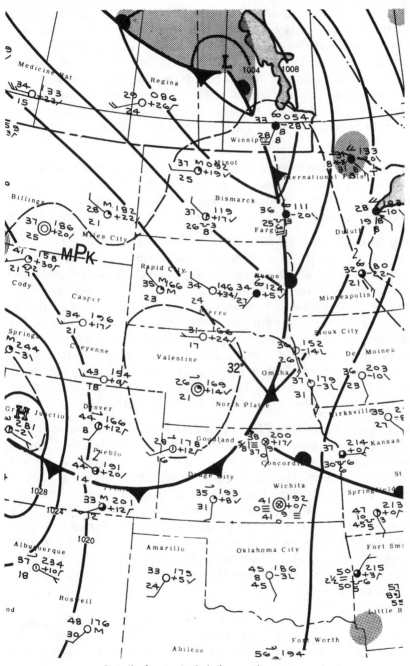

Detail of a typical daily weather map.

on the map around the circles which represent the particular stations. Each station is identified by name. In the lower left-hand corner of the main map is a sample station model, which is merely an enlargement and explanation of all the weather information contained in the coded reports on the map.

The main map offers a picture of the weather throughout the U.S. and parts of Canada and Mexico. The smaller maps contain specific weather data and are used in conjunction with the larger map.

WEATHER MAP FOR 1:00 P.M. This map shows the location of the high and low pressure areas, isobars (lines of equal barometric pressure), location of weather fronts and areas of rain or snow during the 12 hours preceding the time of the main map.

500-MILLIBAR CONSTANT PRESSURE CHART. This map shows the results of radiosonde observations made from high-flying balloons which carry weather-recording instruments and transmit the data back to ground stations. At sea level the standard atmospheric pressure is 1013.2 millibars, and with increasing altitude the standard pressure decreases. A pressure of 500 millibars is standard at about 18,000 feet. The continuous black lines on this chart represent the actual height in feet of the 500-millibar level during a one-hour period shortly preceding the time of the main map. The same map also shows temperatures and wind directions and velocities at these altitudes.

EXPLANATION OF THE WEATHER MAP. On the back side of the weather map is a complete explanation of the data shown on the face of the map proper. At first acquaintance the symbols and coded information may appear complicated but with a bit of study it becomes clear that there is a logical order and graphic plan for each group of symbols and their corresponding code numbers. As in a cross-word puzzle, all the information to supply the answers is there — it is necessary only to interpret it correctly. Read the explanatory material at the top of the sheet and refer to the maps to see how the codes and symbols are used in actual practice.

For example, a cold front is indicated by the symbol. The map shows a cold front extending from Wichita, Kan., northeastward to Ottawa, Canada. Front movement is in the direction of the triangular points. The paths followed by individual disturbances are called storm tracks, and are indicated by the symbols ⟶ ⊠⟶. The map shows such a storm track from Duluth, Minn., east and slightly north to a point northeast of Quebec. The low pressure cell (identified by the letter L northwest of Quebec) is considered the center of the storm area. Thus the arrows ⟶ ⟶ indicate its path and the ⊠ indicates its location at each six-hour interval prior to the current map.

The information on the back of the map entitled "Symbolic Form of Message" can be ignored here since the information is mainly of concern to weather station personnel. The sample coded message is the means by which map data is sent by tele-typewriter to the Weather Bureau offices.

THE STATION MODEL. The sample station model in the lower left-hand corner of the main weather map explains and identifies all data that can be entered on the map for any given reporting station. In studying the model and the detailed item-by-item explanation that follows here, refer also to a few of the actual

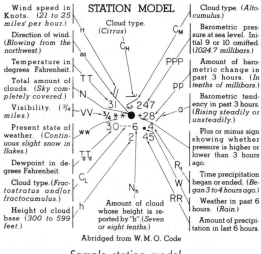

Sample station model.

station reports on the map for practice in interpreting the coded reports. The order of interpretation is, first, the station circle itself (sky coverage), and then counterclockwise around the station.

1. *Sky coverage.* The station circle is shaded to represent the amount of visible sky covered by clouds. See end of the arrow identified by the letter N and explained as "Total amount of clouds *(Sky completely covered)."* For other amounts of cloud cover see table 4 on rear side of map. Example: the main map, at Phoenix, Ariz., the sky is completely covered by clouds. At Abilene, Texas, according to table 4, the sky cover is between seven and eight-tenths.

2. *Wind direction and velocity.* The direction *from* which the surface wind is blowing (arrow dd) is indicated by a shaft extending from the station circle *into* the wind. These wind directions are given only to sixteen points of the compass. The direction of the shaft relative to true north (upward when reading a chart or map) indicates the true direction of the wind.

Wind velocities are coded in knots and plotted as feathers and half-feathers representing 10 and 5 knots, respectively, on the end of the shaft that indicates the wind direction. At the end of the arrow (ff) it states "Wind speed in knots, (21 to 25 miles per hour)." The wind speed here is converted into statute miles per hour. See table 6 on the back for other wind speed values.

Example: On the main map, Phoenix reports the wind from the east at 5 to 8 mph or 3 to 7 knots. Medford, Ore., reports a calm wind since there is no wind shaft and feathers but a double circle. See table 6 for explanation.

3. *Temperature.* The current temperature on the model is shown as 31. These are in degrees Fahrenheit, on the surface at the station. Example: The temperature at Cheyenne, Wyo., is 55° F.

4. *Visibility.* To left of the station circle, the value $\frac{3}{4}$ is the horizontal visibility in miles — in this case, $\frac{3}{4}$ of a mile. Example: Denver reports a visibility of 5 miles. When the visibility at a station is greater than 10 miles the actual visibility is omitted, as in the case of Portland, Ore., on the main map.

5. *Present state of the weather.* The two snowflake symbols ** to the left of the circle indicate continuous slight snow. There are distinctive symbols for all weather phenomena. You needn't memorize the complete list but you should be familiar with the more common ones shown in the accompanying illustration. (See also table 5 on the back of the map.) Example: Boise, Idaho, reports slight rain showers. Washington, D.C., reports haze.

Most commonly used weather symbols.

6. *Dewpoint.* The current dewpoint is shown as 30. This is expressed in degrees Fahrenheit. Dewpoint is the temperature at which a given air will become saturated with moisture. When the temperature and dewpoint are the same value at a given station, saturated air (fog) can be present. Example: The dewpoint at Bismarck, N.D., is 32° F. Since the temperature is 38° there is no indication of saturated air here. At Alma, Ga., the temperature and dewpoint are both 62°, and sure enough, there's fog at Alma, as indicated by the symbol for light fog at the left of the station circle. (See table 5 on the back of the map.)

7. *Cloud type (lower layer).* The low cloud symbol (in this case three dashes) is always located under the station circle. It is described at the end of arrow CL as fractostratus and/or fractocumulus. (See table 1 on the back of the map for low cloud symbols.)

Example: The low clouds at Reno, Nev., are Sc, or stratocumulus, not formed by spreading out of cumulus. (See column at extreme right of table 1.)

8. *Height of cloud base (from the surface of the station).* The 2 is a code figure for the height of the cloud base. At the end of arrow h you find "Height of cloud base (300 to 599 feet)." See table 3 rear side of map for explanation. Example: At Salt Lake City the code figure 5 is indicated. According to table 3, the height of the low cloud base at Salt Lake City is 2,000 to 3,499 feet above the station surface.

9. *Amount of cloud (lower layer only).* The 6 is code for the amount of low clouds covering the sky as observed from the station. At the end of arrow Nh is explained "Amount of cloud whose height is reported by h (seven or eight tenths)." See

table 4 for explanation. Note also the symbols, previously referred to, that indicate the *total* sky cover in the station circle. Example: At Cody, Wyo., the code 2 indicates a low cloud cover of two and three-tenths as shown in table 4.

10. *Amount of precipitation*. At the end of arrow RR this is explained as "Amount of precipitation in last 6 hours." The amount is given in hundredths of an inch, and thus .45 indicates that .45 hundredths of an inch of precipitation has fallen in the last 6 hours at this station. Example: At Little Rock, Ark., the .03 indicates that .03 of an inch of rain has fallen in the last 6 hours. At Miami, Fla., the T indicates only a *trace* of precipitation. (The shaded areas on the map indicate where precipitation is occurring at the time of observation.)

11. *Weather in past six hours*. At the end of arrow W read: "Weather in past 6 hours *(Rain)*." The black dot is the symbol for rain, as shown in table 8 on the back of the map. This is interpreted to mean that the past weather has consisted of rain, and the present weather (symbols to left of station circle) consists of continuous slight snow in flakes. Example: The past weather at Oklahoma City has consisted of a thunderstorm (see table 8 for thunderstorm symbol).

12. *Time precipitation began or ended*. The figure 4 at the end of arrow Rt is code for "Time precipitation began or ended" — in this case, three to four hours ago, as explained in table 2. Example: At Miami the code is 6, and since there is no indication of present weather, the 6 means that precipitation ended there five to six hours ago.

13. *Plus or minus sign indicating pressure change*. At the end of the arrow pointing to the plus sign read: "Plus or minus sign showing whether pressure is higher or lower than 3 hours ago." These signs indicate whether the pressure has risen or fallen in the past three hours. In general, rising pressure indicates better weather, falling pressure worse weather. Example: At Winslow, Ariz., the pressure has risen, and at Albuquerque, N.M., the pressure has fallen during the past three hours.

14. *Barometric tendency in past three hours*. This symbol (see table 7) indicates the general trend of the atmospheric pressure during the three-hour period preceding the time of the map. Example: At Jacksonville, Fla., the symbol indicates the pressure was steady or rising, then falling, during the past three hours. At Galveston, Tex., the pressure rose then steadied.

15. *Amount of barometric change in the past three hours.*
This is recorded in whole units and tenths of millibars. Thus,
the 28 at the end of arrow pp on the sample station model
indicates a change of 28 tenths, or 2.8 millibars, in the past three
hours. Example: At Portland, Ore., the pressure has changed
17 tenths or 1.7 millibars during the three-hour period preceding
the time of the map.

16. *Barometric pressure at sea level.* Arrow PPP points to
the figures 247 which indicates a barometric pressure of 1024.7
millibars. The initial 9 or 10 (as the case may be) is omitted.
In reading this pressure it is necessary to supply a decimal in
front of the last digit. Since the 9 or 10 is omitted, the pressure
as recorded could be either 924.7 or 1024.7 millibars. Normally,
however, the pressure seldom drops below 975 millibars or rises
above 1035 millibars. To supply the missing 9 or 10, use the one
which is closer to the standard sea level pressure of 1013.2 millibars. Example: The pressure at Casper, Wyo., is reported as
088. This would be interpreted as 1008.8 millibars. The alternate
interpretation of 908.8 millibars is obviously incorrect since it is
below the normal pressure range. Also, 1008.8 is much closer to
standard pressure than 908.8 millibars.

17. *Cloud type (middle layer).* The middle cloud symbol
(arrow CM) is located immediately above the station circle. The
symbol shown at the arrow point is explained at the end of the
arrow line CM as "Cloud type. *(Altocumulus)*." For other middle
cloud symbols and explanations see table 1 under column headed
CM (middle section of table). Example: At Spokane, Wash., the
middle clouds are Ac (Altocumulus) formed by the spreading
out of Cu (Cumulus). This symbol is number 6 in the column CM
in the table.

18. *Cloud type (high layer).* The high cloud symbol, shown
by the arrow CH, is located above the station circle at a higher
position than the middle cloud symbol. For high cloud symbols
and explanations see table 1 under column headed CH (right side
of table). Example: At Casper, Wyo., the high clouds are veils
of Cs (cirrostratus) covering the entire sky. This symbol is
number 7 in the column CH of the table.

19. *Missing data.* Whenever pertinent weather data is
omitted from the station circle it is indicated by the letter M.
There is no missing data in the sample station model. At Albuquerque, N.M., the M to the left of the station circle indicates

C_L	LOW CLOUDS Description (Abridged From I.M.O. Code)	C_M	MIDDLE CLOUDS Description (Abridged From I.M.O. Code)	C_H	HIGH CLOUDS Description (Abridged From I.M.O. Code)	Cloud Abbreviation
*	Cu with little vertical development and seemingly flattened.	*	Thin As (entire cloud layer semitransparent).	*	Filaments of Ci, scattered and not increasing.	St or Fs-Stratus or Fractostratus
*	Cu of considerable development, generally towering, with or without other Cu or Sc bases all at same level.	*	Thick As, or Ns.		Dense Ci in patches or twisted sheaves, usually not increasing.	Ci-Cirrus
*	Cb with tops lacking clear-cut outlines, but distinctly not cirriform or anvil-shaped, with or without Cu, Sc, or St.	*	Thin Ac; cloud elements not changing much and at a single level.	*	Ci, often anvil-shaped, derived from or associated with Cb.	Cs-Cirrostratus
	Sc formed by spreading out of Cu, Cu often present also.		Thin Ac in patches; cloud elements continually changing and/or occurring at more than one level.		Ci, often hook-shaped, gradually spreading over the sky and usually thickening as a whole.	Cc-Cirrocumulus
*	Sc not formed by spreading out of Cu.	*	Thin Ac in bands or in a layer gradually spreading over sky and usually thickening as a whole.		Ci and Cs, often in converging bands, or Cs alone; the continuous layer not reaching 45° altitude.	Ac-Altocumulus
*	St or Fs or both, but not Fs of bad weather.		Ac formed by the spreading out of Cu.		Ci and Cs, often in converging bands, or Cs alone, the continuous layer exceeding 45° altitude.	As-Altostratus
*	Fs and/or Fc of bad weather (scud) usually under As and Ns	*	Double-layered Ac or a thick layer of Ac, not increasing, or As and Ac both present at same or different levels.	*	Cs covering the entire sky.	Sc-Stratocumulus
	Cu and Sc (not formed by spreading out of Cu) with bases at different levels		Ac in the form of Cu-shaped tufts or Ac with turrets.		Cs not increasing and not covering entire sky; Ci and Cc may be present.	Ns-Nimbostratus
*	Cb having a clearly fibrous (cirriform) top, often anvil-shaped, with or without Cu, Sc, St, or scud.		Ac of a chaotic sky, usually at different levels; patches of dense Ci are usually present also.	*	Cc alone or Cc with some Ci or Cs, but the Cc being the main cirriform cloud present.	Cb-Cumulonimbus

* MOST COMMON - KNOW THEM.

Cloud symbols.

the dewpoint is missing or not reported. At Rock Springs, Wyo., the M immediately above the station circle indicates the type or description of the middle clouds is missing or not reported.

20. *Amount of data placed around the station circle.* The amount of weather data around the station circles depends on the extent of the conditions found by observation at the time of the map issuance. If there are no clouds, obscuration, etc., and the visibility is unlimited, the station map data will be at a minimum, as in the case of Roswell, N.M. If there are clouds, obscuration, poor visibility, precipitation, etc., there will be a maximum amount of station information on the map, as shown at Fort Worth.

READING THE STATION MODELS. Let's put in practice what you have learned in the art of reading station weather information. Referring to the main weather map, read *all* of the weather at the following stations. Don't hesitate to flip the map over, and use the tables when necessary.

Fresno, Calif., New Orleans, Miami, Pittsburgh, Portland, Wichita, Minneapolis, and Boise, Idaho.

You are probably pleasantly surprised now at the amount of weather map data you have learned. Try several other stations each time you have a few minutes to spare.

SURFACE WEATHER MAP ANALYSIS

After the station weather data is entered on the map, the meteorologist proceeds with the analysis of the information. The isobars, fronts, air masses, etc., are located and plotted on the map. Their identification is noted by standard symbols and abbreviations. Once the map is completed, the overall picture reveals a good deal more about the weather than is evident from a study of the separate station reports.

ISOBARS. These are heavy lines on the map drawn to connect points having the same sea level barometric pressure. Isobars outline the pressure system and aid in locating the areas of relatively high and low pressure. Note that on the main weather map the isobars in the north central section of the U.S. outline the high pressure area near Fargo, N.D. Note also that a low pressure area, identified by the letter L, is outlined near Las Vegas, Nev. Isobars show the pressure gradient in much the same way that contour lines on a navigation chart indicate the steepness or flatness of the terrain. The closer the isobars, the higher the wind speeds.

FRONTS. A front, as explained in Chapter 8, is the dividing line between two air masses of different temperature, moisture, density, and wind velocity. When two air masses of different characteristics come together they will not mix but instead remain separate entitities. Fronts are prominently shown on weather maps by heavy black lines with triangular or half-circle symbols aligned along either side of the line, as the case may be.

On the main weather map, the front line extending from Mexico northeastward to the Atlantic ocean can be easily identified by front symbols (see back of map, at top center, for front symbol legends). The section from Mexico north to El Paso is a cold front (triangular black symbols on the same side of the front line) at the surface. From here the front lies to the east and then runs sharply to the north to Oklahoma City. This is a stationary front at the surface (triangular and half-circle black symbols on alternate sides of the front line).

Continuing northeastward, the front runs just beyond Ottawa, Canada. This is a cold front as indicated by the black triangular symbols on the same side of the front line. From this point, one section of the front swings to the northwest ending at the L, which is the center of the low pressure area. The symbols on this section are triangles and half-circles on the same side of the front line. This identifies the short section as an occluded front.

From just north of Ottawa another front swings to the east and then curves to the south over the Atlantic. This is a warm front as indicated by the half-circle symbols on the same side of the front line.

Cold and warm fronts move in the direction the map symbols point to. The cold front in Mexico is moving to the east, and the warm front that extends into the Atlantic is moving to the north and east.

As an exercise, identify the fronts that run from western to eastern Canada at the top of the map.

FRONTOGENESIS. This is a condition in which the front is increasing in intensity or building up. It is indicated on the map by the word "Frontogenesis" placed along the affected front line. This condition does not appear on our particular reference map.

FRONTOLYSIS. A condition in which the front is decreasing in intensity or dissipating. It is indicated on the map by the word "Frontolysis" placed along the affected front line. This condition does not appear on the reference map.

PRECIPITATION AREAS. Areas on the map in which precipitation (rain, snow, drizzle) is occurring are shaded. Examples: Fort Worth, Wichita, and Boise, Idaho.

AIR MASSES. An air mass is a huge body of air having nearly the same characteristics of temperature, pressure, etc. They are classified according to the latitudes and the nature of the surface over which they form, and the relative temperature of the air and the surface over which they are moving. These various classifications, together with additional symbols denoting transition stages, etc., are shown on the back of the reference map at top center. Examples of air masses on the reference map: An mP air mass is shown south of Las Vegas, Nev. The m indicates it was formed over a maritime source (north Pacific) and the P indicates the air mass has moved southward from the Polar region. The cP air mass northeast of Duluth, Minn., has a continental source (Canada) and was formed in the Polar region.

ISOTHERMS. These are lines connecting all points of equal temperature, but are rarely included on the surface weather map. The freezing temperature isotherm is usually drawn on these maps as a line of dashes (— — —) with the word "freezing" at both ends. Note that a freezing isotherm is shown on the reference map and runs from central to eastern Canada.

SQUALL LINE. When a series of thunderstorms are occurring along a front or over the ridges of mountains they form a squall line. The squall is indicated on the weather map by a series of thunderstorm symbols at stations in the same general area. An example on the reference map is the series of thunderstorms along the front from Fort Worth to Oklahoma City. Note the thunderstorm symbols that appear at these stations.

STORM TRACKS. A storm track is clearly visible on the reference map, extending from Fargo, N.D., to the present low pressure center northeast of Quebec.

TELETYPE SEQUENCES

As a private pilot you should know how to read and understand hourly sequence reports. These reports are transmitted via teletype to all FSS weather briefing offices and also broadcast at 15 minutes past each hour by nearly all VOR stations with voice facility. An ability to read and interpret teletype reports enables you to understand the total weather picture. Moreover, you will be required to analyze several such reports in your FAA written examination.

Each hour on the hour, at several hundred stations across the country, observations are taken by personnel of the National Weather Service. The observations are transmitted to the National Meteorological Center near Washington, D.C., where the data from all reporting points are gathered, refined and then sent out to the FSS and Weather Service airport stations for dissemination to pilots.

The surface aviation weather report contains some or all of the following elements, in the same order:

(1) *Station designator.* Each reporting station is identified by a three-letter location identifier. The letters usually provide a clue but if you still can't identify the station the weather briefing personnel will gladly help.

(2) *Type and time of report.* There are two basic types of reports: (a) *recorded observations* taken on the hour, transmitted in sequenced series and identified by sequence numbers preceding the reports; and (b) *special reports* of observations taken when needed to report significant changes in the weather and identified by the letters *SP* following the station designator; any hourly surface weather reports transmitted out of sequence must carry the time and type of observation.

(3) *Sky condition and ceiling.* Sky cover symbols have been replaced by contractions in teletype weather reports but you may occasionally run across the old symbols in some outdated context. The first seven contractions in the accompanying sky cover table are used to report either clear skies or layers of clouds or obscuring phenomena aloft. A layer is defined as clouds or obscuring phenomena with the base at approximately the same level. Height of the base of a layer precedes the sky cover designator. Height is in hundreds

SUMMARY OF SKY COVER CONTRACTIONS

NEW CONTRAC- TION	FORMER SYMBOL	MEANING		SPOKEN
CLR	○	Clear (Less than 0.1 sky cover)		CLEAR
SCT	⦶	Scattered layer aloft (0.1 through 0.5 sky cover)		SCATTERED
BKN*	⦷	Broken layer aloft (0.6 through 0.9 sky cover)		BROKEN
OVC*	⊕	Overcast layer aloft (More than 0.9, or 1.0 sky cover)		OVERCAST
-SCT	-⦶	Thin scattered	At least 1/2 of the sky cover aloft is trans-	THIN SCATTERED
-BKN	-⦷	Thin broken	parent at and below the level of the layer	THIN BROKEN
-OVC	-⊕	Thin overcast	aloft.	THIN OVERCAST
X*	X*	Surface based obscuration (All of sky is hidden by surface based phenomena)		SKY OBSCURED
-X	-X	Surface based partial obscuration (0.1 or more, but not all, of sky is hidden by surface based pheno- mena)		SKY PARTIALLY OBSCURED
V		V preceding BKN or OVC indicates variable ceiling heights		

*This sky condition may constitute a ceiling layer.

of feet *above ground level (AGL)*. When more than one layer is reported, the layers are separated by a space after each of the contractions. A minus sign preceding *SCT, BKN,* or *OVC* indicates a thin layer. To be classified as "thin" a layer must be half or more transparent. When the sky is hidden by a surface-based phenomena such as precipitation, fog, dust or blowing snow, the symbols —× and × are used for partial and total obscuration respectively. When a

CEILING DESIGNATORS		
CODED	MEANING	SPOKEN
M	Measured. Determined by ceilometer or ceiling light or by the unobscured portion of a landmark protruding into ceiling layer.	MEASURED CEILING
R	Radar. Determined by cloud detection radar.	MEASURED CEILING
A	Aircraft. Reported by pilot of an aircraft.	PILOT REPORTS CEILING
B	Balloon. Determined by timing the ascent of a balloon into the ceiling layer.	BALLOON CEILING
E	Estimated. Determined by any method, but height may be too uncertain to be classified as M, A, B, or R.	ESTIMATED CEILING
W	Indefinite. Vertical visibility into a surface-based obscuration. Regardless of method of determination, vertical visibility is classified as an indefinite ceiling.	INDEFINITE CEILING

ceiling is indicated by any of the designators in the accompanying table, that ceiling is the height of the lowest layer of clouds or obscuring phenomena aloft reported as broken or overcast and not classified as thin. The ceiling also might be the vertical visibility into a surface-based obscuration that hides all the sky.

A ceiling designator always precedes the height of the ceiling layer. As shown in the table, the designator identifies the method by which the height was determined, or, in the instance of *W*, it indicates that the ceiling is vertical visibility into a total obscuration.

The sky cover and ceiling as determined from the ground observations represent as nearly as possible what the pilot will actually experience in flight. For example, a pilot flying above a reported broken ceiling layer should see less than half the ground surface below. The pilot descending through a surface-based total obscuration should first see the ground directly below his airplane from the height reported as vertical visibility into the obscuration.

The letter *V* appended to the ceiling height indicates variable ceiling; the range of this variance is shown in the remarks. Variable ceiling is reported only when it is critical to terminal operations.

(4) *Visibility*. Prevailing visibility at the reporting station, which follows sky and ceiling in the report, is the greatest distance objects can be seen and identified through at least 180° of the horizon. It is reported in statute miles and fractions. *V* is added when visibility varies, a condition reported only when it is critical to aircraft operations.

WEATHER DESIGNATORS			
CODED	SPOKEN	CODED	SPOKEN
TORNADO	TORNADO	ZL	FREEZING DRIZZLE
FUNNEL CLOUD	FUNNEL CLOUD	A	HAIL
WATERSPOUT	WATERSPOUT	IP	ICE PELLETS
T	THUNDERSTORM	IPW	ICE PELLET SHOWERS
T+	SEVERE THUNDERSTORM	S	SNOW
R	RAIN	SW	SNOW SHOWERS
RW	RAIN SHOWER	SP	SNOW PELLETS
L	DRIZZLE	SG	SNOW GRAINS
ZR	FREEZING RAIN	IC	ICE CRYSTALS

(5) *Weather and obstructions to vision*. The term *weather* as used in teletype sequences refers only to those conditions listed in the accompanying table of weather designators. Following the weather designator (if any), the intensity of precipitation is indicated like this: -- very light; - light; (no sign) moderate; + heavy. A severe thunderstorm (T+) is one in which the surface wind is 50 knots or more and/or hail is ¾″ or more in diameter. Obstructions to vision include the phenomena listed in the accompanying table.

OBSTRUCTIONS TO VISION			
CODED	SPOKEN	CODED	SPOKEN
BD	BLOWING DUST	F	FOG
BN	BLOWING SAND	GF	GROUND FOG
BS	BLOWING SNOW	H	HAZE
BY	BLOWING SPRAY	IF	ICE FOG
D	DUST	K	SMOKE

(6) *Sea level pressure.* Sea level pressure, separated from the preceding elements by a space, is transmitted as three digits, and given to the nearest tenth of a millibar with the decimal point omitted. Since the sea level pressure usually is greater than 960.0 millibars and less than 1050.0, the first 9 or 10 is omitted. To read the pressure, prefix a 9 or 10, whichever brings it closer to 1000.0 millibars. For example, at a station reporting 106 in its sequence the pressure would be 1010.6 millibars.

(7) *Temperature and dew point.* Temperature and dew point, stated in whole degrees Fahrenheit, are separated from the preceding elements by a space. Temperature and dew point themselves are separated by a slash. A minus sign precedes temperature or dew point when either is below 0°F. The spread between temperature and dew point is important: when it narrows to 3° or 4° you are likely to encounter fog or low stratus conditions.

(8) *Wind.* Wind follows dew point and is separated from it by a slash. Average wind direction and speed are given in four digits, the first two being the direction from which the wind is blowing. The direction is in tens of degrees referenced to true north. For example, 01 is 10°, 21 is 210°, 36 is 360°. The second two digits are speed in knots. A calm wind is reported as 0000. When gusts are present, a *G* follows the average speed, followed by the *peak* speed, both in knots. For example, 1522G37 indicates a wind from 150°, 22 knots, with gusts to 37 knots.

(9) *Altimeter setting.* The altimeter setting follows wind direction and speed, separated by a slash. The last three digits are transmitted with the decimal point omitted. To decode, prefix either a 2 or a 3, whichever brings the value closer to 30.00 inches. Since the normal range of altimeter settings is between 28.00 and 31.00 inches, decode as follows: If the sequence reads 996, you would simply add a two (29.96). If the sequence reads 013, you would add a 3 and read 30.13 inches.

(10) *Remarks.* Remarks, if any, follow the altimeter setting, and are usually separated from it by either an arrow or a slash. Remarks may include notices to airmen or other pertinent material for that station, such as runway visual range during periods of critical IFR weather.

Study the accompanying sample sequence reports and the interpretation of each.

SEQUENCE REPORTS (SA)

JFK M26OVC 4ØBKN 5 R-K 186/46/4Ø/3217/ØØ8

Interpretation

Station identifier: John F. Kennedy Airport.

Type and time of report: omitted since this is not a
special or out-of-sequence report. The omission identifies
this as a scheduled record observation for the hours specified in the sequence heading.

Sky Condition and ceiling: measured 2,600 feet overcast,
4,000 broken.

Visibility: 5 miles.

Weather and obstructions to vision: light rain, smoke.

Sea level pressure: 1018.6 millibars.

Temperature and dew point: temperature 46°F., dew point
40°F.

Wind: from 320° at 17 knots.

Altimeter setting: 30.08 inches of mercury.

ELP 12ØBKN 3ØØBKN 2Ø Ø9Ø/5Ø/27/151Ø/991

Interpretation

El Paso, 12,000 feet broken, 30,000 broken, visibility 20 miles,
pressure 1009.0 millibars, temperature 50°F., dew point 27°F.,
wind 150° at 10 knots, altimeter 29.91 inches of mercury.

LAX M42OVC 8 1Ø5/57/49/Ø9Ø6/984

Interpretation

Los Angeles International, measured 4,200 feet overcast, 8 miles
visibility, pressure 1010.5 millibars, temperature 57°F., dew
point 49°F., wind 090° at 6 knots, altimeter 29.84 inches of
mercury.

IN-FLIGHT WEATHER ADVISORIES

In-flight advisories are unscheduled forecasts to advise enroute aircraft of the development of potentially hazardous weather. They are also excellent aids in preflight planning and weather briefing. Ceiling heights are always above ground level (AGL). There are three types of advisories: (a) SIGMET, coded *WS,* (b) AIRMET, coded *WA,* and (c) continuous AIRMETs, coded *WAC.*

SIGMET (WS). Serves to advise all aircraft of potentially hazardous weather conditions, specifically: (a) tornadoes, (b) lines of thunder-

---

IN-FLIGHT WEATHER ADVISORIES

MKC WS 271645
271645Z-272100Z

SIGMET ALFA 2.   FLT PRCTN.   CHC MDT CAT 260-380 WYO NEB
PNHDL WRN SDAK ASSOCD WITH JTSTR.   CONT SIGMET BYD 21Z.

Interpretation

Kansas City SIGMET issued on the 27th at 1645Z, valid from 1645Z
on the 27th until 2100Z on the 27th.

SIGMET Alfa 2.   Flight precaution.   Chance of moderate clear air
turbulence between 26,000 and 38,000 feet Wyoming, Nebraska
Panhandle, western south Dakota, associated with jetstream.
Continuing beyond 2100Z.

MKC WA 271550
271550Z-272000Z

AIRMET BRAVO 4.   FLT PRCTN.   OVR PTNS SE SDAK NE AND CNTRL NEB
WRN KANS AND E CNTRL COLO CIGS FQTLY BLO 1 THSD FT VSBYS LCLLY
BLO 3 MI IN PCPN AND OR FOG WITH OCNL MDT ICG IN CLDS.   CONDS
IPVG SLOLY AND WL BCM LCL IFR BY 20Z.   CNL AIRMET AT 20Z.

Interpretation

Kansas City AIRMET issued on the 27th at 1500Z, valid from 1550Z
on the 27th until 2000Z on the 27th.

AIRMET Bravo 4.   Flight precaution.   Over portions of southeast
South Dakota and central Nebraska, western Kansas and eastern
central Colorado.   Ceilings frequently below 1 thousand feet with
visibilities locally below 3 miles in precipitation and/or fog
with occasional moderate icing in clouds.   Conditions slowly
improving and will become locally IFR by 2000Z.   AIRMET cancelled
at 2000Z.

storms (squall lines), (c) embedded thunderstorms, (d) hail ¾″ or greater in diameter, (e) severe and extreme turbulence, (f) severe icing, (g) widespread sandstorms/duststorms lowering visibilities to below 3 miles.

AIRMET (WA). Warns of weather that may be hazardous to single-engine and light aircraft and in some cases to other aircraft as well, specifically, (a) moderate icing, (b) moderate turbulence, (c) sustained winds of 30 knots or more at or within 2,000 feet of the surface, (d) onset of extensive areas of visibility below 3 miles and/or ceilings less than 1,000 feet, including mountain ridges and passes.

Continuous AIRMETs (WAC). Issues for (a) continued moderate turbulence over mountainous terrain, (b) continued ceilings below 1,000 feet and/or visibilities less than 3 miles over an extensive area.

Valid periods. The valid periods for AIRMETs and SIGMETs are specifically stated in the heading. WACs remain valid until cancelled.

Message identifier. Each in-flight advisory is identified by a phonetic identifier (Alfa, Bravo, Charlie, Etc.). Advisories for each hazardous area are numbered sequentially (Alfa 1, Alfa 2, etc., or Bravo 1, Bravo 2, etc.). When a new advisory of the same alphabetic series is issued by the same reporting station, all preceding advisories of the same series are automatically cancelled. For example, Alfa 2 would cancel Alfa 1, Bravo 3 would cancel Bravo 2, etc. However, a new issuance by one reporting station does not cancel an advisory issued by another station unless specifically stated. For instance, an Alfa 2 issued by Kansas City would *not* cancel Alfa 1 issued by Fort Worth.

WINDS ALOFT FORECASTS

During pre-flight planning you will want to refer to the winds and temperatures aloft forecasts (identified FD in teletype code), which provide the wind and temperature information you need to select the most efficient cruising altitudes. A typical FD is illustrated. The heading indicates the time of the data from which the forecast is composed, along with the times during which the FD is valid (1800-0300Z on the 16th day). Since temperatures above 24,000 feet are always negative, the minus signs are omitted above this level.

Forecast levels. The line labelled *FT* shows the nine standard FD levels for all wind aloft forecasts. Note that some lower-level wind and temperature data are omitted: winds at levels lower than 1,500 feet above the station are not forecast, nor are temperatures for the 3,000-foot level or for any level lower than 2,500 feet above the station.

WINDS/TEMPERATURES ALOFT REPORTS (FD)

```
FD WBC 151745
BASED ON 151200Z DATA
VALID 160000Z FOR USE 1800-0300Z.   TEMPS NEG ABV 24000
```

FT	3000	6000	9000	12000	18000	24000	30000	34000	39000
ALS			2420	2635-08	2535-18	2444-30	245945	246755	246862
AMA		2714	2725+00	2625-04	2531-15	2542-27	265842	256352	256762
DEN			2321-04	2532-08	2434-19	2441-31	235347	236056	236262
HLC		1707-01	2113-03	2219-07	2330-17	2435-30	244145	244854	245561
MKC	0507	2006+03	2215-01	2322-06	2338-17	2348-29	236143	237252	238160
STL	2113	2325+07	2332+02	2339-04	2356-16	2373-27	239440	730649	731960

Decoding. These forecasts are relatively simple to read. The four-digit group of numbers represents wind direction, referenced to true north, and wind speed. The first two digits are the direction, in tens of degrees, and the second two the speed in knots. For example, the forecast for 12,000 feet over Denver is a wind from 250° at 32 knots (2532). If the first digit is either a 5, 6, 7 or 8 you are alerted to the fact that the wind speed is greater than 100 knots. To decode, subtract 50 from the direction digits, and add 100 to the speed digits. For example, the STL forecast for 34,000 feet is coded 730649. Subtracting 50 from the direction digits (73) tells you that the wind direction is 230°. By adding 100 to the speed digits (06) you determine that at 34,000 feet the forecast wind is from 230°, speed 106 knots. The last two digits in the group—the temperature—should be read as −49°C. When the wind speed is forecast to be less than 5 knots the coded group is given as "9900" and should be read as light and variable.

Interpolating for intermediate levels. Sometimes it's necessary to determine the wind and temperature at an altitude other than the standard levels included in the FD forecasts. For example, assume your cruising altitude in the vicinity of HLC will be 7,500 feet. The HLC winds are given for the 6,000 and 9,000-foot levels in the forecast illustrated. Since 7,500 feet is half way between 6,000 and 9,000, the direction of the wind at 7,500 could be assumed to be 190° (210° at 9,000 − 170° at 6,000 = 40°; ½ of 40 = 20, and 20 + 170 = 190). By the same reasoning, the wind speed at 7,500 feet is determined to be 10 knots (13 knots at 9,000 feet − 7 knots at 6,000 = 6 knots; ½ of 6 = 3, and 3 + 7 = 10 knots). The forecast wind at 7,500 feet is therefore interpolated as 190°/10 knots. A glance at the forecast temperatures for 6,000 and 9,000 feet over HLC indicates a temperature of −2° at 7,500 feet. Ordinarily you can do this sort of interpolating by simple mental arithmetic, but it's advisable to work it out precisely on paper when taking your FAA written exams.

TERMINAL FORECASTS

Scheduled terminal forecasts (coded FT) covering a period of 24 hours are issued three times daily. The format is essentially the same as the hourly sequence. Each forecast is for a specific airport terminal, including the area within a five-mile radius of the runway complex.

TERMINAL FORECAST (FT)

```
FT 152140

DCA 152222 10SCT C18BKN 5SW-- 3415G25 OCNL C 8X1SW.

12Z C50OVC 3212G22.

BRF C20BKN 4SW. 16Z MVFR CIG BCMG VFR AFT 21Z.
```

Interpretation

FT 152140: Terminal forecast 15th day of month, transmitted at 2140Z (GMT).

Station identifier: DCA (Washington, D.C.)

Date and time: The forecast is valid for the 15th day of the month beginning at 2200 GMT (Z) and ending the next day at 2200 GMT.

Sky and ceiling: Each forecast cloud layer is separated from the layer above by a space after each contraction. A forecast ceiling or obscuration is indicated by *C*. The DCA forecast indicates a 1,000-foot scattered cloud layer with an 1,800-foot broken ceiling.

Visibility: In statute miles and fractions. This value is omitted when the visibility is forecast to be over 6 miles. In this forecast the visibility is 5 miles.

Weather and obstructions to vision: These elements use the same contractions as those in the hourly sequence reports and are entered only when expected. *SW--* following the visibility indicates very light snow showers.

Wind: 3415G25 means forecast wind from 340°/15 knots gusting to 25.

Remarks: OCNL C8X1SW means occasional ceiling 800 feet, sky obscured, visibility 1 mile in snow showers.

Expected changes: When changes are expected, the preceding conditions are followed by a period and the time and conditions of the expected changes. *12Z C50OVC 3212G22 BRF C20BKN 4SW. 16Z MVFR CIG BCMG VFR AFT 21Z.* This means that by 1200Z the ceiling will be 5,000 feet overcast, wind 320°/12 knots gusting to 22 knots. Briefly ceiling 2,000 feet broken, 4 miles visibility in snow showers. By 1600Z marginal VFR ceiling becoming VFR after 2100Z.

Both terminal and area forecasts use ceiling and visibility contractions as follows:

LIFR (low IFR): Ceiling less than 500 feet and/or visibility less than 1 mile.

IFR: Ceilings 500 to less than 1,000 feet and/or visibility 1 to less than 3 miles.

MVFR (marginal VFR): Ceiling 1,000 to 3,000 feet and/or visibility 3 to 5 miles inclusive.

VFR: Ceilings greater than 3,000 feet and visibility greater than 5 miles; includes clear sky.

These contractions are used for the outlook portions of the forecasts extending beyond 18 hours. They enable the forecaster to describe more realistically expected conditions in the outlook period, primarily for advanced flight planning. If winds or gusts of 25 knots or greater are forecast for the outlook period, the word *wind* is also included for all categories including VFR. Some examples:

LIFR CIG: low IFR owing to low ceilings.

IFR F: IFR owing to visibility restricted by fog.

MVFR CIG HK: Marginal VFR because both ceiling and visibility restricted by haze and smoke.

IFR CIG R WIND: IFR owing to both low ceiling and visibility restricted by rain; wind expected to be 25 knots or more.

AREA FORECASTS

Area forecasts, coded *FA,* cover conditions over several states. They are used mainly to determine enroute weather and the weather at those airports for which no terminal forecasts are issued. FA are scheduled every 12 hours, each covering an 18-hour period with an additional 12-hour outlook. All times are in GMT. Distances are in nautical miles, visibilities in statute miles.

AREA FORECAST (FA)

```
MIA FA 200040
01Z FRI - 19Z FRI
OTLK 19Z FRI-072 SAT

FLA E OF 85 DEGS GA AND CSTL WTRS

HGTS ASL UNLESS NOTED

SYNOPSIS...STNRY HI PRES RDG NCAR CST EWD OVR ATLC.  E TO
SE FLO CONTG OVR FLA AND GA.

SIGCLDS AND WX...

NRN AND CNTRL GA.
40 SCT VRBL BKN LYRD TO 140.  AFT 07Z OCNL CIGS BLO 10
VSBYS BLO 5HK.  CONDS IMPVG BY 15Z TO CIGS ABV 15 VSBY
5HK.  OTLK.  VFR.

E CST SECS CNTRL SRN FLA AND ADJ CSTL WTRS.
GENLY 25 SCT VRBL BKN TOPS 100-120.  SCT SHWRS OVR WTRS
DRFTG WWD OCNLY MOVG ONSHR CSTL AREAS WITH CONDS LCLY CIG
25 BKN 2RW TOPS 180.  OTLK.  VFR.

SRN GA AND RMNDR FLA AND ADJ WTRS.
NO SIGCLD AND WX.  OTLK.  VFR.

ICG...LCL MDT IN TCU/RW.  FRZG LVL 110 N GA TO 140 S FLA.
```

Interpretation of the area forecast:

Heading: Miami is the reporting station, 20th day of the month, reporting at 0040 GMT, valid from 0100 to 1900 GMT Friday, with outlook for the period 1900 Friday to 0700 GMT Saturday.

Forecast area: Contractions identifying states and any adjacent waters. This sample FA covers Florida east of 85°, Georgia, and coastal waters.

Height statement: All heights above sea level (ASL) unless otherwise noted. In the FA sample, for *NRN AND CNTRL GA* the forecast is *40 SCT VRBL BKN LYRD TO 140,* meaning 4,000 feet scattered, variable to broken clouds layered to 14,000 feet (ASL). This in turn means that terrain above 4,000 feet will be obscured by clouds. Both tops and bases of clouds are always ASL.

Height exception: FAs sometimes include heights above *ground* level, which is indicated in either of two ways: (1) ceiling by definition is above ground level; in the sample, *FA AFT 07Z OCNL CIGS BLO 10 VSBYS BLO 5HK* means that after 0700 GMT ceilings are expected below 1,000 feet (above ground level is here implied), with visibilities below 5 miles in haze and smoke; (2) alternatively, by including the abbreviation *AGL* (above ground level) after the height.

Synopsis: The synopsis briefly summarizes locations and movements of fronts, pressure systems, and circulation patterns. It also may indicate moisture and stability conditions. Interpreting the sample synopsis: Stationary high pressure ridge North Carolina coast eastward over Atlantic. East to southeast flow continuing over Florida and Georgia.

Significant clouds and weather (SIGCLDS AND WX): Significant, that is, to flight operations. Obstructions to vision are included when the forecast visibility is 6 miles or less. Expected precipitation and thunderstorms are always included. An outlook *(OTLK)* is included for each area. Example: *OTLK. VFR BCMG MVFR CIG F AFT 09Z,* meaning VFR weather becoming marginal VFR because of low ceiling and to visibility restricted by fog after 0900Z.

Icing: Coded *ICG,* with location, type and extent of expected icing. The freezing level in hundreds of feet ASL is included. The FA sample here is interpreted: Locally moderate icing in towering cumulus and rain showers. Freezing level at 11,000 feet in northern Georgia to 14,000 feet in southern Florida.

STUDYING THE WEATHER IN FLIGHT

If the pilot has adequately checked the weather prior to beginning a cross-country flight he will have in mind the sequence of weather changes he may expect to observe as his flight progresses. Since weather can and often does change rapidly, and since forecasts of the weather are sometimes not as accurate as the pilot and the meteorologist would like them to be, it is definitely to the pilot's advantage to acquire the habit of continually observing the weather about him, and to make mental comparisons between that which he sees and that which he had expected. In this way he will be making a running check of the weather and thereby be better able to evaluate any important deviations from the expected weather. He will be better able to analyze what is happening and to what extent these weather changes will affect his flight.

Clouds are excellent aerial signposts for the pilot who is checking the weather as he flies. For example, the location of localized convective air currents may be plainly marked by cumulus clouds since convection is usually the cause of this type of cloud. Heavy cumulus having sharply defined outlines are usually growing clouds, indicating

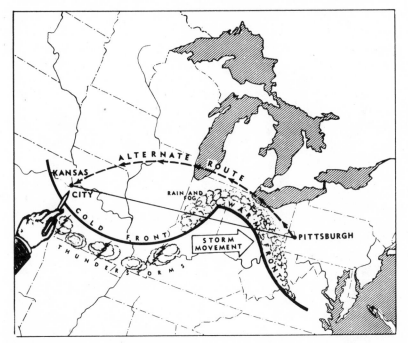

Weather reports and forecasts help the pilot to plan an alternate course around bad weather.

that their tops may still be rising and that they may in time grow into cumulonimbus, the thunderstorm cloud. Well-defined stratocumulus clouds usually have bases high enough for VFR flight below, except in mountainous country where they become banked against the ridges or hills. Clouds appearing to have twisting or turning motions are almost invariably associated with heavy turbulence.

Watching the visibility trends can be equally helpful. It is not unusual to find a reduction in visibility in the vicinity of industrial areas because of the smoke and other impurities that are released into the atmosphere. While these localized conditions can seriously reduce the in-flight visibility, they are not in themselves forerunners of further deterioration of the weather. On the other hand, a reduction in visibility due to fog or precipitation can be very significant.

Scattered thunderstorms along the flight route are usually circum-navigable, but pilots should learn to distinguish them from the almost solid lines of thunderstorms known as squall lines.

10. Cross-country navigation

N AVIGATION is one of the most enjoyable aspects of private flying. There is probably no need to emphasize its importance in safely getting an aircraft from A to B, regardless of whether B is 15 or 1,500 miles away. It is basically a skill — a skill which you must develop and improve from the very beginning of pilot training. At first it may all seem rather obscure to you, but you will probably be surprised at how quickly you pick up the fundamentals.

Your first acquaintance with navigation will come on your first flight. The problem will be a simple one — something so simple as learning to identify your home airport from the air. From that you will go on to such problems as finding your way back to the airport after training maneuvers a few miles away. These may seem like pretty elementary problems, but they are the first steps in learning to navigate by *pilotage,* that is, locating your position by reference to features on the ground.

Pilotage is only one of the four main types of air navigation, but it is the one most widely used in private flying — by far. Of course pilotage requires good visibility so that man-made objects and terrain features can be seen and identified. Unless you are intimately familiar with the area over which you are flying, it also requires an up-to-date air navigation chart, which uses symbols to show landmarks and topography.

The three other methods of navigation are dead reckoning, radio and electronic navigation, and celestial navigation.

Dead reckoning is the determination of position by advancing a previous position on the basis of speed, time, and direction. When you plot your course on a chart, establish a heading to fly, and estimate the time it will take you to get from departure to destination, you're using dead reckoning. When you establish

Pilotage — the identification of landmarks on the ground (left, a city; right, a rural area).

your groundspeed between two cities over which you fly, and then set an ETA (estimated time of arrival) for your destination, you're also using dead reckoning. The system requires an accurate record of time, speed, heading, distance, and fuel, and a means of multiplying and dividing the factors involved, either mathematically, or, more simply and quickly, with the aid of a mechanical computer. To a greater or less extent all other systems of navigation are dependent on dead reckoning.

Radio and electronic navigation is the determination of course or position by reference to radio transmitters on the ground and receivers in the aircraft. (There are some electronic navigation systems in which the transmitters are actually carried in the aircraft itself, but we shall not be concerned here with them or with other specialized systems such as loran, consol and Doppler.) Radio navigation makes instrument flying possible, but of course it can also be used to great advantage (and is) in good weather. Private pilots are expected to know at least the fundamentals of radio navigation.

Celestial navigation is the determination of position (and incidentally heading) by reference to the sun, stars, planets, and moon. It is used almost exclusively by navigators in transoceanic flying.

Still another specialized system of navigation is *pressure pattern flying*, which is actually not a method of position-finding at all but rather a means of obtaining a course which will result in the least flying time between departure point and destination. It combines dead reckoning with the measured difference between pressure and absolute altitudes, and in the technically correct sense can be used only in over-water flying.

For all practical purposes, private pilots need concern themselves only with pilotage, elementary dead reckoning, and the fundamentals of radio navigation. The latter was covered in Chapter 7. This chapter has to do with pilotage and dead reckoning.

THE EARTH'S SURFACE

Regardless of the kind of navigation a pilot uses, unless he is a space man he is travelling from one point to another over the earth's surface. The earth is not a true sphere, being slightly flattened at the poles, but for navigational purposes no significant errors are introduced if it is *considered* a true sphere. The navigation charts we use are simply flat representations of parts of the surface of this sphere. On these charts, north is always toward the top, south to the bottom, east to the right, and west to the left.

GREAT CIRCLES. If a plane were passed through the center of the earth, it would divide the earth into two equal halves. Regardless of the direction, the plane's intersection with the surface forms a great circle.

EQUATOR. Once each 24 hours the earth rotates around its axis, which intersects the surface at the true north and south poles. The equator divides the earth into equal halves, the northern and southern hemisphere.

LATITUDE. The equator is the base from which latitude is measured. Every point on the equator is exactly 90° from the poles, and any point located between the equator and the poles will be a certain number of degrees north or south of the equator. On navigation charts the parallels of latitude run east and west to the extreme edges of the chart. Degrees of latitude are numbered on the left and right sides of the chart and elsewhere on the chart proper. The lowest latitude is at the bottom of the chart and the highest latitude at the top. This of course applies to charts of the northern hemisphere. In the southern hemisphere the lowest latitude is at the top and the highest at the bottom. Each degree of latitude is divided into 60 minutes, and each

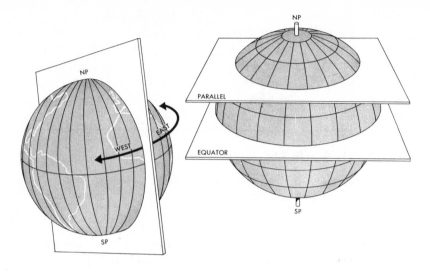

Longitude (left) is measured east and west of the Greenwich meridian. Latitude (right) is measured north and south of the equator.

minute of latitude (signified by the sign ′) is equal to one nautical mile. Each minute of latitude is divided into 60 seconds (″). Thus the exact statement of the latitude of a given point is expressed, for example, as 44°18′22″ North.

MERIDIANS. An imaginary plane passing through the center of the earth and through the north and south poles forms a great circle on the surface of the earth. This great circle is called a meridian. Every place on earth is located on a meridian, which also establishes true directions for that place since the meridians are also true north lines. Meridians run north and south on navigation charts. The primary purpose of meridians is to measure longitude (see below) and for that reason the degrees of longitude are numbered at the top and bottom edges of the charts. In the United States the longitude increases from the right side of the chart to the left.

LONGITUDE is the angle formed at the north pole between the Greenwich meridian and any other meridian. The meridian which passes through Greenwich, England, is the prime meridian (0 degrees) from which longitude is measured, both east and west to 180°. The prime meridian and its extension around the other side of the earth (the 180° meridian) divide the earth into western and eastern hemispheres. Longitude is therefore measured from 0 to 180° west and 0 to 180° east, depending upon whether it is east or west of the Greenwich meridian. The longitude of any point or place is equal to the angle formed by the Greenwich meridian and the meridian of the point or place. Each degree of longitude is divided into 60 minutes (60′) and each minute is divided into 60 seconds. Except along the equator, however, one minute of longitude, because of the convergence of the meridians toward the poles, is less than a nautical mile. It varies decreasingly in length from the equator northward to the poles. All meridians converge at the poles, and so of course one minute of longitude here has no length at all.

RELATION OF TIME AND LONGITUDE. The earth rotates through 360° every 24 hours, so that to an observer on earth the sun appears to move from east to west at the rate of 15° of longitude per hour. This allows a convenient division of the earth into 24 standard time zones, each roughly 15° of longitude wide. In the U.S. there are four time zones — Eastern, Central, Mountain, and Pacific. You won't have any trouble converting time from one zone to another if you remember that the sun appears to travel from east to west, and therefore any place to the east will have any given time earlier.

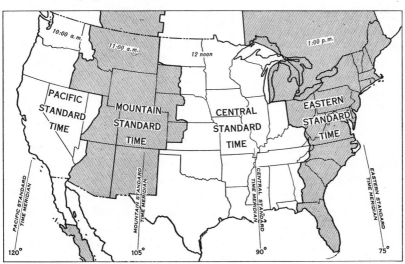

Standard time zones in the U. S.

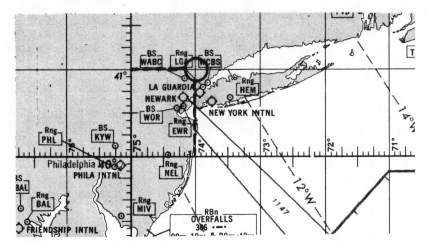

Locating New York's approximate position on a chart.

LOCATING POSITIONS. To locate any point on a chart by reference to geographical coordinates, it is necessary to know both the latitude and longitude of that point. Longitude is the east-west measurement, latitude the north-south measurement. A given longitude and a given latitude can intersect at only one point on the earth's surface, and conversely any given point can have only one value of longitude and latitude. New York City, for example, is located at *approximately* 41° north latitude, 74° west longitude. To find this position on a Sectional aeronautical chart, locate at the side of the chart the parallel of latitude marked 41°, and follow it across to the point where it intersects the meridian of longitude marked 74°. Actually this is a point in New Jersey across the Hudson River from the northern suburbs of New York City, but for most practical purposes whole degrees of longitude are enough to locate a large and prominent metropolitan area.

NAUTICAL AND STATUTE MILES. One of the first and most important lessons in navigation is learning how to measure distances on charts. An error in determining the distance between two points can result in a miscalculation in the amount of fuel required for a given flight with a possible forced or unscheduled landing. The standard unit of distance measurement in private flying is the statute mile. The airlines and the military services, on the other hand, work almost exclusively with nautical miles. Nearly all navigation charts, however, contain scales graduated

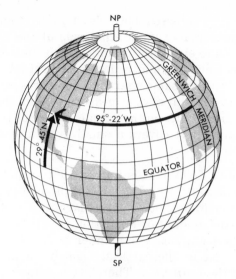

Locating Houston on a world globe.

in both statute and nautical miles, and most private pilots prefer the statute mile since this is the unit of measurement with which they are most familiar. Either unit is permissible in flight plans and position reports within the U.S.

The statute mile is 5,280 feet long, as compared to 6,080 feet for the nautical mile. Since the nautical mile is longer than the statute mile, there will be fewer nautical than statute miles in a given distance. To convert from statute to nautical miles, or vice versa, these formulas can be solved arithmetically:

$$\text{Nautical miles} = \frac{\text{Statute miles}}{1.15}$$

$$\text{Statute miles} = \text{nautical miles} \times 1.15.$$

All navigation computers contain a statute-nautical-mile conversion scale which is much simpler and faster to use than the formulas.

CHARTS AND CHART READING

First, what's the difference between a map and a chart? A map is considered to be any representation of the earth's surface, usually (but not always) on a flat piece of paper, while a chart is simply a map intended primarily for navigation.

The scale is expressed both fractionally and in terms of miles to the inch. For example, the scale of the Sectional chart series is one inch to eight statute miles. This means that one inch on the chart is equal to eight miles on the actual surface of the earth. The scale of the same chart is also expressed as 1:500,000. This means that one unit of any measurement on the chart equals 500,000 of the same units on the actual surface of the earth.

A large-scale chart covers a small area, a small-scale chart covers a large area.

CHART PROJECTIONS. It is impossible to represent perfectly the curved surface of the earth on a flat piece of paper. A certain distortion is inevitable, but on the large-scale charts used in private flying the amount of distortion is very small and the resulting error is negligible. The manner in which the features on the curved surface of the earth are shown on the flat piece of paper is called the *projection*. There are a number of projections used in aeronautical charts but the most common one by far is the Lambert conformal. The Lambert projection can be considered as a cone placed over the earth, with the axis of the cone coinciding with the axis of the earth. The cone intersects the earth along two selected parallels of latitude — in the U.S., for example, at 33° N. and 45° N. The meridians appear as straight lines which converge toward a point beyond the top of the chart in the northern hemisphere. The parallels appear as concentric circles with a common center at the point where the extended meridians would meet.

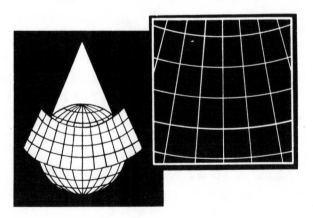

Lambert conformal chart projection.

Some of the advantages of the Lambert chart are:

1. Very little distortion, even in the areas most remote from the standard parallels.

2. A straight line drawn on a Lambert chart is very close to a great circle, which is the shortest course between any two points.

3. All courses and bearings measured on the chart are accurate.

4. The same distance scale can be used anywhere on the chart with no measurable error.

5. Adjoining charts of the same scale can be fitted together to form strips over relatively long distances with no appreciable error.

6. Since radio waves travel over the earth in a great circle path, radio bearings can be plotted without error on the Lambert chart as straight lines.

U.S. CHARTS. The principal air charts for VFR flying in the U.S., all published by the National Ocean Survey and sold over the counter at hundreds of shops and airports around the country, are Sectionals and World Air Charts (WAC's).

SECTIONALS. The contiguous 48 states are covered by 38 Sectionals on a scale of 1:500,000 (1 inch = 8 statute or 6.86 nautical miles). They show all important topographic details such as roads, railroads, populated areas and drainage, as well as radio aids. Alaska is covered by 15 Sectionals, the Hawaiian Islands by one.

WORLD AIR CHARTS cover the land areas of the world in a uniform series at a scale of 1:1,000,000 (1 inch = 16 statute or 13.7 nautical miles). For use mainly in moderate speed aircraft. Depict cities and towns, distinctive landmarks, railroads, airways, radio aids. Complete coverage of the contiguous states in 11 charts, Alaska in 8, Hawaii in one.

VFR TERMINAL AREA CHARTS (scaled 1/250,000 or 1 inch = 4 statute or 3.43 nautical miles) depict the airspace within the terminal control areas (TCA's) of major U.S. airports in considerable detail, with both radio and visual aids.

EL PASO

SECTIONAL AERONAUTICAL CHART
SCALE 1:500,000

Lambert Conformal Conic Projection Standard Parallels 25°20′ and 30°40′
Topographic data corrected to November

22 ND EDITION *February*
Includes airspace amendments effective *February*
and all other aeronautical data received by January
Consult appropriate NOTAMs and Flight Information
Publications for supplemental data and current information.
This chart will become *OBSOLETE FOR USE IN NAVIGATION* upon publication of
the next edition scheduled for *AUGUST*

PUBLISHED IN ACCORDANCE WITH INTER-AGENCY AIR CARTOGRAPHIC COMMITTEE
SPECIFICATIONS AND AGREEMENTS. APPROVED BY:
DEPARTMENT OF DEFENSE ★ FEDERAL AVIATION ADMINISTRATION ★ DEPARTMENT OF COMMERCE

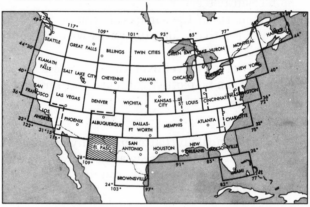

CONTOUR INTERVAL

500 feet

Intermediate contours shown at 250 feet

———500———   ———250———
Basic   Intermediate

HIGHEST TERRAIN elevation is
10180 feet
located at 28°15′N-107°36′W

Critical elevation - - - - - - - - - - - - - - •4254

Approximate elevation - - - - - - - - - - ×3200

Doubtful locations are indicated by omission
of the point locator (dot or "x")

——————— ATTENTION ———————
THIS CHART CONTAINS MAXIMUM ELEVATION FIGURES (MEF).
The Maximum Elevation Figures shown in quadrangles bounded by ticked
lines of latitude and longitude are represented in THOUSANDS and
HUNDREDS of feet above mean sea level. The MEF is based on
information available concerning the highest known feature in each
quadrangle,including terrain and obstructions (trees,towers,antennas,etc.).

Example: 12,500 feet **12⁵**

CONVERSION OF ELEVATIONS
FEET (Thousands)   0 2 4 6 8 10 12 14 16 18 20 22 24 26 28 30
METERS (Thousands) 0   1   2   3   4   5   6   7   8   9

Published at Washington, D.C.
U.S. Department of Commerce
National Oceanic and Atmospheric Administration
National Ocean Survey

CHART SYMBOLS & INTERPRETATION. A well-printed and carefully planned aeronautical chart is a remarkable piece of paper and one of the biggest values available considering the amount of graphic information it offers. It would take a book of at least 100 pages to provide the same amount of information contained on one 27 x 18-inch World Aeronautical Chart. The reason so much material can be compressed into such a small area is the use of standardized symbols. The shape, color, or size of many of these symbols suggest the features they represent. In order to derive the most value from aeronautical charts, a working knowledge of these symbols is called for. An interpretation or key to the symbols is printed on the reverse side, or in the margins, of nearly all charts.

USING CHARTS IN FLIGHT. Select the chart or charts to be used for the flight, and check the dates of issue to make certain they are current. If both departure point and destination are on the same chart, draw a straight pencil line connecting them and measure the true course. If two or more charts are required for the flight, use a small-scale planning chart of some sort for drawing in the course, and then transfer this course to the required flight charts.

Regardless of the size of the cockpit of the aircraft it is next to impossible to use charts properly unfolded and opened out. It is much simpler to fold them before takeoff in such a way that the course line falls along the center, with the top and bottom folds at least 50 or 60 miles on either side of the course.

Dead reckoning should always be used in conjunction with pilotage or flying by visual reference. Plot the expected position ahead of the current position, and then note the anticipated landmark on the chart and try to visualize it as it will appear from the air. Hold the chart so that you are looking ahead down the course line; that is, so that you bear the same directional relationship to the course line on the chart that the aircraft does to the actual flight path. Landmarks then appear in the same relative direction on both the chart and the earth's surface.

When the landmark becomes visible, observe it carefully and compare it closely with its symbols or representation on the chart. When you are over or abeam the landmark, note the time and write it on the chart alongside its symbol. If you fly directly

EL PASO

LEGEND

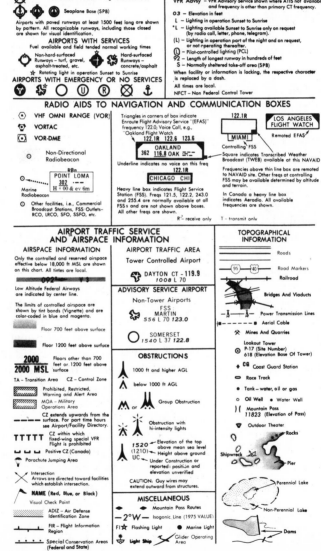

over the landmark you have a *pinpoint fix* at the moment when it is below the aircraft. If the landmark is to the left or right of course you can estimate your bearing and distance from it.

Estimating distance from the air is a minor skill that comes only with experience. In the first place, the altitude of the aircraft determines the distance at which objects or landmarks are visible. The higher the altitude the farther you can see, and consequently the shorter all distances will appear. The best way to acquire this skill is to measure on the chart the distance between two landmarks along the route, and then compare this known distance with the way it appears in reality.

NAVIGATION BY PILOTAGE

Pilotage in its simplest form is a means of navigating from one point to another by visual reference to landmarks or checkpoints on the ground. These may be railroad tracks, highways, cities, towns, rivers, mountains, shorelines, dams, racetracks, or any of the scores of other prominent features on the earth's surface which can be seen and identified from the air. All that's required for this basic kind of navigation is good visibility, an up-to-date chart, and an ability to organize your procedures in a systematic way. It sounds easy, and it actually is — if you don't try to fly in doubtful weather and if you plan your flight.

Experienced pilots place a lot of emphasis on pre-takeoff planning for a cross-country flight. Planning is, in fact, an integral part of cross-country flying, as you will see in the next few pages, which constitute a step-by-step guide to a flight by pilotage under VFR weather conditions.

(1) THE CHART. Obtain the latest edition of the chart that covers the area of your planned flight. An obsolete chart may contain information that is hazardous. Sectional charts, to repeat, are best for short and medium-range cross-country flights.

(2) PLOTTING THE COURSE. Lay the chart on a table or other flat surface, and draw a straight line from your point of departure to the destination (airport to airport). This can be done with a plain ruler or, better, with a navigation plotter such as the Weems Mark II. Mark off the distance in 10- or 20-mile intervals. Use a sharp pencil, making sure the line is straight

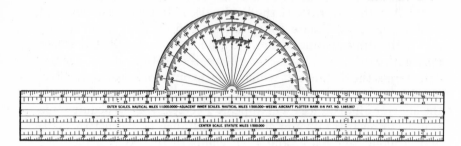

Mark II-N navigation plotter.

and that it intersects the center of the airport symbol. Make a careful study of the intervening country and decide whether to fly direct or whether a detour may be desirable in order to avoid flying over large bodies of water, mountains, or other hazardous terrain. Note whether landing fields are available enroute for refueling or use in case of an emergency. Using an appropriate groundspeed and the actual distance to destination, estimate your time enroute. You should know the range (in fuel hours) of the aircraft you intend to fly. From this you can determine whether or not you can make the flight without fueling stops. Be sure to allow at least a 45-minute reserve fuel supply at your destination or at any intermediate fueling stop.

(3) CHECKPOINTS. Now that you have established a definite course from departure to destination, study the terrain on the chart and choose suitable checkpoints. These can be distinctive patterns of railroad tracks or highways, sharp bends in rivers, race tracks, quarries, small lakes, etc. As your flight progresses, the checkpoints will be used to maintain the correct course and to estimate the groundspeed. Your checkpoints need not be on your direct line of flight, but should be near enough to be easily seen. For this part of the pre-flight planning it is essential that you know the chart symbols (explained on the back of the chart) in order to recognize the many landmarks available as checkpoints.

(4) ENCLOSING THE COURSE. This consists of using an easily recognizable feature on the terrain which lies parallel to

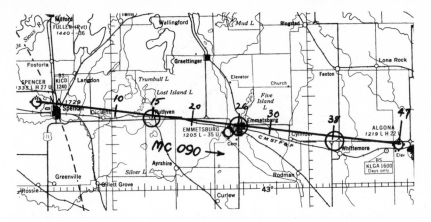

Plot the course and then select suitable checkpoints, indicating the distances from departure or to destination.

your course. It may serve as a guide line or bracket, and may be a river, railroad track, or a prominent highway. The ideal arrangement would be to have a continuous guide line on each side of the route five to 10 miles from the line of flight. It is seldom that two can be found, but one will usually serve satisfactorily. If you should temporarily lose your checkpoints, you can fly to this chosen guide line and reset course. Another landmark should be used as an end-of-course check to prevent flying beyond your destination should you miss it or actually fly directly over it.

(5) TRUE COURSE. Having plotted your course and made an accurate listing of checkpoints and the distances between them, measure the true course to find the number of degrees your true course will lie, counting clockwise from true north. Use the meridian (north-south) line approximately midway between departure and destination. Your true course can be measured with a common protractor, or better still with a navigation plotter such as the Weems Mark II.

For a number of reasons which will become apparent later, it's not likely that your aircraft will follow the precise true course between departure point and destination. A distinction is made therefore between *true course,* which is the direction of *intended* flight, and the *track,* which is the *actual* flight path of the aircraft over the ground. Like course, the track may be either true, magnetic, or compass track, depending upon whether

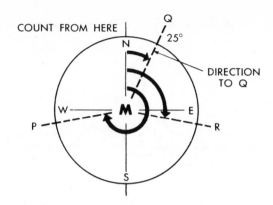

Measuring true course. The line N-M-S is a meridian pointing to the north and south geographical poles. The direction of Q from M is the angle from north clockwise to the line M-Q. The direction of Q is 25°, or, to put it another way, the true course between M and Q is 25°. The direction of R from M is 100°, and the direction of P from M is 260°.

or not magnetic variation and compass deviation have been applied. Most commonly, however, we work with true track since the winds aloft are stated in true directions and the difference between course and track is usually attributable to variations in wind direction or velocity.

(6) APPLYING VARIATION TO TRUE COURSE. The magnetic compasses used in aircraft refer all directions to *magnetic* north rather than to true north, which is the reference for directional measurement on the chart. At most places in the world, magnetic and true north do not coincide. This difference between magnetic and true north is called *variation,* and it is either westerly or easterly variation depending upon whether magnetic north lies to the west or to the east of true north. The amount of the magnetic variation at any locality is shown on all aeronautical charts by means of lines of equal variation known as isogonic lines. In the northeastern U. S. the variation is westerly (that is, the magnetic compass points west of true north) and in the rest of the country it is easterly (that is, the magnetic compass points east of true north). The dividing line between easterly and westerly variation is the agonic line, or line of no variation, where magnetic north and true north are the same.

Since we measure courses from a chart with reference to true north and then try to fly this course by means of a magnetic

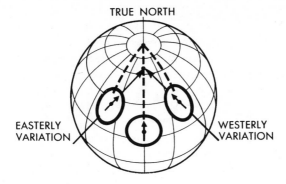

TRUE NORTH

EASTERLY
VARIATION

WESTERLY
VARIATION

Variation is the difference between true north and magnetic north.

compass, it is necessary to apply the variation to the true course to determine magnetic course. To convert a true course to magnetic course, *always add westerly variation, subtract easterly variation.* There is no exception to this rule, one of the single most important rules in navigation. To apply variation incorrectly is to court disaster.

$$\textit{True course} \underset{- \textit{ easterly variation}}{\overset{+ \textit{ westerly variation}}{\Big\langle}} \Big\rangle = \textit{magnetic course.}$$

Here are two sample problems in determining magnetic course:

1. You plan to fly from Airport A to Airport B. The true course is 130°. The variation as shown on the chart by the nearest isogonic line is 12° east (12° E). Applying the rule of subtracting easterly variation and adding westerly variation, the magnetic course is 130° — 12° = 118°.

2. Airport B to Airport C: true course = 285°, variation = 11° west, magnetic course = 296°.

(7) HEADINGS BETWEEN CHECKPOINTS. Assume that you have taken off on your flight, climbed to cruising altitude, and then arrived over your first checkpoint. Between this checkpoint and the second one, you should make allowance for the approximate drift of your aircraft due to the effect of the wind. In pilotage, correction for wind drift is made by noting whether or not your plane is drifting to the right or left of your intended true course. Should you note a right drift it will be necessary to correct to the left. The amount of correction will be determined

by the amount of observed drift and where you actually are in relation to your intended course. If you note an approximate 10° left drift after passing over your first checkpoint, it will be necessary to correct 10° to the right in order to remain on course. Drift of the airplane can be observed if you note landmarks such as a highway, railroad, or section lines which are approximately parallel to your course. In flying one of these lines the plane's drift to right or left can be determined roughly.

It is important that between the first and second checkpoints you have noted the reading on your compass. The compass (assuming no instrument error) should now read the sum of your true course, plus or minus variation, and plus or minus your wind correction angle. This is the magnetic heading, and should be maintained on your compass from one checkpoint to another so long as you remain on course.

Your computations for magnetic heading should be:
Airport A to Airport B:

True course	130°
Variation	12° E
Magnetic course	118°
Wind correction angle 10° Right	
Magnetic heading	128°

Thus, you have a magnetic heading from first to second checkpoint. You would hold this magnetic heading of 128° so long as you remain on course toward the next checkpoint.

In working out headings, several abbreviations are customarily used:

TC = true course.
WCA = wind correction angle.
TH = true heading.
Var. (or VAR) = magnetic variation.
MH = magnetic heading.
DEV (explained below) = compass deviation.

Summarizing the computations for heading:
Airport A to Airport B:

TC	130°
VAR.	12° E.
MC	118°
WCA	10° R.
MH	128°

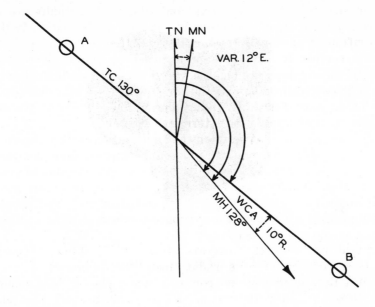

In actual practise it is customary to apply the wind correction angle to the true course before applying the variation. Thus:

TC	130°
WCA	10° R.
TH	140°
VAR.	12° E.
MH	128°

If your calculations are correct, if your estimate of the drift angle is close enough, and if you hold the magnetic heading of 128°, then you will actually make good the true course of 130° between Airports A and B. Remember that in correcting your compass for variation and wind effect you are simply setting up a compass reading calculated to keep you on your intended true course.

(8) COMPASS DEVIATION is technically defined as the angle between the magnetic meridian and the axis of a compass card, expressed in degrees east or west (in the same way that variation is) to indicate the direction in which the northern end of the compass is offset from magnetic north. Less technically, deviation is compass error. It is caused by a number of things, but mostly by instruments and equipment within the aircraft itself

Standard aircraft magnetic compass.

— metal parts of the aircraft structure, flashlights, cockpit heaters, electrical circuits, radios, metal tools, cigarette lighters. Even a Boy Scout's pocket compass, when placed close enough, can throw an aircraft compass off as much as 50°. The point is, however, that the error in a compass caused by the permanent equipment in an aircraft is not important if the amount of error is *known*. Some error can be removed by qualified instrument mechanics adjusting the compass magnets. This is called compass compensation. To determine the amount of error left after compensation, the compass can be "swung." The aircraft is

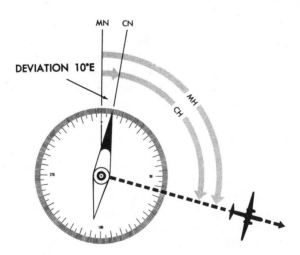

Deviation is the difference between magnetic north and compass north.

placed in straight and level flight attitude in the center of a large circle oriented exactly to magnetic north and usually painted on the ramp or parking apron of an airport. Sometimes the aircraft engine is started up and the radio equipment is turned on to simulate as closely as possible actual flight conditions. The aircraft is then turned within the circle until it is aligned with magnetic north, and the difference between the reading of the aircraft compass and 000* (magnetic north) is the deviation for that heading. The process is repeated every 30° around the compass rose. A record of the deviation is made on each of the 12 headings, and is then entered on a compass correction card which is placed near the compass installation in the cockpit for the pilot's reference.

Example: When aligned with magnetic north on the compass rose an aircraft's compass reads 005°. In other words, the compass reads 5° too high. The deviation is 5° *west,* since the compass indicates that compass north is 5° west of magnetic north, as shown by the compass rose. Obviously, then, in order to steer a heading of 000° or magnetic north with this aircraft, it will be necessary to add 5° to the magnetic heading.

To determine a compass heading or course, deviation is applied to the magnetic heading or course exactly the same way that variation is applied to the true heading or course — add westerly deviation, subtract easterly. In actual practise, however, the fact that deviation is westerly or easterly is usually ignored since most pilots prefer to use a compass correction card such as that shown in the illustration. On this particular card, for

FOR (MH)	0	30	60	90	120	150	180	210	240	270	300	330
STEER (CH)	0	29	58	86	115	146	179	212	244	276	304	332

Compass deviation card.

example, it is indicated that in order to hold a magnetic heading of 120° it is necessary to steer a compass heading of 115°. The deviation is 5° east, but the card presents the information to the pilot with the correction already made.

Note that no correction is given for a magnetic heading of 128° (the heading referred to in step No. 7 for your flight from

* In both air and marine navigation, headings are usually stated in three figures in order to avoid possible confusion with other angular measurements expressed in degrees, such as radio bearings, magnetic variation, and drift angle. Thus 005°, 067°, 225°, 318°.

Airport A to B). It does, however, list the deviation for 120°, which is the closest to your magnetic heading of 128°. If you use this same deviation and apply it to your magnetic heading you determine a compass heading of 123° (MH 128° –5°).

Thus far, since measuring the true course on the chart you have corrected it for wind drift angle, variation, and deviation, and arrived at a compass heading. As long as you hold this compass heading (and as long as the wind doesn't change) you will make good the true course between departure point and destination.

To return for a moment to the problem of deviation, suppose the deviation were westerly instead of easterly. In this case the compass correction card would read:

FOR MH   120

STEER CH   125

In the example from Airport A to B above, then, the compass heading would be 133° (MH 128° +5° westerly deviation = CH 133°).

The standard procedure for converting a true course into a compass heading takes the following form. As long as you fly you will be solving this basic navigation problem, and you should know the step-by-step process as well as you know your own age.

True course ± wind correction angle = true heading.

True heading ± variation = magnetic heading.

Magnetic heading ± deviation = compass heading.

Here are a few sample problems in determining compass heading from true course:

TC	WCA	TH	VAR.	MH	Dev.	CH
281°	5° R.	286°	4° E.	282°	5° W.	287°
015°	10° L.	005°	10° W.	015°	3° E.	012°
161°	0°	161°	15° E.	146°	2° E.	144°
324°	6° R.	330°	2° E.	328°	6° W.	334°
352°	2° L.	350°	12° W.	002°	5° E.	357°
085°	5° L.	080°	9° E.	071°	0°	071°

Remember that in the above problems you are working from left to right, from true course to compass heading. In all of these cases, westerly variation and deviation are always added, easterly variation and deviation subtracted. And the difference between true course and true heading is simply the wind correction angle. When the wind is calm (and there is no wind correction angle) course and heading are the same.

(9) COMPUTING GROUNDSPEED, ELAPSED TIME, AND FUEL CONSUMPTION. To obtain this information on your flight, it is necessary to know some facts about the airplane. The computations of course and headings to this point could apply to any airplane. Operating data for the mythical airplane is as follows:

> Type and description—Avion 85, two-place tandem, registration N1278H.
>
> Indicated airspeed—90 mph.
>
> Fuel octane—80.
>
> Fuel capacity—22 gallons.
>
> Fuel consumption—6 gallons per hour (6 gph).
>
> Oil capacity—6 quarts ($1\frac{1}{2}$ gallons), placed in engine crankcase.
>
> Range in flying hours—3.67 or 3 hours and 40 minutes (fuel capacity of 22 gallons divided by fuel consumption of 6 gallons per hour.)

You actually take off from Airport A at 1200 o'clock noon and climb to your cruising altitude of 5,000 feet above sea level (predetermined as a safe altitude over the particular terrain). Arriv-

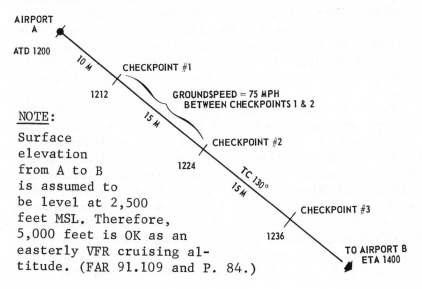

AIRPORT A

ATD 1200

10 M

CHECKPOINT #1

1212

GROUNDSPEED = 75 MPH
BETWEEN CHECKPOINTS 1 & 2

15 M

CHECKPOINT #2

1224

TC 130°

15 M

CHECKPOINT #3

1236

TO AIRPORT B
ETA 1400

NOTE:

Surface elevation from A to B is assumed to be level at 2,500 feet MSL. Therefore, 5,000 feet is OK as an easterly VFR cruising altitude. (FAR 91.109 and P. 84.)

ing over your first checkpoint (a distance of 10 miles on course from Airport A) you note the time of 1212 in your log. It has taken 12 minutes, from actual takeoff at Airport A, to climb to 5,000 feet altitude and arrive over your first checkpoint.

Flying toward your second checkpoint you immediately note a 10° wind drift to the left for which you correct 10° to the right. This correction, along with your calculations for a 12° E. variation and 5° E. deviation (as previously computed), places you on a compass heading of 123°.

Continuing toward your second checkpoint (a distance of 15 miles) with the compass reading 123°, you are aware that your true course of 130° is being made good, and the terrain over which you are flying matches the chart data as previously plotted and studied.

You arrive over your second checkpoint and note the time as 1224. It has taken you 12 minutes to fly the 15 miles between checkpoints. By simple mathematics (groundspeed equals distance divided by time flown), or by using your computer, you establish your groundspeed as 75 mph. Should the wind remain the same, you can now estimate your time of arrival over the third checkpoint (also a distance of 15 miles) as 12 minutes, or a clock time of 1236. Noting your estimated time of arrival (ETA) over the third checkpoint in your log, you now have a good basis for an ETA at destination, Airport B, which you had previously found to be 150 miles on course from point of departure.

With the groundspeed of 75 mph and the known distance to destination of 150 miles, you establish a total elapsed time of two hours to destination from your point of departure, and note in your log an ETA at Airport B of 1400 (1200 at A plus two hours enroute).

During pre-flight planning you roughly estimated the total time enroute from Airport A to B as 1:30. This was based on a true airspeed (TAS) of 99 mph and forecast winds directly off the wingtip which would result in neither headwind nor tailwind. The approximate true airspeed you determined by adding 2% of the indicated airspeed (IAS) for each thousand feet of altitude above sea level. The airplane operating manual showed that at your selected cruising altitude of 5,000 feet and with standard power setting the indicated airspeed would be 90 mph. Two percent for each 1,000 feet of altitude to 5,000 feet = 10%, and 10% of 90 mph IAS = 99 mph TAS. The distance from A to B is 150 miles. With a groundspeed of 99 mph (same as the TAS) the time in flight was therefore estimated to be approximately 1:30.

Now in flight, however, you have calculated your ground-speed between checkpoints as 75 mph. This means that you have a headwind component of 24 mph, and since you still have to crab the airplane to the right to stay on course it also means the wind is blowing from the right front quarter.

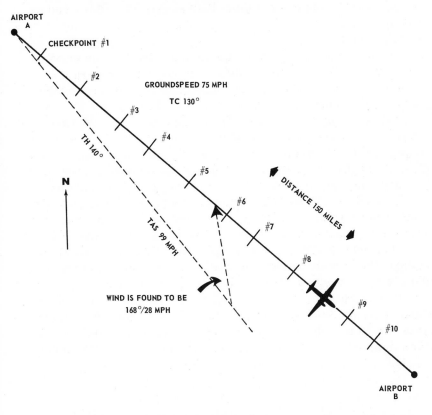

With the newly determined groundspeed of 75 mph you re-estimate your time in flight between A and B (150 miles) as two hours. However, you still don't have to revise your original plan to make the flight non-stop since the aircraft has a maximum fuel range of 3:40. Nevertheless your ETA will be a half-hour later than the flight plan ETA.

Since your aircraft consumes fuel at the rate of six gallons an hour and the estimated time enroute is two hours, it is evident that you will use 12 gallons of fuel. With a capacity of 22 gallons it is also evident that 10 gallons of fuel should remain in the tanks at destination. This is a safe enough margin even if you run into still stronger headwinds or bad weather that makes a landing at an alternate airport advisable. For flight under VFR conditions an alternate airport is not required but since it provides an added margin of safety it is recommended. An alternate is mandatory for flight under IFR conditions.

In the course of the preceding pilotage flight, the purpose of which was to point up the step-by-step planning and navigation, all data such as takeoff time, headings, altitude, time over checkpoints, groundspeeds, ETAs, and fuel consumed should have been entered on a simple flight log. The sole purpose of this log is to make it easier for you to navigate your aircraft from departure to destination with the maximum safety and efficiency. When you jot the figures down in the proper column on a flight log you are eliminating guesswork and the possibliity of confusion.

The following illustration shows a sample log for the pilotage flight above from Airport A to Airport B. This includes the pre-flight planning data as well as the actual flight data determined enroute. Study the log carefully, and check the data shown against the enroute navigation outlined in the nine steps above. Note also that under the TIME column in the flight log four minutes extra are added for the time necessary to climb to altitude from takeoff, as well as another four minutes for letdown at destination. This adds eight minutes to the actual time enroute for a total of 2 :08, and an actual fuel consumption of 12.8 gallons, as shown in the summary at the bottom of the log.

FLIGHT LOG

TRIP __A-B__   ALT. __5000__   DIST. __150 S.M.__

DATE __15 September__   PILOT __E. BROOKS__   (VFR)/IFR

FROM	TO	ALT.	TEMP	TAS	TC	WCA	TH	VAR	MH	DEV	CH	DIST.	GS	TIME	FUEL CONS.	ETA	ATA
A	CHKPT #1	5000	+5C	99	130	10R	140	12E	128	5E	123	10	75	climb 4+8	1.2	1212	1212
#1	#2	"	"	"	"	"	"	"	"	"	"	15	"	12	1.2	1224	1224
#2	#3	"	"	"	"	"	"	"	"	"	"	15	"	12	1.2	1236	1236
#3	#4	"	"	"	"	"	"	"	"	"	"	10	"	8	.8	1244	1244
#4	#5	"	"	"	"	"	"	"	"	"	"	15	"	12	1.2	1256	1256
#5	#6	"	"	"	"	"	"	"	"	"	"	15	"	12	1.2	1308	1308
#6	#7	"	"	"	"	"	"	"	"	"	"	10	"	8	.8	1316	1316
#7	#8	"	"	"	"	"	"	"	"	"	"	15	"	12	1.2	1328	1328
#8	#9	"	"	"	"	"	"	"	"	"	"	20	"	16	1.6	1344	1344
#9	#10	"	"	"	"	"	"	"	"	"	"	10	"	8	.8	1352	1352
#10	B	"	"	"	"	· "	"	"	"	"	"	15	"	L TONY +12	1.6	1408	1408
									TOTALS			150		2:08	12.8	1408	1408

SUMMARY

TOTAL DISTANCE __150__   TOTAL TIME __2ʰ8ᵐ__   TOTAL FUEL __12.8__

NOTES: WEATHER, ETC.

ATD = 1200

CAVU OVER ENTIRE ROUTE — ALT. 30.02

DEAD RECKONING

Pilotage, as we have seen, is a means of navigating from one point to another solely by reference to identifiable landmarks. As such, it is limited to periods of good visibility and to routes with landmarks prominent and distinctive enough to be identified from the air. Proceeding a step in navigation beyond pilotage we come to dead reckoning, which, to oversimplify, is a system of determining where an aircraft *should* be on the basis of where it *has been*. In other words, it is literally reckoning by deduction, which is where the name came from (deduced reckoning = ded., or dead, reckoning). Actually, dead reckoning (or DR, as it is commonly referred to) depends on two factors: (1) readings of the flight instruments such as airspeed indicator, altimeter, and compass; (2) the forecast or observed winds.

All other systems of navigation are dependent upon DR to a greater or less extent, even pilotage. When you measure a course on a chart, or determine your groundspeed between two fixes, or establish an ETA for your destination, you are practising DR. There are three main problems in all navigation, regardless of whether the aircraft is a 65 horsepower trainer or an intercontinental jet transport. These are (1) to know the aircraft's position at all times, (2) to know the direction in which to turn the aircraft to reach any given point, and (3) to know the time at which that point will be reached. Dead reckoning is the means of solving all three.

As a pilot you will be expected to know at least the fundamentals of DR, and what's even more important you will find that when you use DR on a cross-country flight you can save time, make your flying safer, and have more fun in the process.

What follows here is the account of a typical flight by dead reckoning, with emphasis on the practical rather than the theoretical.

A FLIGHT BY DEAD RECKONING

On Thursday February 11 you plan to take off at 0900 hours on a flight from Airport A to Airport B, a distance of 220 miles on a true course of 090°. In the pilot's lounge of the airport at A, where there are facilities for you to plan your flight, you lay out your navigation chart on the big plotting table, along with two or three sharpened pencils, your Weems plotter for measuring courses and distances, your navigation computer (probably the Mark 8C or the Dalton E-6B), and some note paper. At the top of the notepaper you write down the performance figures for your aircraft:

Type: Avonna, two-place, side-by-side, single-engine lightplane.

Identification number: N2314B.

Fuel octane: 80.

Fuel capacity: 28 gallons.

Fuel consumption: 5 gallons per hour.

Oil capacity: 6 quarts.

Total range in flying time: 5.6 hours (5h36m), computed on the basis of 28 gallons fuel capacity divided by fuel consumption of 5 gph.

Airport A to Airport B, distance 220 miles, true course 090°. A cruising altitude of 4,000 feet is established since the terrain is fairly level and the highest hill is 2,500 feet above sea level. Your estimated time of departure is 10:00 AM (ETD 1000). Calling the local weather station, you are given a forecast for your intended route which indicates the weather will be VFR all the way to Airport B. The reported wind at 4,000 feet is from 45° at 40 mph (wind direction is always given as the direction *from* which the wind is blowing). Comparing the TC of 090° with the wind direction from 45° establishes that the wind will be coming from the front left quarter of the airplane. It will drift you to the right of your course if not corrected for, and since it is a headwind it will reduce your groundspeed. This wind will therefore increase the time required to fly from departure to destination and will also increase the total amount of fuel consumed.

With this data you can now draw a simple wind triangle, establish your wind correction angle (WCA), and determine groundspeed. From these two values you can find compass heading, time to destination, and amount of fuel you will need.

For this part of preflight planning it is best to draw the wind vector on a blank sheet of paper, and on the same sheet compute all enroute data. In this way your navigation chart will remain clear except for the line of your true course and the marks indicating your checkpoints.

APPLICATION OF THE WIND TRIANGLE. Understanding the construction and use of the wind triangle in dead reckoning is probably the most difficult single accomplishment for the private pilot. The trouble lies not so much in the student's inability to construct the triangle as in the efforts to mechanically complete the wind vectors and still not fully understand its relationship with the actual flight of the airplane. When completed, the wind triangle tells you where the airplane is going under the particular wind conditions.

Now let's construct the wind triangle for the flight from A to B and follow each step to its conclusion. In pilotage you apply the principles of the wind triangle in obtaining the correct headings, but without drawing a diagram, as you do in DR.

You now have the following additional facts about your flight from A to B:

ETD: 1000 (10:00 AM).

True course: 090°.

Distance: 220 statute miles.

Wind at 4,000': From 45° at 40 mph.

Flight altitude: 4,000'.

Indicated airspeed: 88 mph.

True airspeed: 95 mph (IAS + 2% per each thousand feet of altitude, or IAS + 8% = 88 + 7 for a TAS of 95 mph).

Variation: 18° east (from the chart).

Deviation: 5° east (from the compass card in the airplane).

In order to complete the preflight data for the flight we must find:

Groundspeed (from which the time enroute can be established, also ETA at Airport B, and fuel needed).

Wind correction angle (from which compass headings can be established).

SOLUTION OF THE WIND TRIANGLE. You know the true course, true airspeed, and the wind direction and velocity of your intended flight and want to find the groundspeed and wind correction angle. In turn these will enable us to find the time enroute, ETA, fuel needed, and compass heading.

Step 1. On a plain sheet of paper draw a vertical line to represent true north and south directions. Since your flight is to the east, the wind triangle will be drawn to the east. The north-south line should be to the left of the paper to provide space for the triangle. It is not necessary to have a sheet large enough to plot the entire distance to Airport B since you are interested only in solving the triangle on the basis of one-hour increments for the wind speed and true airspeed. If you plot the wind triangle on a chart, the north-south line should be drawn through the airport of departure and parallel to the closest meridian.

Step 2. Mark a dot about midway on the north-south line to represent your airport of departure, and identify it as part of the triangle of velocities by labeling it E. Placing the plotter's center hole over the dot, line the plotter up parallel to the north-south line on the paper and make a temporary mark at 45° for the wind direction, and also at 090° for the true course. It is important that you always start your measurement in degrees from true north (0° or 360°) and read in a clockwise direction, i.e., 45°, 90°, 180°, etc. Now line up the straight edge of the plotter with E (point of departure) and the 90° temporary mark. Draw the true course line from E through the 90° mark to an indefinite length.

Step 3. Place the straight edge of the plotter at E and line up with the 45° mark (direction the wind is *from*). Draw wind line away from E to the southwest a distance equal to 40 miles. The length of this wind line is usually measured in the units on the bottom scale of the plotter. Regardless of what kind of units are used to measure the wind line the same units must also be

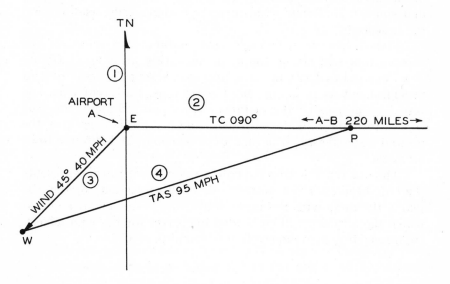

used for other measurements in completing the triangle of velocities. Since the wind is from 45° at 40 mph, the line representing the wind direction and length is now shown in correct relationship to your intended true course of 90°. From analysis of the wind triangle thus far it can be seen that the wind is coming from your left (as viewed from the airplane moving along the 90° true course) and will drift the airplane to the *right* of the course. You can see also that the wind is blowing from the airplane's left front quarter, and is in effect a headwind. This will result in a groundspeed which is less than your true airspeed of 95 mph.

At this point in the computations you can establish two important facts: (1) to correct for wind drift you will have to head the airplane (or crab into the wind) to the *left* of your true course, and (2) since you have a headwind component the groundspeed will be *less* than the true airspeed.

Before going on to the next step, place an arrow at the end of the wind line (at the 40-mile mark) and identify this point on the triangle as W.

Step 4. From W at the end of the wind line (and using the same unit of measurement as before), draw the true airspeed a distance equal to 95 mph, with the 95-mile unit on your plotter intersecting the 90° true course line that you had drawn in Step 2. Label the point of intersection as P. The intersection of the true course and true airspeed lines naturally will be to the east of E, the departure point. The wind triangle is now completed, and you can find your wind correction angle, true heading, and groundspeed.

Step 5. The wind triangle now contains two velocities (or forces) that will act on the airplane during an hour of flight: (1) the wind and (2) the true airspeed. Using the same unit of measurement as in laying out the triangle, the groundspeed is found by measuring the distances from point E along the true course to point P. This represents the actual distance over the ground and along the true course for one hour, and is found to be 62 miles.

The line representing the true airspeed (WP) also represents the true heading (true course with wind correction) of the airplane. Its angle with the north-south line is the actual angle at which the airplane will be headed to correct for the wind effect. On measuring, the true heading is found to be 073°.

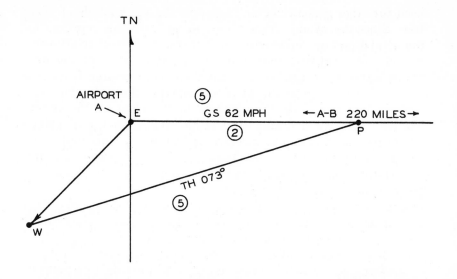

The true heading of 073° can be quickly checked for accuracy since the angle formed by the true course and true heading (lines PE and PW) is the actual wind correction (in this case 17°) which must be applied to the true course. It was previously established that the wind will drift the airplane to the right of true course, and therefore you must crab into the wind 17° to the left of the true course. Visualizing the direction of flight, it is evident that if you are to make good a true course over the ground of 090° and correct for the wind by turning the airplane 17° to the left, the nose of the airplane will be headed in a direction of 073° from north. Thus you are flying a true heading of 073°.

On the standard log form set your figures up as follows:

TC	WCA	TH
090°	17° L	073°

Now that you have completed the wind triangle for the proposed flight, and know the groundspeed, wind correction angle, and true heading, it is possible to complete your preflight data, check the airplane, and get ready for takeoff.

SUMMARIZING THE PREFLIGHT DATA. Using the data above, the compass heading for the flight can be determined:

TC	WCA	TH	VAR	MH	DEV	CH
090°	17° L	073°	18° E	055°	5° E	050°

With the known groundspeed of 62 mph and the distance of 220 miles from Airport A to Airport B, the estimated time in flight can be found:

$$\text{Time} = \frac{\text{Distance}}{\text{Groundspeed}} = \frac{220 \text{ miles}}{62 \text{ mph}} = 3.55 \text{ hours or } 3 \text{ hours } 33 \text{ min.}$$

Convert .55 hours to minutes by multiplying .55 hours × 60. Better still, use a computer, and conversion will be unnecessary. Set the GS, 62 mph, against the one-hour index, and then opposite 220 miles on the outer scale read 3 hours 33 minutes, estimated time enroute, on the inner scale.

The ETA at Airport B can now be found. Your estimated time of departure from Airport A is 1000 hours, and 1000 plus 03h33m equals 1333 (01:33 PM), your ETA at Airport B. The fuel required for the flight can be found by multiplying the fuel consumption rate of 5 gph x 3.55 hours, which equals 17.8 gallons. If you use a computer to obtain the amount of fuel, the time is set in as 3 hours and 33 minutes.

ATD *1000*

FROM	TO	ALT.	TEMP	TAS	TC	WCA	TH	VAR.	MH	DEV.	CH	DIST.	GS	TIME	FUEL CONS.	ETA	ATA
A	B	4,000	7℃	95	090	17L	073	18E	055	5E	050	220	62	3:33	17.8	1333	
A	CHKPT #1																
CHKPT #1	CHKPT #2																
ETC																	

Log entries for determining time enroute and fuel required.

The preflight data as determined above can now be entered at the top of your flight log as shown in the illustration. In brief, this information gives you an advance picture of the navigation details of your flight.

Complete your flight log by choosing some good checkpoints between Airport A and Airport B from your navigation chart, enter them in the log, and determine the distance, time, fuel,

ETA, etc., as you would in pilotage navigation. Once in flight, if you discover that the wind has changed from the original estimate obtained from the weather bureau, it will be necessary to make revised corrections and adjust the data in your flight log accordingly.

PLANNING THE RETURN FLIGHT

You can also pre-plan the return trip from Airport B to Airport A in much the same way you planned the flight from A to B. You will use some of the same data to determine an ETA back at your home airport, compass heading, WCA, etc., but the true course for the return trip naturally will be the reciprocal (opposite) of the outbound course. This can be measured on the navigation chart or determined simply by adding 180° to the outbound true course of 090° (090° + 180° = 270°). In computing a reciprocal course or heading, when the total is greater than 360° the 180° should be subtracted rather than added. *Example:* For an outbound true course of 220°, the reciprocal is 40° (220° - 180° = 040°).

The wind correction angle will be approximately the same number of degrees as for the outbound course, but since the wind will now be from the opposite side of the airplane (from the right) the correction will also be to the right. Remember, always correct *into* the wind. In this case the WCA must be added to the true course to obtain the true heading:

TC	WCA	TH
270°	17°R	287°

Assuming the magnetic variation and compass deviation to be the same as on the outbound course, you can complete your computations and find the compass heading for the return flight:

TC	WCA	TH	VAR	MH	DEV	CH
270°	17°R	287°	18°E	269°	5°E	264°

To find the groundspeed for the return trip it will be necessary to plot another wind triangle the same as for the outbound flight. In sequence, draw the north-south line and establish point E, which in this case will represent Airport B, point of departure for the return flight. Plot the true course of 270° to an indefinite length and then the wind line should be marked W, as

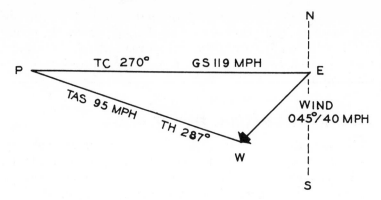

Plotting the wind triangle for the inbound or return flight.

before. From *W* plot the true airspeed of 95 mph to its point
of intersection with the true course, and note as point P. The
return wind triangle is now complete, and you can find the
groundspeed inbound by measuring along the true course line
from E to P. This represents one hour of flight over the ground.
The groundspeed measures 119 mph and is greater than the true
airspeed of 95 mph. This is due to the fact that the wind on the
return flight is a tailwind, whereas on the outbound flight it
was a headwind.

Both the outbound and inbound wind triangles can be combined to save time in drawing the inbound triangle. On the
outbound triangle consider the point E as the starting point for
the return flight and extend the true course line in the direction
opposite to the outbound true course, that is, the reciprocal
course, or 270°. The wind line is then in proper relationship to
the inbound flight and does not have to be redrawn. The true
airspeed line (95 units long) can then be drawn from the point
of the wind line (W) to intersect the return-trip course line.
This intersecting point can be indicated by P_1 for identification
purposes. The distance measured from point E to point P_1 along
the return true course line gives the groundspeed of 119 mph
for the return flight to Airport A.

It is suggested that you draw individual wind triangles in
your initial dead reckoning work until you have a complete
understanding of what each step of the triangle is accomplishing.
Then later combine the triangles for saving time.

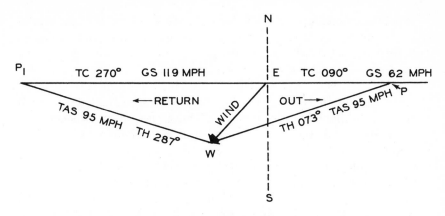

Combining the inbound and outbound wind triangles.

From the information obtained in drawing the return-flight triangle you can now find the estimated time enroute, fuel needed and ETA back at Airport A. You can also complete your flight log for the return flight, using the same checkpoints in reverse order and noting the time between checkpoints in accordance with the faster groundspeed.

Drawing the wind triangle may seem slow and tedious, but it is the only proper way to plan a cross-country flight and get a complete picture of what you can accomplish. With practice, preflight planning becomes simple, and after learning the principles of the wind triangle considerable time can be saved by the use of navigation computers.

PLOTTING AND COMPUTING IN FLIGHT

In the preceding section we were concerned with finding in advance the time enroute, fuel consumption, and compass heading for an anticipated flight. This part tells you what you can do in flight to compensate for unpredicted changes in wind and aircraft performance in order to make good your intended true course, and how to determine the position of the airplane at all times.

Plotting and drawing on the chart in flight is not practical in light planes of the kind used in private flying. The pilot navigator of a small aircraft normally has to content himself with pre-flight plotting before takeoff on cross-country trips.

But if he makes up an accurate flight log showing the true course, checkpoints, distances, time, fuel consumption, and headings, before departure, minor changes enroute can be estimated and corrected for in order to remain on course.

It may seem that additional plotting of the airplane's track and position in flight shouldn't be necessary if all data is correctly established before take-off. This is not so, because changes in wind speed and direction, plus the difficulty of holding a compass heading within one degree, may cause the plane to depart some distance from its intended course. It may be that after passing over a checkpoint you realize that you are off course, and the only information you have to work with is the compass heading, the approximate drift of the aircraft, and the elapsed time from your last known position. In order to establish a new true course while enroute it will be necessary to reverse the procedures in determining the true course in preflight planning.

In flight, you start with the compass heading and work back to a true course, a procedure known as rectifying. It becomes necessary to reverse the add and subtract rules because you are literally "taking away" items from the compass heading. Previously you *added* west variation, west deviation, and right wind correction angles to determine the compass heading from the true course. In rectifying you reverse the rule and subtract

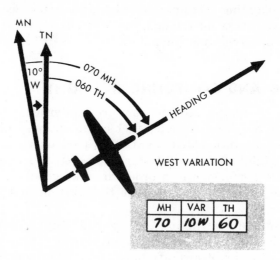

Rectifying the magnetic heading.

west variation, west deviation, and right wind correction angles when working from the compass heading back to true course (or track). Similarly, you now *add* east variation, east deviation, and left wind correction angles.

The steps in rectifying are as follows:

(1)   Jot down the reading of the magnetic compass.

(2) Find the magnetic heading by rectifying the compass heading for deviation.

(3) Find the true heading by rectifying the magnetic heading for variation.

(4) Find the true track made good over the ground by rectifying the true heading for the wind correction angle. To establish the WCA, note the present drift of the airplane.

(5) Plot the now known track on the chart and fix your position by approximating the distance you have flown since your last known position.

From the information obtained by rectifying, you can now re-plot your true course to destination, making the necessary corrections to establish a new compass heading. In step 4, when drift observations are not possible because of restricted visibility, the true heading can be rectified by means of a wind triangle or computer. Use the wind direction and velocity as given in weather reports or as last determined in your in-flight plotting and computing.

The following problem is an example of rectifying the compass heading to find the true track and a new position.

Point A in the illustration on page 220 marks the last known position of the airplane. Other data:

Compass heading in flight: 055°

Groundspeed (approximate): 110 mph

Elapsed time: 1:20

Drift angle (wind from the left, correct to the left): 10°L

Compass deviation for heading of 055°: 3°W

Magnetic variation: 7°E

The true track is found by rectifying in accordance with rules previously given:

055° — Compass heading in flight.

−3° — Deviation (it is westerly, but in rectifying it is subtracted).

052° — Magnetic heading.

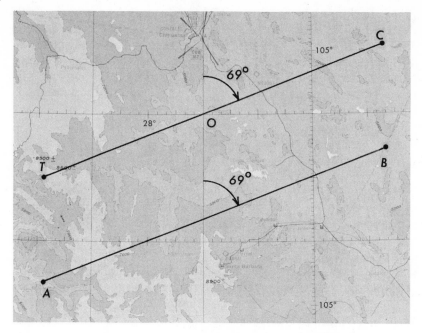

Plotting the track (actual ground path) on the chart.

+7° — Variation (it is easterly, but in rectifying it is added).

059° — True heading.

+10 — Drift (wind from the left, drift to the right, so angle must be added in rectifying).

069° — True track actually made good over the ground.

The approximate distance covered in 1:20 at a groundspeed of 110 mph is 147 miles. By checking the chart, it is noted that 147 miles on a true track of 069° crosses approximately 3° of longitude. The track angle of 069° is measured at the meridian nearest halfway at any convenient intersection, point 0, and the line TC obtained. The line AB, drawn from A parallel to TC, is the dead reckoning track made good. Point B, on the track line 147 miles distant from A, marks the position of the airplane by dead reckoning.

In the air, as the pilot of a small airplane you will have little opportunity for this kind of plotting. Instead, it is assumed that you have plotted your route carefully before taking off, and that you have subdivided it into 10- or 20-mile intervals, from checkpoint to checkpoint. If the intended true course was determined as 072° then the true track actually made good (069°) lies about 3° to the north. Estimating the distance of 147 miles along the plotted route (seven-tenths of the distance between the 140- and 150-mile ticks), a point is marked on the chart along a line at an angle of 3° to the plotted route, and the time noted.

In estimating small angles it may be of some help to remember the formula that an angle of 1° is represented by an offset of 1 in 60. In other words, if you draw a line 60 inches in length, and at one end a perpendicular line 1 inch long is erected, a line from the top of the perpendicular to the far end of the 60-inch line will meet at an angle of 1°. When you are off course 1° after flying 60 miles you are off course one mile.

Applying this principle to the above problem (an angle of 3° at 147 miles), an angle of 1° has an offset of 1 mile in a distance of 60 miles, two miles in 120, $2\frac{1}{2}$ miles in 150, and three miles in 180 miles. An angle of 3° will have an offset three times as great, or $7\frac{1}{2}$ miles in 150 miles flown. A point about $7\frac{1}{2}$ miles north of the plotted route line and 147 miles distant from your starting point represents the dead reckoning position.

In practice, it must be realized that there are a number of sources of possible error in a position so determined. For example, due to irregularities in handling the airplane, pilots are seldom able to fly a given heading closer than one or two degrees. The determination of drift can only be considered as correct within two or three degrees due to variable winds and problems of observation. Moreover, the groundspeed can only be considered approximate at times.

On some flights these various errors tend to cancel out, but on others they accumulate and become serious if not corrected after a reasonable time enroute. The dead reckoning position plotted above should not be taken as the actual position but as the center of an "error circle" somewhere within which lies the actual or true position.

For example, after an hour of flight at an estimated groundspeed of 120 mph, it is believed that the total course error may be 3°. An error of 1° is represented by 1 mile in 60, or 2 miles in 120 miles flown. An error of 3° would be 6 miles in 120, from which an error circle with a radius of 6 miles is drawn around the dead reckoning position. If landmarks on the chart are not seen at the end of the hour near the plotted position, they probably can be found somewhere within the circle of error. Often you are able to identify your position quicker by placing the error limit on the chart area within which to look for landmarks beneath you in the particular area.

After establishing your new DR position, you can now adjust your computations, reset true course to destination, and continue the flight with confidence that the time and effort spent in learning dead reckoning is paying off.

The following summary may help to fix in your mind the procedures for (1) finding compass heading in preflight planning, and (2) rectifying back to the true course while in flight.

A. *True course to compass heading.*

Step 1. Measure true course on chart from departure to destination.

Step 2. Plot the wind triangle and obtain the wind correction angle. If a right WCA, add to true course; if left, subtract from true course to obtain true heading.

Step 3. Find variation on the chart. Add west variation and subtract east from true heading to obtain magnetic heading.

Step 4. Find deviation from the compass card in the particular airplane. Add west deviation and subtract east from magnetic heading to obtain compass heading.

After taking off, clearing the airport, and climbing toward your cruising altitude, turn the airplane until the desired compass heading appears at the lubber line of the magnetic compass. You should now be making good the true course found in step 1 above. Be alert to evidence that you are staying on course.

B. *Compass heading to true course or track:*

Step 1. Observe the compass heading and jot it down on your flight log.

Step 2. Find deviation from the compass card for this particular compass heading. For west deviation *subtract* and for east deviation *add* to the compass heading to obtain magnetic heading.

Step 3. Find variation from the chart in the locality of your flight. For west variation *subtract* and for east variation *add* to the magnetic heading to obtain true heading.

Step 4. Observe wind drift and determine the wind correction angle. For a right wind correction angle *subtract* and for a left wind correction angle *add* to the true heading to obtain the true track.

Step 5. Plot the track on the chart and establish your present position over the ground as explained in the preceding text.

ADDITIONAL WIND VECTORS

Each of the following wind vectors is very useful to the private pilot and each serves a particular purpose. As mentioned previously, plotting in flight is limited in small aircraft, but the principles learned in these wind vectors will be of considerable help in your dead reckoning calculations. The explanations will be brief and to the point since you should now be familiar with all the terms involved.

A. *Find:* True course and groundspeed.

Given: True heading, true airspeed, and wind direction and velocity.

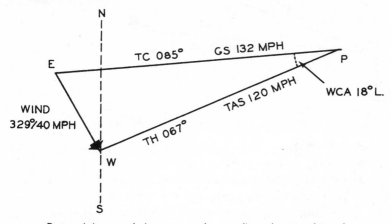

Determining track (course made good) and groundspeed.

Solution: (Refer also to the accompanying illustration.)

1. Draw the north-south line (N-S).

2. Establish point W on N-S line and draw the true heading line (WP in illustration) to the length of the true airspeed.

3. Draw wind line (EW) with W (head of the wind arrow, which indicates direction) to join the TH line at W. The length of the wind line EW will be determined by the wind velocity.

4. Draw the true course line from E (tail of the wind arrow) to P (the TH line at one hour of TAS).

5. Measure the true course.

6. Measure distance from E to P for the groundspeed being made good.

7. Measure the angle formed by lines PW and PE to obtain the wind correction angle.

8. The solution of this wind triangle makes it possible also to find the compass heading, time enroute, fuel consumption, and estimated time of arrival.

B. *Find:* The wind direction and velocity.

Given: True course, groundspeed, true heading, and true airspeed.

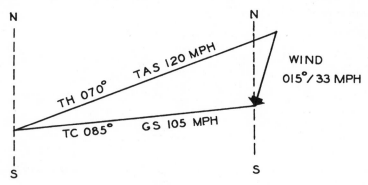

Determining the wind direction and velocity.

Solution: (Refer also to the accompanying illustration).

1. Draw the N-S line.

2. Establish a point on the N-S line, and from this point draw the TC to the length of the GS.

3. From this same point draw the TH to the length of the TAS (TH line in the same direction as the TC).

4. Draw the wind line connecting the hour points on the TC and TH lines. This forms the triangle from which the wind data can be obtained.

5. Establish the head of the wind line at the TC point. This is obvious since the wind always blows *from* the TH to the TC.

6. With your plotter, measure the direction the wind is blowing from and also its velocity, measuring in units the length of the wind line from the TH to TC hour points. To measure the wind direction construct another N-S line parallel to the first N-S line and adjacent to the wind line.

LOST PROCEDURE (PILOTAGE)

It seems that all who fly cross-country are destined to lose their way or become temporarily misplaced at one time or another. Therefore, the beginning pilot should give some forethought to procedures and practices that can be used to lead wandering birdmen out of the wilderness. Confining our problems to the typical VFR dilemma, we can start with the general and proceed to more specific rules, as set forth by the FAA in an *Exam-O-Gram*.

GENERAL:

Don't fight the problem — try to solve it! Stay loose and don't hit the panic button, thus virtually assuring that all the thinking gears will grind to a halt.

Analyze and evaluate as to fuel available and consumption rate. In other words, how much longer can you fly insofar as fuel is concerned? Be conservative, not hopelessly optimistic.

Weather — good, bad, improving, or deteriorating?

Equipment — is everything functioning? Do you have lights (cockpit, landing, navigation, etc.) or survival gear of any description?

Terrain — is it open and flat country, mountains, marshes, semi-desert, sparsely or thickly populated?

Daylight — hours remaining (if any). Have you had night or instrument flying experience? Once you have made a reasoned assessment of the situation you are better prepared to make vital decisions. One of the first is to decide if help is available or are you on your own?

SPECIFIC:

Condition one: (a) low on fuel, (b) weather deteriorating, (c) inadequate experience and darkness imminent, and (d) engine or equipment malfunctioning. While (d) is not necessarily associated with being lost, the solution which follows would certainly apply if the situation were serious enough. *Get it on the ground!* Most accidents are the product of mistakes which have multiplied over a period of time. Getting lost is no exception. *Don't push your luck.* It may well be that in doing so you have made your final mistake. If terrain or other conditions make it impossible at the moment, don't search too long for an exceptionally good landing place. Anything *usable* will do. Remember, most people on the ground know where they are.

Never fly until the petrol runs out. There are few things so nerve shattering as the rustle of the wind when an engine has coughed its last. *Never* fly until the sun slowly sinks in the golden west. *Never* fly until the weather deteriorates.

Condition two: (a) plenty of fuel, (b) plenty of daylight, and (c) plenty of good weather, but still lost. *Establish an error semicircle* as follows:

1. Straighten out your course. Establishing a course by hunch or because you have a "feeling" is for the birds. Don't wander aimlessly.

2. Use knowledge of last known position, elapsed time, approximate wind and ground speed (airspeed is better than nothing) to establish how far you may have traveled since your last checkpoint.

3. Using this distance as a radius, draw a semicircle ahead of your last known position on the chart. For example, you estimate your groundspeed at 120 mph. If you have been flying 20 minutes since your last checkpoint, then the no-wind radius of your semicircle is 40 miles projected along the direction of your estimated track. If you believe your wind is from the right, then you are most probably in the left quadrant of your semicircle. Of course, unless you were sure about the wind, you could not ignore the right quadrant. The use of a simple computer can materially reduce the effort required in solving problems of speed, time, distance, and fuel consumption.

4. If you have been flying a steady compass heading and keeping a reasonably accurate navigation log, it's not likely you will have too much difficulty.

5. Don't overlook the possibility of being lost and yet being right on course or nearly so. First, look for something big on the surface. Don't concern yourself with the minute checkpoint unless that is all that is available. Often there will be linear features such as rivers, mountain ranges, or prominent highways and railroads easy to spot and identify. Double check all landmarks. Compare and analyze them to the fullest.

Remember this point: be sure you have up-to-date charts, including those adjacent to the one in use. Everything which appears on the chart will usually be on the ground, but no standard chart is so detailed that everything you can see on the ground can also be found on the chart.

LOST PROCEDURE (RADIO)

A pilot in any emergency phase (uncertainty, alert, or distress) should take three steps to obtain assistance:

1. If equipped with a radar beacon transponder, and if unable to establish voice communications with an air traffic control facility, switch to Mode A/3 and Code 7700.

2. Contact controlling agency and give nature of distress and pilot's intentions. If unable to contact controlling agencies, attempt to contact *any* agency on assigned frequency or the following emergency frequency (both transmit and receive): 121.5 mHz. The effective range will be generally limited to radio line-of-sight. Those stations which will most likely hear you include: all military towers, most civil towers, VHF direction finding stations, radar facilities, FSS's, and ocean station vessels. The message should include the following: (1) "MAYDAY, MAYDAY, MAYDAY" (if distress), or "PAN, PAN, PAN" (if uncertainty or alert); (2) aircraft identification repeated three times; (3) type of aircraft; (4) position or estimated position (stating which); (5) heading, true or magnetic (stating which); (6) true airspeed or estimated true airspeed (stating which); (7) altitude; (8) fuel remaining in hours and minutes; (9) nature of distress; (10) pilot's intentions (bailout, ditch, crash landing, etc.); (11) assistance desired (fix, steer, bearing, escort, etc.); (12) two 10-second dashes with mike button followed by aircraft identification (once) and then say, "OVER." *Note:* While you are holding the mike button, the DF stations will be plotting a fix of your position.

3. Comply with information and clearance received. Accept the "communications control" offered to you by the ground radio station, silence interfering radio stations, and do not shift frequency or shift to another ground station unless absolutely necessary.

Direction finding (DF) equipment has long been used to locate lost aircraft, to guide aircraft to areas of good weather or to airports, and now at most DF equipped airports, DF instrument approaches may be given to aircraft in emergency.

Experience has shown that a majority of actual emergencies requiring DF assistance involve pilots with a minimum of flight experience, particularly IFR experience. With this in mind, a DF approach procedure provides for maximum flight stability in the approach by utilizing small degrees of turn, and descents when the aircraft is in a wings-level attitude. The DF specialist will give the pilot headings to fly and tell him when to begin descent.

DF instrument approach procedures are for emergency use, and will not be given in IFR weather conditions unless the pilot has declared an emergency.

To become familiar with the procedures and other benefits of DF, pilots are urged to request practice guidance and approaches in VFR weather conditions. DF specialists welcome the practice and, workload permitting, will honor such requests.

DOWNED AIRCRAFT

The rapidity of rescue on land or water will depend on how accurately your position may be determined. If a flight plan has been followed and your position is on course, rescue will be expedited. For ditching or crash landing, if there is no additional risk of fire and if circumstances permit, radio should be set for continuous transmission. If it becomes necessary to ditch, distressed aircraft should make every effort to ditch near a surface vessel. If time permits, the position of the nearest vessel can be obtained from a Coast Guard Rescue Coordination Center through the FAA facility. Unless you have good reason to believe that you will not be located by search aircraft, it is better to remain near your aircraft and prepare means for signalling whenever aircraft approach your position.

The pilot should remember the four C's: Confess predicament to any ground radio station. Do not wait too long. Give SAR (search and rescue) a chance. (2) *Communicate* with ground link and pass as much of the distress message on first transmission as possible. (3) *Climb* if possible for better radar DF detection. If flying at low altitude, the chance for establishing radio contact is improved by climbing; also, chances of alerting radar systems are sometimes improved by climbing. (4) *Comply* with advice and instructions received.

When you are doubtful of your position, or apprehensive for your safety, do not hesitate to request assistance. Search and Rescue facilities, including radar, radio, and DF stations, are ready and willing to help. There is no penalty for their use.

CROSS-COUNTRY FLYING

Cross-country flying is the goal of all your training as a private pilot. You will learn early that each phase of the ground and flight program you complete is moving you that much closer to your first solo cross-country. How much you already know, plus what you learn on this flight and how well you conduct it, will determine to a large extent whether or not your instructor certifies you for your license. Certainly you want him to approve your cross-country techniques, so once again let's briefly summarize the material covering cross-country flight, much of which we have already discussed in detail.

CERTIFICATES AND LICENSES. You are required to have your pilot and medical certificates with you at all times when you are serving as a pilot. It is also your responsibility to determine that the aircraft you fly is properly certificated and airworthy. The aircraft must carry a registration certificate showing the name of the registered owner, an airworthiness certificate showing the date to which the plane is considered airworthy, and an operations limitations record or airplane flight manual which shows loading of the airplane, allowable speeds, performance, etc.

WEATHER. During training and after you become a private pilot, you are allowed to fly cross-country only when VFR (visual flight rules) weather prevails. It is your responsibility to make sure the weather *is* VFR. For the latest information, a local

Weather Bureau Office or FAA Flight Service Station (FSS) is within easy reach by telephone wherever you do your flying. Of course, a Private Pilot with an Instrument Rating can fly according to the Instrument Flight Rules (IFR) providing he has accomplished his recent instrument flying experience requirements and has an airplane that is properly instrumented and equipped for IFR flight.

The FAA states that a pilot seeking a weather briefing may be compared to a buyer shopping for goods or services. If the buyer can clearly identify and state his needs, he is more easily and adequately served. The telephone weather briefing can be completely adequate if the pilot knows how to get the information. *The briefer needs to know the following information:* (1) estimated time of departure (ETD); (2) estimated time enroute (ETE) or estimated time of arrival (ETA); (3) destination; (4) route to be flown; (5) type of flight plan (VFR or IFR); (6) type of aircraft. *The pilot needs to know the following:* (1) present weather conditions at destination and along the route of flight; (2) trend and forecast at destination and also at the alternate airport if required; (3) trend and forecast of weather conditions along the proposed route of flight; (4) freezing level, icing conditions, and turbulence; (5) present and forecast thunderstorm activity; (6) winds aloft at appropriate altitudes; (7) escape routes, that is, areas of good or improving weather; (8) notices to Airmen: *meteorological* (SIGMETS, AIRMETS, and PIREPS), and *facilities* (NOTAMS and AIRADS, the latter being NOTAMS given only local dissemination).

WINDS. Wind velocities are given in knots (nautical miles per hour). If necessary, convert these velocities to statute miles per hour to make them correspond with your airspeeds, groundspeed, and distance measured on the chart. The private pilot generally uses statute miles for distances and speeds, but the trend is toward the nautical scale in commercial flying. You will find it simple to convert to the nautical with the aid of any navigation computer. Wind directions are *true* directions in weather reports, but when you are given instructions from the control tower for takeoff and landing the wind direction is *magnetic* to correspond with the magnetic direction of the runways.

RADIO EQUIPMENT. There may or may not be radio equipment in your airplane, depending on whether you are operating from a controlled or non-controlled airport. Two-way radio is required for operation to and from controlled fields. If you have no radio in your airplane, naturally you will limit your cross-country flights to non-controlled airports.

The advantages of being equipped with good communications and navigation radios far outweigh the cost. An investment in quality comm/nav gear is rather like investing in insurance against having an emergency. Additional radio equipment can always be used to advantage.

AIRMAN'S INFORMATION MANUAL. This publication is an invaluable aid to the cross-country pilot and should be in his possession for pre-flight reference and in the airplane for in-flight data. It lists all airports in the U.S. by state and airport name. This information also includes radio facilities, airport locations, runway lengths, fuel available, etc. In addition, the Notices to Airmen section keeps you up to date on airport changes, frequency revisions, and other related information.

SPEEDS IN CROSS-COUNTRY FLYING. Your estimate of time and fuel consumption in cross-country flying are dependent upon a correct analysis of airplane speed. The indicated airspeed (IAS), as recorded by the airspeed indicator, is a true value only at sea level under standard temperature conditions. At altitudes above sea level it is necessary to correct the IAS for the less dense air in order to determine the true airspeed (TAS). The TAS, plus or minus the tailwind or headwind component respectively, equals the aircraft's groundspeed. To convert IAS to TAS is a simple matter. It can be done mathematically, by allowing for a standard increase in true airspeed at the rate of 2% per 1,000 feet of altitude above sea level. Although this is only a rough approximation of the true airspeed since it doesn't take into consideration variations in air temperature, it is usually accurate enough at the relatively slow speeds of light training planes. For the sake of simplicity and greater accuracy, however, a computer should be used.

To correct for true airspeed in the mathematical conversion, read the IAS on the airspeed indicator and add 2% of the IAS for each 1,000 feet of altitude. Example: Your cruising altitude is 5,000 feet, the IAS is 100 mph. At 5,000 feet the TAS is 10% (5 × 2%) greater than the IAS. 10% of 100 mph IAS = 10 mph, and therefore the TAS = 100 + 10 or 110 mph. From this the groundspeed is determined by applying the headwind or tailwind component, as derived from the solution of the wind triangle, to the TAS.

Strictly speaking, indicated airspeed should also be corrected for instrument error when the amount of error has been determined. Indicated airspeed ± instrument error = calibrated airspeed (CAS). In lightplane private flying, however, the instrument error is usually so small that it is ignored, and IAS and CAS are therefore considered the same.

TIME. In pre-flight planning, estimates of time enroute must be made to establish fuel stops, to determine if a day flight might turn into a night flight, or to meet a schedule. Estimated time of arrival (ETA) is based on the estimated flying time from departure to destination, enroute stops for fuel, sightseeing, or changes in weather conditions. Actual time of departure (ATD) is the local time at which the airplane wheels break contact with the ground on takeoff. If a flight plan has been filed, the ATD should be reported to the local FAA station handling your flight plan. This can be done by the pilot via direct radio contact with FAA. For flight plan purposes it is important to report your actual time of arrival (ATA) at destination. This report is immediately transmitted back to your departure point and closes out your flight plan. The net flying time is the total time you are airborne between departure and destination. Elapsed time enroute includes the net flying time plus the time for fueling or other stops between departure and destination.

FUEL DATA. If you don't know or aren't sure of the fuel capacity and consumption of the particular aircraft you take on a cross-country flight, check with the local operations office, or look in the aircraft for the exact data. It can be found in the operation limitations record or flight manual, either of which should be in the airplane at all times. Fueling stops enroute are determined by the range in fuel hours of the airplane. For example, the fuel capacity of a particular airplane is 24 gallons and the rate of consumption is six gallons per hour. The total range of this airplane is four hours. In VFR flight you should maintain at least a 45-minute fuel reserve for possible bad weather and navigation error. This leaves 3:15 of actual flight fuel-hours. Your pre-flight planning will have to show that you can arrive at destination within that time, 'or that there is a satisfactory alternate airport with proper fuel within the same range of the departure airport.

RESTRICTED AREAS. During cross-country pre-flight planning be sure that your intended course does not take you over

PROHIBITED AREA Flight of aircraft prohibited Only the reserved airspace effective below 18,000 feet MSL are shown The type of area shall be spelled out in large areas if space permits	PROHIBITED P-56
DANGER, RESTRICTED OR WARNING AREA Invisable hazards to air navigation Refer to the tabulation shown on the border for additional information	D-300 OR R-300 OR W-300

areas where there are restrictions of flight. These effected areas are plainly shown on navigation charts and are fully explained on the back of each chart. Unauthorized flight is not permitted within a Prohibited Area, or within a Restricted Area during the time of use and between the altitudes noted on the back of the particular chart. Flight within Caution Areas is not restricted, but pilots are advised to exercise extreme caution when flying over such areas.

ALTIMETER SETTINGS. The sensitive altimeter is an atmospheric pressure-measuring instrument which must be corrected before takeoff and landing, and during flight. Altimeter settings are provided by control towers as a part of the takeoff and landing instructions. They are also transmitted during regular weather broadcasts and are available to the pilot at any time on request. A current altimeter setting means a corrected altitude indication for approach and landing, and assures adequate terrain clearance.

FAR requires that you maintain your cruising altitudes (VFR or IFR) by reference to your altimeter. *(See the FAR booklet in the pocket.)* Remember this phrase also: *"WHEN*

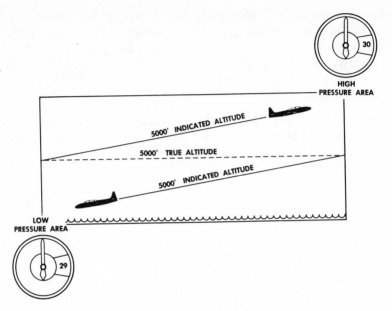

The effect of pressure on altitude.

FLYING FROM A HIGH TO A LOW OR FROM HOT TO COLD, LOOK OUT BELOW!" If you are flying in air that is colder than standard for that particular altitude, you should expect your aircraft to be actually lower than the altitude indicated on your altimeter, even when it is properly set according to regulation. This is because the cold air is more compacted and the pressure levels that an altimeter senses are actually closer to each other and closer to the earth. Moreover, when you fly from a high pressure area to an area of lower pressure without resetting your altimeter, the particular pressure level to which your altimeter has been set in reference will now be closer to the earth and you will automatically descend in attempting to maintain a constant altimeter indication.

A majority of pilots confidently expect that the current altimeter setting will compensate for irregularities in atmospheric pressure. Unfortunately, this is not always true. Remember that the altimeter setting broadcast by ground stations is the station pressure corrected to mean sea level. It does not reflect distortion at higher levels, particularly the effect of nonstandard temperature.

WEIGHT AND BALANCE. The private pilot need not know the technicalities of airplane weight and balance, but he should know what it is, how it is established, and how to check to make sure the plane is not overloaded or improperly loaded. In either case, the airplane can become unstable in flight, and under extremely adverse loading conditions can actually be dangerous to fly. There are two important weight and balance items that any pilot can check before takeoff: (1) make sure that the airplane maximum gross load is not exceeded, and (2) make sure that the loading schedule (fuel amount, passenger seating arrangement, and baggage distribution) comes within the limitations of the particular airplane weight and balance data.

Here is the weight and balance data of a typical four-place airplane, as found in the airplane operation limitations or flight manual:

Forward C. G. limit + 8.5
Rearward C. G. limit + 21.9
Max. gross weight   2190 pounds
Empty weight   1320 pounds

	Weight (lbs) $\times$	Arm (") $=$	Moment ("lbs)
Aircraft empty	1320	12.80	16896
Oil (9 qts)	17	−49.00	− 833
Pilot (1) front	170	16.00	2720
Passenger (1) rear	170	48.00	8160
Passenger (1) front	170	16.00	2720
Fuel (40 gallons)	240	22.00	5280
Baggage	100	75.50	7550
Total	2187		42493

Items with no preceding sign are plus (+) values.
Items with a minus (−) sign preceding are minus values.

$$\text{Center of gravity} = \frac{\text{Total Moments}}{\text{Total Weight}} = \frac{42493}{2187} = 19.43$$

The rearmost C. G. limit will be exceeded if two passengers are placed in the rear seat of this airplane per loading as authorized in above weight and balance data.

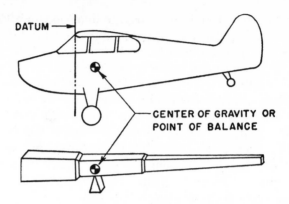

The entire aircraft weight may be considered to be concentrated at the center of gravity. Datum is an imaginary perpendicular line from which horizontal measurements are taken for balance purposes.

Note that the maximum gross weight allowable is 2,190 pounds. The total load as listed is 2,187 pounds. Consequently the total weight of the airplane on this flight is 3 pounds less than the maximum allowable gross, and within safe operating limits.

The loading schedule outlined above starts with "Aircraft empty" and ends with "Baggage." Note that there is listed "Pilot (1) front," "Passenger (1) rear," and "Passenger (1) front." Although this is a four-place airplane, under the loading schedule only one passenger is allowed in the rear seat, where, of course, there is space for two. The reason for this, as noted, is that the rearmost center of gravity (C. G.) limit will be exceeded if two passengers are placed in the rear seat according to the loading authorized in the weight and balance data. Moreover, the maximum gross load would be exceeded and the airplane would be unsafe to fly. If you want to carry a second passenger in the rear seat it will be necessary to reduce the total load to compensate for the additional passenger's weight. There are only two flexible weight items: fuel (40 gallons) and baggage (100 pounds). The baggage can be reduced or eliminated altogether, but if you reduce the fuel load the range of the airplane will be shortened. This can be compensated for by setting up additional fuel stops. As a general rule, alternate loading schedules are provided in the weight and balance data to take care of problems such as this one.

Weights used in airplane loading computations are: (1) fuel, six pounds per gallon, (2) oil, 7.5 pounds per gallon, (3) water, eight pounds per gallon, and (4) occupants (pilot and passengers), 170 pounds each. Exceptions to the standard loading schedule may be made when the pilot's and passengers' actual average weight is less than the 170 pounds allowed. When this occurs and you don't have a positive schedule for the particular airplane to go by, check with a certificated mechanic to make sure that an alternate loading arrangement comes within the weight and balance limitations of the aircraft.

NAVIGATION COMPUTERS

To solve the elementary problems of pilotage and dead reckoning navigation in this chapter we have depended on simple mathematics, and we have drawn the wind triangles by hand. The purpose of this seemingly roundabout process was to help you visualize the problems involved — the effect of wind on the aircraft's heading and speed, the determination of the estimated time enroute, the amount of fuel to be consumed on a given flight, and so on. In actual practise, it is much faster and simpler to use a navigation computer. Virtually all pilots carry a computer of some kind. Regardless of what kind you use, after you've worked with it for a while you'll find that the solutions to your wind and time-speed-distance problems are almost automatic — at least mechanical. If you fully understand the principles of the wind triangle and the rate problems you will no longer need to draw them out by hand, or multiply and divide. The computer will do the work for you.

11. Attitude control by instruments

DURING the actual cross-country flight which climaxes the practical test for the private pilot certificate you will be required to demonstrate your ability to maintain control of the aircraft under emergency conditions by reference only to instruments. You will already have received some basic instrument flight training from your instructor. Chances are that if your instruction has been based on the integrated method of primary flight training you will not have experienced any difficulty at all in maintaining control of the airplane solely by reference to instruments. As a matter of fact, when you learn to use instruments in performing flight maneuvers at the same time you learn the maneuvers by visual reference outside the cockpit, no special instrument training is even needed generally.

The demonstration is conducted under simulated instrument conditions—that is, a curtain, hood, or other device is provided so that all outside references are obscured from your vision and you are forced to rely on attitude information from flight instruments. The instructor or examiner serves as your safety pilot, keeping watch for airborne traffic.

During the test you are required to perform the following maneuvers while flying by instrument reference:

(1) Recovery from the start of a power-on spiral.

(2) Recovery from the approach to a climbing stall.

(3) Normal turns of at least 180° left and right to within plus or minus 20° of a pre-selected heading.

(4) Shallow climbing turns to a predetermined altitude.

(5) Shallow descending turns at reduced power to a predetermined altitude.

(6) Straight and level flight.

Your performance of these maneuvers is evaluated on the basis of coordination, smoothness, and accuracy. Any loss of control which makes it necessary for the examiner to take over in order to avoid stalling or exceeding the operating limits of the airplane is disqualifying.

The demonstration can be accomplished using only a gyroscopic turn indicator and sensitive altimeter (in addition, of course, to the customary required VFR flight instruments such as airspeed indicator, altimeter, and magnetic compass), but the FAA prefers that full IFR flight instrumentation be utilized if available. This would mean the addition (especially) of a gyroscopic bank and pitch indicator (or artificial horizon) and gyroscopic direction indicator (also called directional gyro and heading indicator).

The basic operating principles of the altimeter and airspeed indicator have been explained in Chapter 4. A few paragraphs about the gyroscopic flight instruments follow here, along with some cautions in the use of the magnetic compass.

TURN AND SLIP INDICATOR

The turn and slip indicator (official FAA name for the instrument formerly identified as the turn and bank indicator) was one of the first flight instruments used for controlling an aircraft without visual reference to the ground or horizon. It is actually a combination of two instruments—(1) a ball which is free to move in a curved transparent tube in order to indicate slip or skid, and (2) a needle which indicates the rate of turn of the aircraft. The ball part of the instrument is actuated by natural forces, while the turn indicator depends upon gyroscopic properties for its indications.

THE BALL. The pilot's coordination can be checked by the ball part of the turn-and-bank. The ball is actually a balance indicator since it shows the relationship between the angle of bank and the rate of turn. It indicates to the pilot the *quality* of his turn—whether or not the aircraft has the correct angle of bank for its rate of turn. In a *coordinated turn* the ball assumes a position between the reference markers. In a *skid* the rate of turn is too great for the angle of bank, and the excessive centrifugal force causes the ball to move to the outside of the turn. To correct the aircraft's attitude to coordinated flight it is necessary for the pilot to increase the bank or decrease the rate of turn, or do both. In a *slip* the rate of turn is too slow for the angle of bank, and the lack of centrifugal force causes the ball to move to the inside of the turn. To correct for coordinated flight the pilot must decrease the bank or increase the rate of turn, or do both.

THE TURN NEEDLE. The turn needle indicates the rate (in number of degrees per second) at which the aircraft is turning about its vertical axis. Unlike the gyro horizon, it does not provide a direct indication of the banking attitude of the aircraft. However, for any given airspeed there is a definite angle of bank necessary to maintain a *coordinated* turn at a given rate. The faster the airspeed, the greater the angle of bank required to obtain a given rate of turn. Thus the turn needle gives only an indirect indication of the aircraft's banking attitude or angle of bank.

Because the turn-and-bank indicator is one of the most reliable instruments the pilot has in recovering from unusual attitudes, it's essential that he know how to interpret its indications.

TYPES OF TURN NEEDLES. Both the 2-minute and the 4-minute turn needles are in common use. On a 2-minute turn needle a 360° turn made at a rate indicated by a one-needle-width deflection requires 2 minutes to complete. The aircraft is thus turning at a rate of 3° per second—a standard rate turn. With the 4-minute needle a 360° turn made at a rate indicated by a one-needle-width deflection requires 4 minutes to complete. The aircraft is therefore turning at a rate of $1\frac{1}{2}°$ per second. A standard rate turn of 3° per second would be indicated on this type of turn needle by a two-needle-width deflection. You may find an instrument marked as a 2-minute turn needle but calibrated so that a two-needle-width deflection represents a standard rate of turn of 3° per second.

DIRECTIONAL GYRO

The directional gyro (or heading indicator) is fundamentally a mechanical instrument designed to both supplement and complement the magnetic compass. The compass itself is subject to such errors and limitations that it makes straight flight and precision turns to headings difficult to accomplish, especially in turbulent air. The directional gyro is not affected by the forces that make the magnetic compass difficult to interpret.

To use the directional gyro properly, the pilot must adjust the rotatable card to the desired reading by means of a caging knob. In flight the readings should be checked at regular intervals of about 10 or 15 minutes against the indication of the magnetic compass. Use great care when reading the compass. Set the directional gyro to the magnetic compass indication only when the aircraft is in wings-level, unaccelerated flight.

Straight and level flight.

The panels on this and the following three pages show the indications of each of the attitude instruments during the standard maneuvers of a typical light airplane. The instruments, in the same grouping throughout, are (left to right, top row) airspeed indicator, gyro-horizon, altimeter, and (bottom row) turn-and-slip indicator, directional gyro, rate-of-climb indicator.

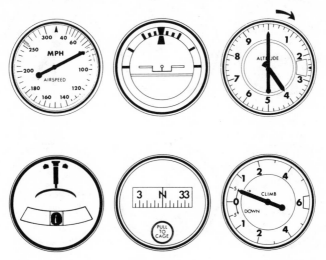

Straight climb.

Straight descent.

Standard-rate level turn to the left.

Climbing turn to the right.

Descending turn to the left.

Steep banked turn to the right.

Approaching stall.

Like the compass, the directional gyro also has its limitations. Its range of operation varies with the particular model, but for the most part the type found in light aircraft is accurate only within 55° of pitch and 55° of bank. When either of these attitude limits is exceeded the instrument "tumbles" or "spills" and no longer provides the correct indication until it is reset. Once the instrument has been spilled it can be reset with the caging knob.

GYRO-HORIZON

The one instrument that gives a literal picture of the attitude of the aircraft is the gyro-horizon (also referred to variously as attitude indicator or artificial horizon). The relationship of the instrument's miniature aircraft to the horizon bar is the same as the relationship of the real aircraft to the actual horizon. This instrument gives an instantaneous indication of even the smallest changes in attitude. It has no lead or lag and is wholly reliable when properly maintained.

The gyro-horizon is provided with an adjustment knob by means of which the pilot can move the miniature aircraft upward or downward inside the case. Normally the miniature aircraft is adjusted so that the wings overlap the horizon bar when the real airplane is in straight and level cruising flight.

Some models of the gyro horizon are equipped with a caging mechanism. These models must be uncaged only during straight and level flight or else they will give inaccurate readings. When uncaging this model it must be uncaged *fully*: otherwise it may tumble at the lower limits.

The pitch and bank limits depend upon the make and model of the instrument. Limits in the banking plane are usually from 100° to 110°, and the pitch limits are usually between 60° and 70°. If any of these limits are exceeded the instrument will tumble or spill and provide erroneous readings until reset with the caging mechanism.

It's absolutely vital for pilots to know how to interpret the gyro-horizon's banking scale. The scale indicator moves in the opposite direction from that in which the plane is actually banked. This can be confusing if you use the indicator to determine the direction of bank. The scale is there for one purpose: to achieve precision. For an indication of the direction of bank of the real aircraft, you must relate the instrument's miniature aircraft to the horizon bar. (By way of an exception, however, there is a gyro-horizon on the market with a banking scale that moves in the same direction as the bank of the aircraft.)

The gyro-horizon, as we said, is a reliable instrument, and certainly the most realistic flight instrument on the light aircraft panel. Its indications are very close approximations of the actual attitude of the aircraft itself.

COMPASS ERRORS

According to the FAA itself, one of the aeronautical subjects in which "consistently large numbers of pilots fare poorly" on the written examinations is the magnetic compass—its limitations, errors, and in-flight characteristics. Although the compass was one of the first instruments to be installed in aircraft, it is still one of the least understood instruments in the cockpit. Most light airplanes are not equipped with any other direction-indicating instrument than the compass. Mechanically, the compass is a simple, self-contained unit, independent of external suction or electrical power for its operation. In standard cross-country flying the compass is likely to be dependable at all times—but only if the pilot understands its inherent errors and limitations.

In Chapter 10, Cross-Country Navigation, we discussed magnetic variation and deviation, the two main sources of compass error for which corrections can be determined relatively easily. We shall review these corrections briefly and then discuss the other sources of compass error.

VARIATION is the angular difference between true north and magnetic north. The amount of variation in all areas is printed on aeronautical charts in degrees east or west of true north. When converting from true headings or courses to magnetic headings or courses, subtract easterly variation and add westerly. When converting from magnetic headings or courses to true headings or courses, the rule applies in reverse: add easterly variation and subtract westerly.

DEVIATION is the deflection of the compass needle from magnetic north as a result of local magnetic disturbances in the aircraft. The compass should be checked periodically for deviation by ground "swinging," and the amount of deviation then reduced by means of the small adjustable magnets with which compasses are equipped. The errors still remaining after compensation should be recorded on a compass correction card which should be installed in the cockpit within easy view of the pilot. The magnetic disturbances set up within the aircraft itself are caused by electrical and radio systems, some varieties of cargo, and metallic objects in the cockpit such as flashlights and aluminum computers. These latter accessories should never be placed on top of the instrument panel near the magnetic compass: they can induce deviation errors of as much as 30° or 40°.

In addition to these errors, the pilot should have a *working knowledge* of the following in-flight errors:

OSCILLATION ERROR is the erratic swinging of the compass card which may be the result of turbulence or rough pilot technique.

MAGNETIC DIP is the tendency of the magnetic compass to point down as well as north in certain latitudes. This tendency is responsible for:

(a) *Northerly turn error*—the most pronounced of the in-flight errors. It is most apparent when turning to or from headings of north and south.

(b) *Acceleration error*—an error that can occur during airspeed changes. It is most apparent on headings of east and west.

As a quick refresher on this instrument's in-flight dip error, we'll take a simulated demonstration flight around the compass rose. Unless otherwise noted, we will limit our bank during turns to a *gentle* bank. Also, we will assume that we are in the northern hemisphere because the characteristics which we will observe would not be present at the magnetic equator, and would be reversed in the southern hemisphere.

DEMONSTRATION NO. 1. (Heading—north; error—northerly turn error.) As we start a turn in either direction from this heading, we notice that momentarily the compass *gives an indication of a turn opposite the direction of the actual turn.* (While the compass card is in a banked attitude, the vertical component of the earth's magnetic field causes the north-seeking end of the compass to dip to the low side of the turn, giving the pilot an erroneous turn indication.) If we continue the turn toward east or west, the compass card will begin to indicate a turn in the correct direction, *but will lag behind the actual turn* at a diminishing rate until we are within a few degrees of east or west. While holding a compass indication of north, if we ease into a very gradual shallow banked turn—say 3° or 4° of bank —it is possible to change the actual heading of the aircraft by 20° or more *while still maintaining an indication of north by the compass.*

DEMONSTRATION NO. 2. (Heading—east; error—acceleration error.) The northerly turn error that we previously experienced is not apparent on this heading (or on a west heading). However, let's see what happens when we accelerate and decelerate by changing the airspeed. With the wings level, we *increase* the airspeed by increasing the power setting or by lowering the nose, or both. Result: although we are holding the nose of the aircraft straight ahead, our compass card erroneously indicates a turn toward *north*. On the other hand, if we *decrease* the airspeed by reducing the power setting or raising the nose of the aircraft, or both, the compass gives an erroneous indication of a turn toward *south*. (Because of the pendulous-type mounting, the end of the compass card which the pilot sees is tilted upward during acceleration and downward during deceleration and changes of airspeed. This momentary deflection of the compass card from the horizontal results in an error that is most apparent on headings of east and west.)

DEMONSTRATION NO. 3. (Heading—south; error—northerly turn error.) Again we are presented with the northerly turn error problem that we encountered in Demonstration 1. Although the same set of forces that caused the erroneous indication when we banked the aircraft while on a north heading will be working against us on this heading, the compass indications will appear quite different. For example, as we roll into a turn in either direction, the compass gives us an indication of a turn in the correct direction but at a *much faster rate than is actually being turned*. As we continue our turn toward west or east, the compass indications will continue to precede the actual turn— but at a diminishing rate—until we are within a few degrees of west or east. (It might be noted that the acceleration error is not apparent on this heading or on a north heading.)

DEMONSTRATION NO. 4. (Heading—west; error—acceleration error.) On this heading we encounter the same errors we previously covered on a heading of east in Demonstration 2. When we *increase the airspeed,* we get an erroneous indication of a *turn toward north*. When we *decrease the airspeed,* we will get an erroneous indication of a *turn toward south*. (A memory aid that might assist you in recalling this relationship between airspeed change and direction of the error is the word "ANDS" —*Accelerate—North, Decelerate—South.*)

The points we are trying to get across are these: (1) When taking readings from the magnetic compass while on a northerly or southerly heading (for establishing a course, setting the gyro-driven heading indicator, etc.), remember that it is essential to have the wings perfectly level for several seconds before taking the reading. (2) When you are on an easterly or westerly heading it is important for the airspeed to be constant so that you can get an accurate reading. (3) On an intermediate heading, both of the above conditions should be met. (*Note*: If your aircraft is equipped with a gyro-driven heading indicator, be sure to check it frequently with your magnetic compass.)

TURNS TO HEADINGS

For the pilot who would like a general set of rules for determining his lead point when making turns by reference to the magnetic compass, the following procedures are recommended. In order to minimize dip error, the angle of bank should not exceed 15°.

1. *When turning to a heading of north you must allow, in addition to your normal lead, a number of degrees approximately equal to the latitude at which you are flying. Example*: You are making a left turn to a heading of north in a locality where the latitude is 30° N. You have previously determined your normal lead to be approximately 5° for this particular angle of bank. In this case, you should start your roll-out when the compass reads approximately 35°.

2. *When turning to a heading of south you must turn past your normal lead point by a number of degrees approximately equal to the latitude at which you are flying. Example*: You are making a right turn to a heading of south in a locality where the latitude is 30° N. You have previously determined your normal lead to be approximately 5° for this particular angle of bank. In this case, you should turn past your normal lead point of 175° (180° — 5°) by 30°, and start your roll-out when the compass reads approximately 205°.

3. *The error is negligible during turns to east or west; therefore, use the normal amount of lead during turns to an east or west heading.*

4. *For intermediate headings that lie between the cardinal headings, use an approximation based on the heading's proximity to north or south, the direction of the turn, and your knowledge of the compass's lead and lag characteristics in these areas.* In other words, use an "educated guesstimate."

We won't guarantee you that the above method will roll you out on the exact heading every time. At best it is an approximate method, but it *will* get you reasonably close to your desired heading, and this beats having no method at all.

12.

PILOT SERVICES
AND OPERATING DATA

This chapter provides material on operating data and flight services of a very practical nature to private pilots regardless of whether they fly only locally or use their aircraft for intercity transportation. Keep in mind, though, that the FAA written test is designed to find out if you are qualified to conduct a safe and efficient flight under the widest possible range of conditions. This calls for at least a basic knowledge of (among other subjects) cross-country flying over unfamiliar terrain, the air traffic rules, radio aids, navigation, weather, and the principles of flight. And the next step beyond this knowledge—how to apply it under actual operating conditions.

There are one or more questions in the Private Pilot Test Guide on each of the topics included in this chapter, just as there are on all the other topics in the rest of the manual. You can verify that simply by checking the knowledge requirements set forth in the study outline on pages 8-13 of the FAA Test Guide.

A reminder in answering the test questions: if you don't know or aren't sure of the answer, look up the topic of the question in the index of this manual. For example, a question in the Test Guide concerns the purpose of the Advisory Circulars. Under "Advisory Circulars" in the index of this manual, find a reference to page 251 opposite, which summarizes the AC publication system.

The double-columned material in this chapter is reproduced from the Airman's Information Manual except for the material on weather depiction charts which is from FAA's AC 00-45A, Aviation Weather Services. The material on aircraft and engine performance is from the Cessna Model 172 Owner's Handbook.

FAA ADVISORY CIRCULARS

Advisory Circulars issued by the FAA contain non-regulatory material of interest to (but are not binding upon) pilots and the aviation public in general. Examples include: AC 91-36A, VFR Flight Near Noise-Sensitive Areas, and AC 61-32C, Private Pilot Written Test Guide, a copy of which is included with this manual. Advisory Circulars are published in a numbered-subject system corresponding to the subject areas of the Federal Aviation Regulations. Of most interest to pilots are these AC series:

Series	Subject
00	General
20	Aircraft
60	Airmen
70	Airspace
90	Air Traffic Control and General Operating Rules
150	Airports
170	Navigation Facilities

Some AC's are free of charge and available from the FAA (Dept. of Transportation) Washington, DC 20590, while others are for sale singly or by subscription from the Superintendent of Documents, Washington, DC 20402. Checklists setting forth the price (if any) and status of each published Advisory Circular are available at no charge from the FAA.

AIRPORT LIGHTING AIDS

VISUAL APPROACH SLOPE INDICATOR (VASI)

a. The VASI is a system of lights so arranged to provide visual descent guidance information during the approach to a runway. These lights are visible from 3–5 miles during the day and up to 20 miles or more at night. The visual glide path of the VASI provides safe obstruction clearance within ±10 degrees of the extended runway centerline and to 4 nautical miles from the runway threshold. Descent, using the VASI, should not be initiated until the aircraft is visually aligned with the runway. Lateral course guidance is provided by the runway or runway lights.

b. VASI installations may consist of either 2, 4, 6, 12, or 16 lights units arranged in bars referred to as near, middle, and far bars. Most VASI installations consist of two bars, near and far, and may consist of 2, 4, or 12 light units. Some airports have VASI's consisting of three bars, near, middle, and far, which provide an additional visual glide path for use by high cockpit aircraft. This installation may consist of either 6 or 16 light units. VASI installations consisting of 2, 4, or 6 light units are located on one side of the runway, usually the left. Where the installation consists of 12 or 16 light units, the light units are located on both sides of the runway.

c. Two bar VASI installations provide one visual glide path which is normally set at 3 degrees. Three bar VASI installations provide two visual glide paths. The lower glide path is provided by the near and middle bars and is normally set at 3 degrees while the upper glide path, provided by the middle and far bars, is normally ¼ degree higher. This higher glide path is intended for use only by high cockpit aircraft to provide a sufficient threshold crossing height. Although normal glide path angles are three degrees, angles at some locations may be as high as 4.5 degrees to give proper obstacle clearance. Pilots of high performance aircraft are cautioned that use of VASI angles in excess of 3.5 degrees may cause an increase in runway length required for landing and rollout.

d. The following information is provided for pilots as yet unfamiliar with the principles and operation of this system and pilot technique required. The basic principle of the VASI is that of color differentiation between red and white. Each light unit projects a beam of light having a white segment in the upper part of the beam and red segment in the lower part of the beam. The light units are arranged so that the pilot using the VASIs during an approach will see the combination of lights listed below.

e.
2–BAR VASI

	Light Bar	Color
(1) Below glide path	Far	Red
	Near	Red
(2) On glide path	Far	Red
	Near	White
(3) Above glide path	Far	White
	Near	White

f.
3–BAR VASI

(1) Below both glide paths	Far	Red
	Middle	Red
	Near	Red
(2) On lower glide path	Far	Red
	Middle	Red
	Near	White

(3) On upper glide path	Far	Red
	Middle	White
	Near	White
(4) Above both glide paths	Far	White
	Middle	White
	Near	White

g. When on the proper glide path of a 2–bar VASI the pilot will see the near bar as white and the far bar as red. From a position below the glide path, the pilot will see both bars as red. In moving up to the glide path, the pilot will see the color of the near bar change from red to pink to white. From a position above the glide slope the pilot will see both bars as white. In moving down to the glide path, the pilot will see the color of the far bar change from white to pink to red. When the pilot is below the glide path the red bars tend to merge into one distinct red signal and a safe obstruction clearance may not exist under this condition.

h. When using a 3–bar VASI it is not necessary to use all three bars. The near and middle bars constitute a two bar VASI for using the lower glide path. Also the middle and far bars constitute a 2–bar VASI for using the upper glide path. A simple rule of thumb when using a two-bar VASI is:

    All Red _____ Too Low
    All White _____ Too High
    Red & White __ On Glide Path

i. In haze or dust conditions or when the approach is made into the sun, the white lights may appear yellowish. This is also true at night when the VASI is operated at a low intensity. Certain atmospheric debris may give the white lights an orange or brownish tint; however, the red lights are not affected and the principle of color differentiation is still applicable.

TRI-COLOR VISUAL APPROACH SLOPE INDICATOR

a. Tri-color Visual Approach Indicators have been installed at general aviation and air carrier airports. The Tri-color Approach Slope Indicator normally consists of a single light unit, projecting a three-color approach path into the final approach area of the runway upon which the system is installed. In all of these systems, a below glide path indication is red, the above glide path indication is amber and the on path indication is green.

b. Presently installed Tri-color Visual Approach Slope Indicators are low candlepower projector-type systems. Research tests indicate that these systems generally have a daytime useful range of approximately ½ to 1 mile. Nighttime useful range, depending upon visibility conditions, varies from 1 to 5 miles. Projector-type Visual Approach Slope Indicators may be initially difficult to locate in flight due to their small light source. Once the light source is acquired, however, it will provide accurate vertical guidance to the runway. Pilots should be aware that this yellow-green-red configuration produces a yellow-green transition light beam between the yellow and green primary light segments and an anomalous yellow transition light beam between the green and red primary light segments. This anomalous yellow signal could cause confusion with the primary yellow too-high signal.

VISUAL APPROACH SLOPE INDICATOR (VASI)

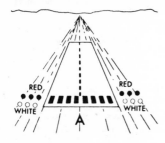

YOU ARE ON THE GLIDE PATH

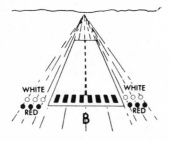

IMPOSSIBLE INDICATION

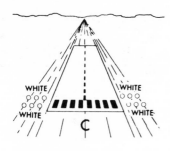

YOU ARE ABOVE THE GLIDE PATH

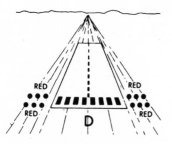

YOU ARE BELOW THE GLIDE PATH

AIRPORT MARKING AIDS

AIRPORT MARKING AIDS

a. In the interest of safety, regularity, or efficiency of aircraft operations, the FAA has recommended for the guidance of the public the following airport marking. (Runway numbers and letters are determined from the approach direction. The number is the whole number nearest one-tenth the magnetic azimuth of the centerline of the runway, measured clockwise from the magnetic north.) The letter or letters differentiate between parallel runways:

For two parallel runways "L" "R"

For three parallel runways "L" "C" "R"

b. Basic Runway Marking—markings used for operations under Visual Flight Rules: centerline marking and runway direction numbers.

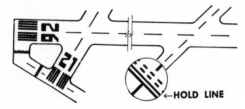

Figure 2–1—BASIC RUNWAY

c. Non-Precision Instrument Runway Marking—markings on runways served by a nonvisual navigation aid and intended for landings under instrument weather conditions: basic runway markings plus threshold marking.

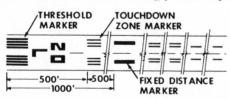

←HOLD LINE

Figure 2–2—NON-PRECISION INSTRUMENT RUNWAY

d. Precision Instrument Runway Marking—markings on runway served by non-visual precision approach aids and on runways having special operational requirements, non-precision instrument runway marking, touchdown zone marking, fixed distance marking, plus side stripes.

Figure 2–3—PRECISION INSTRUMENT RUNWAY

e. Threshold—A line perpendicular to the runway ce terline designating the beginning of that portion of runway usable for landing.

f. Displaced Threshold—A threshold that is not at t beginning of the full strength runway pavement. T paved area behind the displaced runway threshold available for taxiing, the landing rollout, and the take of aircraft.

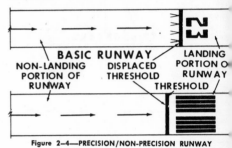

Figure 2–4—PRECISION/NON-PRECISION RUNWAY

g. Closed or Overrun/Stopway Areas—Any surface area which appears usable but which, due to the natu of its structure, is unusable.

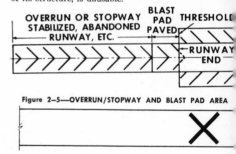

Figure 2–5—OVERRUN/STOPWAY AND BLAST PAD AREA

AUTOMATIC TERMINAL INFORMATION SERVICE (ATIS)

Automatic Terminal Information Service (ATIS) is a continuous broadcast of recorded noncontrol information in selected high activity terminal areas. Its purpose is to improve controller effectiveness and to relieve frequency congestion by automating the repetitive transmission of essential but routine information. Pilots are urged to cooperate in the ATIS program as it relieves frequency congestion on approach control, ground control, and local control frequencies. The Airport Facility/Directory indicates airports for which ATIS is provided.

a. Information to include the time of the latest weather sequence, ceiling, visibility (sky conditions/ceilings below 1000 feet and visibility less than 5 miles will be broadcast; if conditions are at or better than 5000 and 5, sky condition/ceiling and visibility may be omitted) obstructions to visibility, temperature, wind direction (magnetic) and velocity, altimeter, other pertinent remarks, instrument approach and runways in use is continuously broadcast on the voice feature of a TVOR/VOR/VORTAC located on or near the airport, or in a discrete UHF/VHF frequency. The departure runway/s will only be given if different from the landing runway/s except locations having a separate ATIS for departure. Where VFR arrival aircraft are expected to make initial contact with approach control, this fact and the appropriate frequencies may be broadcast on ATIS. Pilots of aircraft arriving or departing the terminal area can receive the continuous ATIS broadcasts at times when cockpit duties are least pressing and listen to as many repeats as desired. ATIS broadcasts shall be updated upon the receipt of any official weather, regardless of content change and reported values. A new recording will also be made when there is a change in other pertinent data such as runway change, instrument approach use, etc.

Sample Broadcast:

DULLES INTERNATIONAL INFORMATION SIERRA. 1300 GREENWICH WEATHER. MEASURED CEILING THREE THOUSAND OVERCAST. VISIBILITY THREE, SMOKE. TEMPERATURE SIX EIGHT. WIND THREE FIVE ZERO AT EIGHT. ALTIMETER TWO NINER NINER TWO. ILS RUNWAY ONE RIGHT APPROACH IN USE.

LANDING RUNWAY ONE RIGHT AND LEFT. DEPARTURE RUNWAY THREE ZERO. ARMEL VORTAC OUT OF SERVICE. ADVISE YOU HAVE SIERRA.

b. Pilots should listen to ATIS broadcasts whenever ATIS is in operation.

c. Pilots should notify controllers that they have received the ATIS broacast by repeating the alphabetical code word appended to the broadcast.
EXAMPLES: "INFORMATION SIERRA RECEIVED."

d. When the pilot acknowledges that he has received the ATIS broadcast, controllers may omit those items contained in the broadcast if they are current. Rapidly changing conditions will be issued by Air Traffic Control and the ATIS will contain words as follows:

"LATEST CEILING / VISIBILITY / ALTIMETER / WIND/(OTHER CONDITIONS) WILL BE ISSUED BY APPROACH CONTROL/TOWER."

The absence of a sky condition/ceiling and/or visibility on ATIS indicates a sky condition/ceiling of 5000 feet or above and visibility of 5 miles or more. A remark may be made on the broadcast, "The weather is better than 5000 and 5," or the existing weather may be broadcast.

e. Controllers will issue pertinent information to pilots who do not acknowledge receipt of a broadcast or who acknowledge receipt of a broadcast which is not current.

f. To serve frequency-limited aircraft, Flight Service Stations (FSS) are equipped to transmit on the omnirange frequency at most en route VORs used as ATIS voice outlets. Such communication interrupts the ATIS broadcast. Pilots of aircraft equipped to receive on other FSS frequencies are encouraged to do so in order that these override transmissions may be kept to an absolute minimum.

g. While it is a good operating practice for pilots to make use of the ATIS broadcast where it is available, some pilots use the phrase "Have Numbers" in communications with the control tower. Use of this phrase means that the pilot has received wind, runway and altimeter information ONLY and the tower does not have to repeat this information. It does indicate receipt of the ATIS broadcast and should never be used for this purpose.

RADAR ASSISTANCE TO VFR AIRCRAFT

a. Radar equipped FAA Air Traffic Control facilities provide radar assistance and navigation service (vectors) to VFR aircraft provided the aircraft can communicate with the facility, are within radar coverage, and can be radar identified.

b. Pilots should clearly understand that authorization to proceed in accordance with such radar navigational assistance does not constitute authorization for the pilot to violate Federal Aviation Regulations. In effect, assistance provided is on the basis that navigational guidance information issued is advisory in nature and the job of flying the aircraft safely, remains with the pilot.

c. In many cases, the controller will be unable to determine if flight into instrument conditions will result from his instructions. To avoid possible hazards resulting from being vectored into IFR conditions, pilots should keep the controller advised of the weather conditions in which he is operating and along the course ahead.

d. Radar navigation assistance (vectors) may be initiated by the controller when one of the following conditions exist:

(1) The controller suggests the vector and the pilot concurs.

(2) A special program has been established and vectoring service has been advertised.

(3) In the controller's judgment the vector is necessary for air safety.

e. Radar navigation assistance (vectors) and other radar derived information may be provided in response to pilot requests. Many factors, such as limitations of radar, volume of traffic, communications frequency, congestion, and controller workload could prevent the controller from providing it. The controller has complete discretion for determining if he is able to provide the service in a particular case. His decison not to provide the service in a particular case is not subject to question.

AERONAUTICAL ADVISORY STATIONS (UNICOM)

a. UNIÇOM is a non-government air/ground radio communication facility which may provide airport advisory service at certain airports. Locations and frequencies of UNICOMs are shown on aeronautical charts and publications.

b. THIS SERVICE SHALL NOT BE USED FOR AIR TRAFFIC CONTROL PURPOSES, except for the verbatim relay of ATC information limited to the following:

(1) Revision of proposed departure time.

(2) Takeoff, arrival, or flight plan cancellation time.

(3) ATC clearance *provided* arrangements are made between the ATC facility and UNICOM license to handle such messages.

c. The following listing depicts the frequencies which are currently designated by the Federal Communication Commission (FCC) for use as Aeronautical Advisory Stations (UNICOM).

Frequency	Use
122.700	uncontrolled fields
122.725	private airports (not open to public)
122.750	private airports (not open to public) and air-to-air communications
122.800	uncontrolled airports
122.950	airports with a control tower
122.975	high altitude
123.000	uncontrolled airports
123.050	heliports
123.075	heliports

TERMINAL RADAR PROGRAMS FOR VFR AIRCRAFT

Stage III Service (Radar Sequencing and Separation Service for VFR Aircraft).

(1) This service has been implemented at certain terminal locations. The service is advertised in the Airport/Facility Directory and the publication Graphic Notices and Supplemental Data. The purpose of this service is to provide separation between all participating VFR aircraft and all IFR aircraft operating within the airspace defined as the Terminal Radar Service Area (TRSA). Pilot participation is urged but it is not mandatory.

(2) If any aircraft does not want the service, the pilot should state NEGATIVE STAGE III, or make a similar comment, on initial contact with approach control or ground control, as appropriate.

(3) TRSA charts and a further description of the Services Provided, Flight Procedures, and ATC Procedures are contained in the publication Graphic Notices and Supplemental Data.

(4) While operating within a TRSA, pilots are provided Stage III service and separation as prescribed in this chapter. In the event of a radar outage, separation and sequencing of VFR aircraft will be suspended as this service is dependent on radar. The pilot will be advised that the service is not available and issued wind, runway information, and the time or place to contact the tower. Traffic information will be provided on a workload permitting basis.

(5) Visual separation is used when prevailing conditions permit and it will be applied as follows:

(a) When a VFR flight is positioned behind the preceding aircraft and the pilot reports having that aircraft in sight, be will be directed to follow it. Upon being told to contact the tower, radar service is automatically terminated.

(b) When IFR flights are being sequenced with other traffic and the pilot reports the aircraft he is to follow in sight, the pilot may be directed to follow it and will be cleared for a "visual approach."

(c) If other "non-participating" or "local" aircraft are in the traffic pattern, the tower will issue a landing sequence.

(d) Departing VFR aircraft may be asked if they can visually follow a preceding departure out of the TRSA. If the pilot concurs, he will be directed to follow it until leaving the TRSA.

(6) Until visual separation is obtained, standard vertical or radar separation will be provided.

(a) 1000 feet vertical separation may be used between IFR aircraft.

(b) 500 feet vertical separation may be used between VFR aircraft, or between a VFR and an IFR aircraft.

(c) Radar separation varies depending on size of aircraft and aircraft distance from the radar antenna. The minimum separation used will be 1½ miles for most VFR aircraft under 12,500 pounds GWT. If being separated from larger aircraft, the minimum is increased appropriately.

(7) Pilots operating VFR under Stage III in a TRSA—

(a) Must maintain an altitude when assigned by ATC unless the altitude assignment is to maintain at or below a specified altitude. ATC may assign altitudes for separation that do not conform to FAR 91.109. When the altitude assignment is no longer needed for separation or when leaving the TRSA, the instruction will be broadcast, "Resume Appropriate VFR Altitudes." Pilots must then return to an altitude that conforms to FAR 91.109 as soon as practicable.

(b) When not assigned an altitude should coordinate with ATC prior to any altitude change.

(8) Within the TRSA, traffic information on observed but unidentified targets will, to the extent possible, be provided all IFR and participating VFR aircraft. At the request of the pilot, he will be vectored to avoid the observed traffic, insofar as possible, provided the aircraft to be vectored is within the airspace under the jurisdiction of the controller.

(9) Departing aircraft should inform ATC of their intended destinaton and/or route of flight and proposed cruising altitude.

PILOTS RESPONSIBILITY: THESE PROGRAMS ARE NOT TO BE INTERPRETED AS RELIEVING PILOTS OF THEIR RESPONSIBILITIES TO SEE AND AVOID OTHER TRAFFIC OPERATING IN BASIC VFR WEATHER CONDITIONS, TO MAINTAIN APPROPRIATE TERRAIN AND OBSTRUCTION CLEARANCE, OR TO REMAIN IN WEATHER CONDITIONS EQUAL TO OR BETTER THAN THE MINIMA REQUIRED BY FAR 91.105. WHENEVER COMPLIANCE WITH AN ASSIGNED ROUTE, HEADING AND/OR ALTITUDE IS LIKELY TO COMPROMISE SAID PILOT RESPONSIBILITY RESPECTING TERRAIN AND OBSTRUCTION CLEARANCE AND WEATHER MINIMA, APPROACH CONTROL SHOULD BE SO ADVISED AND A REVISED CLEARANCE OR INSTRUCTION OBTAINED.

MEDICAL FACTS FOR PILOTS

FITNESS FOR FLIGHT

a. Medical Certification

(1) All pilots except those flying gliders and free air balloons must possess valid medical certificates in order to exercise the privileges of their airman certificates. The periodic medical examinations required for medical certification are conducted by designated Aviation Medical Examiners, who are physicians with a special interest in aviation safety and training in aviation medicine.

(2) The standards for medical certification are contained in Part 67 of the Federal Aviation Regulations. Pilots who have a history of certain medical conditions described in these standards are mandatorily disqualified from flying. These medical conditions include a personality disorder manifested by overt acts, a psychosis, alcoholism, drug dependence, epilepsy, an unexplained disturbance of consciousness, myocardial infarction, angina pectoris and diabetes requiring medication for its control. Other medical conditions may be temporarily disqualifying, such as acute infections, anemia, and peptic ulcer. Pilots who do not meet medical standards may still be qualified under special issuance provisions or the exemption process. This may require that either additional medical information be provided or practical flight tests be conducted.

(3) Student pilots should visit an Aviation Medical Examiner as soon as possible in their flight training in order to avoid unnecessary training expenses should they not meet the medical standards. For the same reason, the student pilot who plans to enter commercial aviation should apply for the highest class of medical certificate that might be necessary in the pilot's career.

Caution: The Federal Aviation Regulations prohibit a pilot who possesses a current medical certificate from performing crewmember duties while the pilot has a known medical condition or increase of a known medical condition that would make the pilot unable to meet the standards for the medical certificate.

b. Illness

(1) Even a minor illness suffered in day-to-day living can seriously degrade performance of many piloting tasks vital to safe flight. Illness can produce fever and distracting symptoms that can impair judgment, memory, alertness, and the ability to make calculations. Although symptoms from an illness may be under adequate control with a medication, the medication itself may decrease pilot performance.

(2) The safest rule is not to fly while suffering from any illness. If this rule is considered too stringent for a particular illness, the pilot should contact an Aviation Medical Examiner for advice.

c. Medication

(1) Pilot performance can be seriously degraded by both prescribed and over-the-counter medications, as well as by the medical conditions for which they are taken. Many medications, such as tranquilizers, sedatives, strong pain relievers, and cough-suppressant preparations, have primary effects that may impair judgment, memory, alertness, coordination, vision, and the ability to make calculations. Others, such as antihistamines, blood pressure drugs, muscle relaxants, and agents to control diarrhea and motion sickness, have side effects that may impair the same critical functions. Any medication that depresses the nervous system, such as a sedative, tranquilizer or antihistamine, can make a pilot much more susceptible to hypoxia (see below).

(2) The Federal Aviation Regulations prohibit pilots from performing crewmember duties while using any medication that affects the faculties in any way contrary to safety. The safest rule is not to fly as a crewmember while taking any medication, unless approved to do so by the FAA.

d. Alcohol

(1) Extensive research has provided a number of facts about the hazards of alcohol consumption and flying. As little as one ounce of liquor, one bottle of beer, or four ounces of wine can impair flying skills, with the alcohol consumed in these drinks being detectable in the breath and blood for at least three hours. Even after the body completely destroys a moderate amount of alcohol, a pilot can still be severely impaired for many hours by hangover. There is simply no way of increasing the destruction of alcohol or alleviating a hangover. Alcohol also renders a pilot much more susceptible to disorientation and hypoxia (see below).

(2) A consistently high alcohol-related fatal aircraft accident rate serves to emphasize that alcohol and flying are a potentially lethal combination. The Federal Aviation Regulations prohibit pilots from performing crewmember duties within eight hours after drinking any alcoholic beverage or while under the influence of alcohol. However, due to the slow destruction of alcohol, a pilot may still be under influence eight hours after drinking a moderate amount of alcohol. Therefore, an excellent rule is to allow at least 12 to 24 hours between "bottle and throttle," depending on the amount of alcoholic beverage consumed.

e. Fatigue

(1) Fatigue continues to be one of the most treacherous hazards to flight, safety, as it may not be apparent to a pilot until serious errors are made. Fatigue is best described as either acute (short-term) or chronic (long-term).

(2) A normal occurrence of everyday living, acute fatigue is the tiredness felt after long periods of physical

MEDICAL FACTS FOR PILOTS

and mental strain, including strenuous muscular effort, immobility, heavy mental workload, strong emotional pressure, monotony and lack of sleep. Consequently, coordination and alertness, so vital to safe pilot performance, can be reduced. Acute fatigue is prevented by adequate rest and sleep, as well as regular exercise and proper nutrition.

(3) Chronic fatigue occurs when there is not enough time for full recovery between episodes of acute fatigue. Performance continues to fall off, and judgment becomes impaired so that unwarranted risks may be taken. Recovery from chronic fatigue requires a prolonged period of rest.

f. Stress

(1) Stress from the pressures of everyday living can impair pilot performance, often in very subtle ways. Difficulties, particularly at work, can occupy thought processes enough to markedly decrease alertness. Distraction can so interfere with judgment that unwarranted risks are taken, such as flying into deteriorating weather conditions to keep on schedule. Stress and fatigue (see above) can be an extremely hazardous combination.

(2) Most pilots do not leave stress "on the ground." Therefore when more than usual difficulties are being experienced, a pilot should consider delaying flight until these difficulties are satisfactorily resolved.

g. Emotion

(1) Certain emotionally upsetting events, including a serious argument, death of a family member, separation or divorce, loss of job and finaneial catastrophe, can render a pilot unable to fly an aircraft safely. The emotions of anger, depression, and anxiety from such events not only decrease alertness but also may lead to taking risks that border on self-destruction. Any pilot who experiences an emotionally upsetting even should not fly until satisfactorily recovered from it.

h. Personal Checklist

(1) Aircraft accident statistics show that pilots should be conducting preflight checklists on themselves as well as their aircraft, for pilot impairment contributes to many more accidents than failures of aircraft systems. A personal checklist that can be easily committed to memory, which includes all of the categories of pilot impairment of discussed in this section, is being distributed by the FAA in the form of a wallet-sized card.

PERSONAL CHECKLIST
**I'M physically and mentally
SAFE to fly—not being
impaired by**

ILLNESS
    MEDICATION.

STRESS
    ALCOHOL
        FATIGUE
            EMOTION

EFFECTS OF ALTITUDE

a. Hypoxia

(1) Hypoxia is a state of oxygen deficiency in the body sufficient to impair functions of the brain and other organs. Hypoxia from exposure to altitude is due only to the reduced barometric pressures encountered at altitude, for the concentration of oxygen in the atmosphere remains about 21 percent from the ground out to space.

(2) Although a deterioration in night vision occurs at a cabin pressure altitude as low as 5,000 feet, other significant effects of altitude hypoxia usually do not occur in the normal healthy pilot below 12,000 feet. From 12,000 to 15,000 feet of altitude, judgment, memory, alertness, coordination and ability to make calculations are impaired, and headache, drowsiness, dizziness and either a sense of well-being (euphoria) or belligerence occur. The effects appear following increasingly shorter periods of exposure to increasing altitude. In fact, pilot performance can seriously deteriorate within 15 minutes at 15,000 feet.

(3) At cabin pressure altitudes above 15,000 feet, the periphery of the visual field grays out to a point where only central vision remains (tunnel vision). A blue coloration (cyanosis) of the fingernails and lips develops. The ability to take corrective and protective action is lost in 20 to 30 minutes at 18,000 feet and 5 to 12 minutes at 20,000 feet, followed soon thereafter by unconsciousness.

(4) The altitude at which significant effects of hypoxia occur can be lowered by a number of factors. Carbon monoxide inhaled in smoking or from exhaust fumes (see below), lowered hemoglobin (anemia), and certain medications can reduce the oxygen-carrying capacity of the blood to the degree that the amount of oxygen provided to body tissues will already be equivalent to the oxygen provided to the tissues when exposed to a cabin pressure altitude of several thousand feet. Small amounts of alcohol and low doses of certain drugs, such an antihistamines, tranquilizers, sedatives and analgesics can, through their depressant actions, render the brain much more susceptible to hypoxia. Extreme heat and cold, fever, and anxiety increase the body's demand for oxygen, and hence its susceptibility to hypoxia.

(5) The effects of hypoxia are usually quite difficult to recognize, especially when they occur gradually. Since symptoms of hypoxia do not vary in an individual, the ability to recognize hypoxia can be greatly improved by experiencing and witnessing the effects of hypoxia during an altitude chamber "flight." The FAA provides this opportunity through aviation physiology training, which is conducted at the FAA Civil Aeromedical Institute and at many military facilities across the United States. Pilots can apply for this training by contacting the Physiological Operations and Training Section, AAC-143, FAA Civil Aeromedical Institute, P.O. Box 25082, Oklahoma City, Oklahoma 73125.

(6) Hypoxia is prevented by heeding factors that reduce tolerance to altitude, by enriching the inspired air with oxygen from an appropriate oxygen system and by maintaining a comfortable, safe cabin pressure altitude. For optimum protection, pilots are encouraged

MEDICAL FACTS FOR PILOTS

to use supplemental oxygen above 10,000 feet during the day, and above 5,000 feet at night. The Federal Aviation Regulations require that the minimum flight crew be provided with and use supplemental oxygen after 30 minutes of exposure to cabin pressure altitudes between 12,500 and 14,000 feet, and immediately on exposure to cabin pressure altitudes above 14,000 feet. Every occupant of the aircraft must be provided with supplemental oxygen at cabin pressure altitudes above 15,000 feet.

b. Ear Block

(1) As the aircraft cabin pressure decreases during ascent, the expanding air in the middle ear pushes the eustachian tube open and, by escaping down it to the nasal passages, equalizes in pressure with the cabin pressure. But during descent, the pilot must periodically open the eustachian tube to equalize pressure. This can be accomplished by swallowing, yawning, tensing muscles in the throat or, if these do not work, by the combination of closing the mouth, pinching the nose closed and attempting to blow through the nostrils (Valsalva maneuver).

(2) Either an upper respiratory infection, such as a cold or sore throat, or a nasal allergic condition can produce enough congestion around the eustachian tube to make equalization difficult. Consequently, the difference in pressure between the middle ear and aircraft cabin can build up to a level that will hold the eustachian tube closed, making equalization difficult if not impossible. The problem is commonly referred to as an "ear block."

(3) An ear block produces severe ear pain and loss of hearing that can last from several hours to several days. Rupture of the ear drum can occur in flight or after landing. Fluid can accumulate in the middle ear and become infected.

(4) An ear block is prevented by not flying with an upper respiratory infection or nasal allergic condition. Adequate protection is usually not provided by decongestant sprays or drops to reduce congestion around the eustachian tubes. Oral decongestants have side effects that can significantly impair pilot performance.

(5) If an ear block does not clear shortly after landing, a physician should be consulted.

c. Sinus Block

(1) During ascent and descent, air pressure in the sinuses equalizes with the aircraft cabin pressure through small openings that connect the sinuses to the nasal passages. Either an upper respiratory infection, such as a cold or sinusitis, or a nasal allergic condition can produce enough congestion around an opening to slow equalization and, as the difference in pressure between the sinus and cabin mounts, eventually plug the opening. This "sinus block" occurs most frequently during descent.

(2) A sinus block can occur in the frontal sinuses, located above each eyebrow, or in the maxillary sinuses, located in each upper cheek. It will usually produce excruciating pain over the sinus area. A maxillary sinus block can also make the upper teeth ache. Bloody mucus may discharge from the nasal passages.

(3) A sinus bolck is prevented by not flying with an respiratory infection or nasal allergic condition. Adequate protection is usually not provided by decongestant sprays or drops to reduce congestion around the sinus openings. Oral decongestants have side effects that can impair pilot performance.

(4) If a sinus block does not clear shortly after landing, a physician should be consulted.

d. Decompression Sickness After Scuba Diving

(1) A pilot or passenger who intends to fly after Scuba diving should allow the body sufficient time to rid itself of excess nitrogen absorbed during diving. If not, decompression sickness due to evolved gas can occur during exposure to low altitude and create a serious inflight emergency.

(2) The recommended waiting time before flight to cabin pressure altitudes of 8,000 feet or less is at least 2 hours after diving which has not required controlled ascent (non-decompression diving), and at least 24 hours after diving which has required controlled ascent (decompression diving). The waiting time before flight to cabin pressure altitudes above 8,000 feet should be at least 24 hours after any Scuba diving.

HYPERVENTILATION IN FLIGHT

a. Hyperventilation, or an abnormal increase in the volume of air breathed in and out of the lungs, can occur subconsciously when a stressful situation is encountered in flight. As hyperventilation "blows off" excessive carbon dioxide from the body, a pilot can experience symptoms of lightheadedness, suffocation, drowsiness, tingling in the extremities, and coolness—and react to them with even greater hyperventilation. Incapacitation can eventually result from incoordination, disorientation, and painful muscle spasms. Finally, unconsciousness can occur.

b. The syptoms of hyperventilation subside within a few minutes after the rate and depth of breathing are consciously brought back under control. The buildup of carbon dioxide in the body can be hastened by controlled breathing in and out of a paper bad held over the nose and mouth.

c. Early symptoms of hyperventilation and hypoxia are similar. Moreover, hyperventilation and hypoxia can occur at the same time. Therefore, if a pilot is using an oxygen system when symptoms are experienced, the oxygen regulator should immediately be set to deliver 100 percent oxygen, and then the system checked to assure that it has been functioning effectively before giving attention to rate and depth of breathing.

CARBON MONOXIDE POISONING IN FLIGHT

a. Carbon monoxide is a colorless, odorless and tasteless gas contained in exhaust fumes. When breathed even in minute quantities over a period of time, it can significantly reduce the ability of the blood to carry oxygen. Consequently, effects of hypoxia occur (see above).

b. Most heaters in light aircraft work by air flowing over the manifold. Use of these heaters while exhaust fumes are escaping through manifold cracks and seals

MEDICAL FACTS FOR PILOTS

is responsible every year for several non-fatal and fatal aircraft accidents from carbon monoxide poisoning.

c. A pilot who detects the odor of exhaust or experiences symptoms of headache, drowsiness, or dizziness while using the heater should suspect carbon monoxide poisoning, and immediately shut off the heater and open air vents. If symptoms are severe, or continue after landing, medical treatment should be sought.

ILLUSIONS IN FLIGHT

a. Introduction

(1) Many different illusions can be experienced in flight. Some can lead to spatial disorientation. Others can lead to landing errors. Illusions rank among the most common factors cited as contributing to aircraft accidents.

b. Illusions Leading to Spatial Disorientation

(1) Various complex motions and forces and certain visual scenes encountered in flight can create illusions of motion and position. Spatial disorientation from these illusions can be prevented only by visual reference to reliabile, fixed points on the ground or to flight instruments.

(a) The leans—An abrupt correction of a banked attitude, which has been entered too slowly to stimulate the balance organs in the inner ear, can create the illusion of banking in the opposite direction. The disoriented pilot will roll the aircraft back into its original dangerous attitude or, if level flight is maintained, will feel compelled to lean in the preceived vertical plane until this illusion subsides.

(b) Coriolis illusion—An abrupt head movement in a constant-rate turn that has ceased stimulating the balance organs can create the illusion of rotation or movement in an entirely different plane. The disoriented pilot will maneuver the aircraft into a dangerous attitude in an attempt to stop rotation. This most overwhelming of all illusions in flight may be prevented by not making sudden, extreme head movements, particularly while making prolonged constant-rate turns under IFR conditions.

(c) Graveyard spin—A proper recovery from a spin that has ceased stimulating the balance organs can create the illusion of spinning in the opposite direction. The disoriented pilot will return the aircraft to its original spin.

(d) Graveyard spiral—An observed loss of altitude during a coordinated constant-rate turn that has ceased stimulating the balance organs can create the illusion of being in a descent with the wings level. The disoriented pilot will pull back on the controls, tightening the spiral and increasing the loss of altitude.

(e) Somatogravic illusion—A rapid acceleration during takeoff can create the illusion of being in a nose-up attitude. The disoriented pilot will push the aircraft into a nose-low, or dive attitude. A rapid deceleration by rapid reduction of the throttles can have the opposite effect, with the disoriented pilot pulling the aircraft into a nose-up, or stall attitude.

(f) Inversion illusion—An abrupt transition from climb to straight and level flight can create the illusion of tumbling backwards. The disoriented pilot will push

the aircraft abruptly into a nose-low attitude, possibly intensifying this illusion.

(g) Elevator illusion—An abrupt upward vertical acceleration, usually by an updraft, can create the illusion of being in a climb. The disoriented pilot will push the aircraft into a nose-low attitude. An abrupt downward vertical acceleration, usually by a downdraft, has the opposite effect, with the disoriented pilot pulling the aircraft into a nose-up attitude.

(h) False horizon—Sloping cloud formations, an obscured horizon, a dark scene spread with ground lights and stars, and certain geometric patterns of ground light can create illusions of not being aligned correctly with the actual horizon. The disoriented pilot will place the aircraft in a dangerous attitude.

(i) Autokinesis—In the dark, a static light will appear to move about when stared at for many seconds. The disoriented pilot will lose control of the aircraft in attempting to align it with the light.

c. Illusions Leading to Landing Errors

(1) Various surface features and atmospheric conditions encountered in landing can create illusions of incorrect height above and distance from the runway threshold. Landing errors from these illusions can be prevented by anticipating them during approaches, aerial visual inspection of unfamiliar airports before landing, using electronic glideslope or VASI systems when available, and maintaining optimum proficiency in landing procedures.

(a) Runway width illusion—A narrower-than-usual runway can create the illusion of the aircraft being at a greater height. The pilot who does not recognize this illusion will fly a lower approach, with the risk of striking objects along the approach path or landing short. A wider-than-usual runway can have the opposite effect, with the risk of leveling out high and landing hard or overshooting the runway.

(b) Runway and terrain slopes illusion—An upsloping runway, upsloping terrain, or both, can create the illusion of greater height. The pilot who does not recognize this illusion will fly a lower approach. A downsloping runway, downsloping approach terrain, or both, can have the opposite effect.

(c) Featureless terrain illusion—An absence of ground features, as when landing over water, darkened areas and terrain made featureless by snow, can create the illusion of greater height. The pilot who does not recognize this illusion will fly a lower approach.

(d) Atmospheric illusions—Rain on the windscreen can create the illusion of greater height, and atmospheric haze the illusion of greater distance. The pilot who does not recognize these illusions will fly a lower approach. Penetration of fog can create the illusion of pitching up. The pilot who does not recognize this illusion will steepen the approach, often quite abruptly.

(e) Ground lighting illusios—Lights along a straight path, such as a road, and even lights on moving trains can be mistaken for runway and approach lights. Bright runway and approach lighting systems, especially where few lights illuminate the surrounding terrain, may create the illusion of lesser distance. The pilot who does not recognize this illusion will fly a high approach.

MEDICAL FACTS FOR PILOTS

VISION IN FLIGHT

a. Introduction

(1) Of the body senses, vision is the most important for safe flight. Major factors that determine how effectively vision can be used are the level of illumination and the technique of scanning the sky for other aircraft.

b. Vision Uder Dim and Bright Illumination

(1) Under conditions of dim illumination, small print and colors on aeronautical charts and aircraft instruments become unreadable unless adequate cockpit lighting is available. Moreover, another aircraft must be much closer to be seen unless its navigation lights are on.

(2) In darkness, vision becomes more sensitive to light, a process called dark adaptation. Although exposure to total darkness for at least 30 minutes is required for complete dark adaptation, the pilot can achieve a moderate degree of dark adaptation within 20 minutes under dim red cockpit lighting. Since red light severely distorts colors, especially on aeronautical charts, and can cause serious difficulty in focusing the eyes on objects inside the aircraft, its use is advisable only where optimum outside night vision capability is necessary. Even so, white cockpit lighting must be available when needed for map and instrument reading, especially under IFR conditions. Dark adaptation is impaired by exposure to cabin pressure altitudes above 5,000 feet, carbon monoxide inhaled in smoking and from exhaust fumes, deficiency of Vitamin A in the diet, and by prolonged exposure to bright sunlight. Since any degree of dark adaptation is lost within a few seconds of viewing a bright light, the pilot should close one eye when using a light to preserve some degree of night vision.

(3) Excessive illumination, especially from light reflected off the canopy, surfaces inside the aircraft, water, snow, and desert terrain, can produce glare, with uncomfortable squinting, watering of the eyes, and even temporary blindness. Sunglasses for protection from glare should absorb at least 85 percent of visible light (15 percent transmittance) and all colors equally (neutral transmittance), with negligible image distortion from refractive and prismatic errors.

c. Scanning for Other Aircraft

(1) Scanning the sky for other aircraft is a key factor in collision avoidance. It should be used continuously by the pilot and copilot (or right seat passenger) to cover all areas of the sky visible from the cockpit.

(2) Effective scanning is accomplished with a series of short, regularly spaced eye movements that bring successive areas of the sky into the central visual field. Each movement should not exceed 10 degrees, and each area should be observed for at least one second to enable detection. Although horizontal back-and-forth eye movements seem preferred by most pilots, each pilot should develop a scanning pattern that is most comfortable and then adhere to it to assure optimum scanning.

HAND SIGNALS

SIGNALMAN DIRECTS TOWING

SIGNALMAN'S POSITION

FLAGMAN DIRECTS PILOT TO SIGNALMAN IF TRAFFIC CONDITIONS REQUIRE

ALL CLEAR (O.K.)

POINT TO ENGINE TO BE STARTED

START ENGINE

PULL CHOCKS

COME AHEAD

LEFT TURN

RIGHT TURN

SLOW DOWN

STOP

INSERT CHOCKS

CUT ENGINES

NIGHT OPERATION (Uses same hand movements as day operation)

EMERGENCY STOP

WEATHER DEPICTION CHART

The weather depiction chart is prepared from surface aviation (SA) reports to give a quick picture of conditions as of valid time of the chart. Figure 6–1 is a weather depiction chart.

PLOTTED DATA

Shown for each plotted station as appropriate are:

1. Total sky cover
2. Height of cloud or ceiling
3. Weather and obstructions to vision, and
4. Visibility.

Total Sky Cover

Total sky cover is shown by the station circle shaded as in table 6–1.

TABLE 6–1. Total sky cover

Symbol	Total sky cover
O	Sky clear
◑	Less than $\frac{1}{10}$ (Few)
◖	$\frac{1}{10}$ to $\frac{5}{10}$ inclusive (Scattered)
◕	$\frac{6}{10}$ to $\frac{9}{10}$ inclusive (Broken)
◉	$\frac{10}{10}$ with breaks (BINOVC)
●	$\frac{10}{10}$ (Overcast)
⊗	Sky obscured or partially obscured

Cloud Height or Ceiling

Cloud height is entered under the station circle in hundreds of feet—the same as coded in an SA report. If total sky cover is few or scattered, the height is the base of the lowest layer. If total sky cover is broken or greater, the height is the ceiling. Broken or greater sky cover without a height entry indicates *thin* sky cover. Partially or totally obscured sky is shown by the same sky cover symbol. Partial obscuration is denoted by absence of a height entry; total obscuration has a height entry denoting the ceiling (vertical visibility into the obscuration).

Weather and Obstructions to Vision

Weather and obstructions to vision are entered just to the left of the station circle using symbols. Precipitation intensity is not entered. When several types of weather and/or obstructions are reported at a station, only the most significant one or two types are entered. When an SA reports clouds topping ridges, a symbol unique to the weather depiction chart is entered to the left of the station circle:

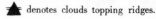 denotes clouds topping ridges.

Visibility

When visibility is less than 7 miles, it is entered to the left of weather and obstructions to vision. It is in miles and fractions.

Table 6–2 shows examples of plotted data.

TABLE 6–2. Examples of plotting on the Weather Depiction Chart

Plotted	Interpreted
◑₈	Few clouds, base 800 feet, visibility more than 6
▽ ◕₁₂	Broken sky cover, ceiling 1,200 feet, rain shower
5∞ ◉	Thin overcast with breaks, visibility 5 in haze
▲ ◕₃₀	Scattered at 3,000 feet, clouds topping ridges
2 O	Sky clear, visibility 2, ground fog or fog
½ ✛ ⊗	Sky partially obscured, visibility ½, blowing snow
¼ ✳ ⊗₅	Sky obscured, ceiling 500, visibility ¼, snow
1 ⚡ ●₁₂	Overcast, ceiling 1,200 feet, thunderstorm, rain, visibility 1

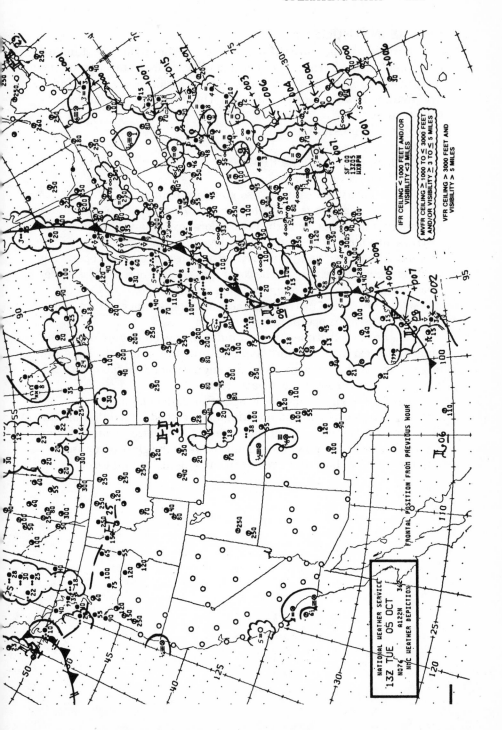

ENGINE INSTRUMENTS

Instruments to measure the performance of the engine are standard equipment in all aircraft. They are generally arranged together on the instrument panel so they can be observed at a glance. Light airplanes are nearly always equipped with the following instruments (illustrated):

1. Manifold pressure gauge.
2. Oil pressure gauge.
3. Tachometer for engine RPM.
4. Oil temperature gauge.

A fuel quantity indicator is also standard equipment.

Instrument markings indicate ranges of operation or minimum and maximum limits, or both. Four colors are generally used in the instrument marking system: red, yellow, blue and green.

A *red line* indicates a point beyond which a dangerous operating condition exists. A *red arc* on the cover glass or face of the dial is sometimes used to indicate a dangerous operating range.

A *yellow arc* on the instrument face indicates a range within which the aircraft is to be operated with caution.

A *blue arc* is sometimes used to indicate special engine operating ranges—for example, on the manifold pressure gauge the blue arc might indicate the range in which the engine can be operated with the carburetor control set at automatic lean.

The *green arc* shows normal range of airplane operation.

When engine instrument markings are etched or painted on the glass cover of the instrument, a white radial is used as an index or slippage mark to show any movement between the glass cover and the instrument case that might result in misalignment and error.

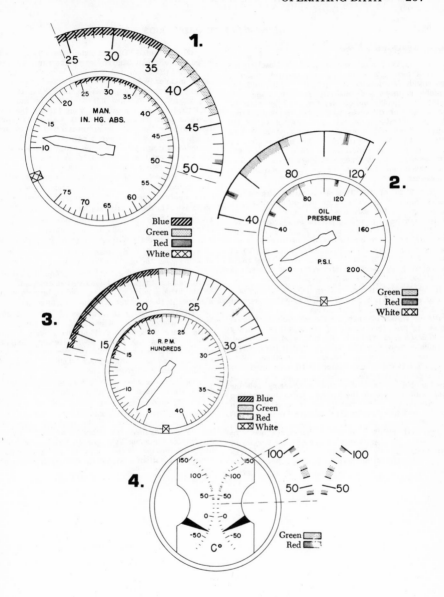

AIR NAVIGATION RADIO AIDS

VOR RECEIVER CHECK

a. Periodic VOR receiver calibration is most import-ant. If a receiver's Automatic Gain Control or modu-lation circuit deteriorates, it is possible for it to display acceptable accuracy and sensitivity close in to the VOR or VOT and display out-of-tolerance readings when lo-cated at greater distances where weaker signal areas exist. The likelihood of this deterioration varies be-tween receivers, and is generally considered a function of time. The best assurance of having an accurate receiver is periodic calibration. Yearly intervals are recommended at which time an authorized repair facility should recalibrate the receiver to the manufacturer's specifications.

b. Part 91.25 of the Federal Aviation Regulations provides for certain VOR equipment accuracy checks prior to flight under instrument flight rules. To comply with this requirement and to ensure satisfactory opera-tion of the airborne system, the FAA has provided pilots with the following means of checking VOR re-ceiver accuracy: (1) FAA VOR test facility (VOT) or a radiated test signal from an appropriately rated radio repair station, (2) certified airborne check points, and (3) certified check points on the airport surface.

(1)The FAA VOR test facility (VOT) transmits a test signal for VOR receivers which provides users of VOR a convenient and accurate means to determine the operational status of their receivers. The facility is designed to provide a means of checking the accuracy of a VOR receiver while the aircraft is on the ground. The radiated test signal is used by tuning the receiver to the published frequency of the test facility. With the Course Deviation Indicator (CDI) centered the omnibearing selector should read 0° with the to-from indication being "from" or the omnibearing selector should read 180° with the to-from indication reading "to". Should the VOR receiver operate an RMI (Radio Magnetic Indicator), it will indicate 180° on any OBS setting when using the VOT. Two means of identifica-tion are used with the VOR radiated test signal. In some cases a continuous series of dots is used while in others a continuous 1020 hertz tone will identify the test signal. Information concerning an individual test signal can be obtained from the local Flight Service Station.

(2) A radiated VOR test signal from an appropriately rated radio repair station serves the same purpose as an FAA VOR signal and the check is made in much the same manner with the following differences: (1) the frequency normally approved by the FCC is 108.0 MHz the repair stations are not permitted to radiate the VOR test signal continuously, consequently the owner/operator must make arrangements with the repair sta-tion to have the test signal transmitted. This service is not provided by all radio repair stations, the aircraft owner/operator must determine which repair station in his local area does provide this service. A representa-tive of the repair station must make an entry into the aircraft logbook or other permanent record certifying to the radial accuracy which was transmitted and the date of transmission. The owner/operator or repre-sentative of the repair station may accomplish the necessary checks in the aircraft and make a logbook entry stating the results of such checks. It will be necessary to verify with the appropriate repair station the test radial being transmitted and whether you should get a "to" or "from" indication.

(3) Airborne and ground check points consist of cer-tified radials that should be received at specific points on the airport surface, or over specific landmarks while airborne in the immediate vicinity of the airport.

(4) Should an error in excess of ±4° be indicated through use of a ground check, or ±6° using the air-borne check, IFR flight shall not be attempted without first correcting the source of the error. CAUTION: no correction other than the "correction card" figures supplied by the manufacturer should be applied in making these VOR receiver checks.

(5) Airborne check points, ground check points and VOTs are included in the Airport/Facility Directory.

(6) If dual system VOR (units independent of each other except for the antenna) is installed in the air-craft, the person checking the equipment may check one system against the other. He shall turn both systems to the same VOR ground facility and note the indicated bearing to that station. The maximum per-missible variations between the two indicated bearings is 4°.

WAKE TURBULENCE

GENERAL

a. Every airplane generates a wake while in flight. Initially, when pilots encountered this wake in flight, the disturbance was attributed to "prop wash." It is known, however, that this disturbance is caused by a pair of counter rotating vortices trailing from the wing tips. The vortices from large aircraft pose problems to encountering aircraft. For instance, the wake of these aircraft can impose rolling moments exceeding the roll control capability of some aircraft. Further, turbulence generated within the vortices can damage aircraft components and equipment if encountered at close range. The pilot must learn to envision the location of the vortex wake generated by large aircraft and adjust his flight path accordingly.

b. During ground operations, jet engine blast (thrust stream turbulence) can cause damage and upsets if encountered at close range. Exhaust velocity versus distance studies at various thrust levels have shown a need for light aircraft to maintain an adequate separation during ground operations. Below are examples of the distance requirements to avoid exhaust velocities of greater than 25 mph:

25 MPH VELOCITY	B-727	DC-8	DC-10
Takeoff Thrust	550 Ft.	700 Ft.	2100 Ft.
Breakaway Thrust	200 Ft.	400 Ft.	850 Ft.
Idle Thrust	150 Ft.	35 Ft.	350 Ft.

c. Engine exhaust velocities generated by large jet aircraft during initial takeoff roll and the drifting of the turbulence in relation to the crosswind component dictate the desireability of lighter aircraft awaiting takeoff to hold well back of the runway edge of taxiway hold line; also, the desirability of aligning the aircraft to face the possible jet engine blast movement. Additionally, in the course of running up engines and taxiing on the ground, pilots of large aircraft in particular should consider the effects of their jet blasts on other aircraft.

d. The FAA has established new standards for the location of taxiway hold lines at airports served by air carriers as follows:

e. Taxiway holding lines will be established at 100 feet from the edge of the runway, except at locations where "heavy jets" will be operating, the taxiway holding line markings will be established at 150 feet. (The "heavy" category can include some B-707 and DC-8 type aircraft.)

VORTEX GENERATION

Lift is generated by the creation of a pressure differential over the wing surface. The lowest pressure occurs over the upper wing surface and the highest pressure under the wing. This pressure differential triggers the roll up of the airflow aft of the wing resulting in swirling air masses trailing downstream of the wing tips. After the roll up is completed, the wake consists of two counter rotating cylindrical vortices.

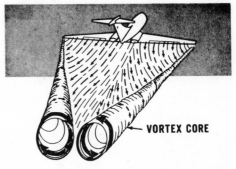

VORTEX CORE

Figure 6-2

VORTEX STRENGTH

a. The strength of the vortex is governed by the weight, speed, and shape of the wing of the generating aircraft. The vortex characteristics of any given aircraft can also be changed by extension of flaps or other wing configuring devices as well as by change in speed. However, as the basic factor is weight, the vortex strength increases proportionately. During a recent test, peak vortex tangential velocities were recorded at 224 feet per second, or about 133 knots. The greatest vortex strength occurs when the generating aircraft is HEAVY—CLEAN—SLOW.

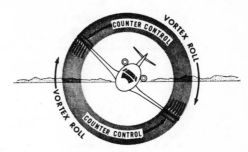

Figure 6-3

b. INDUCED ROLL

(1) In rare instances a wake encounter could cause in flight structural damage of catastrophic proportions. However, the usual hazard is associated with induced rolling moments which can exceed the rolling capability of the encountering aircraft. In flight experiments, aircraft have been intentionally flown directly up trailing vortex cores of large aircraft. It was shown that the capability of an aircraft to counteract the roll imposed by the wake vortex primarily depends on the wing span and counter control responsiveness of the encountering aircraft.

WAKE TURBULENCE

(2) Counter control is usually effective and induced roll minimal in cases where the wing span and ailerons of the encountering aircraft extend beyond the rotational flow field of the vortex. It is more difficult for aircraft with short wing span (relative to the generating aircraft) to counter the imposed roll induced by vortex flow. Pilots of short span aircraft, even of the high performance type, must be especially alert to vortex encounters.

(3) The wake of large aircraft requires the respect of all pilots.

VORTEX BEHAVIOR

a. Trailing vortices have certain behavioral characteristics which can help a pilot visualize the wake location and thereby take avoidance precautions.

(1) Vortices are generated from the moment aircraft leave the ground, since trailing vortices are a by-product of wing lift. Prior to takeoff or touchdown pilots should note the rotation or touchdown point of the preceding aircraft.

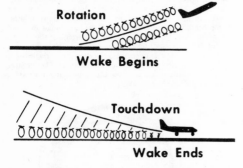

Figure 6—4

(2) The vortex circulation is outward, upward and around the wing tips when viewed from either ahead or behind the aircraft. Tests with large aircraft have shown that the vortex flow field, in a plane cutting thru the wake at any point downstream, covers an area about 2 wing spans in width and one wing span in depth. The vortices remain so spaced (about a wing span apart) even drifting with the wind, at altitudes greater than a wing span from the ground. In view of this, if persistent vortex turbulence is encountered, a slight change of altitude and lateral position (preferably upwind) will provide a flight path clear of the turbulence.

(3) Flight tests have shown that the vortices from large aircraft sink at a rate of about 400 to 500 feet per minute. They tend to level off at a distance about 900 feet below the flight path of the generating aircraft. Vortex strength diminishes with time and distance behind the generating aircraft. Atmospheric turbulence hastens breakup. Pilots should fly at or above the large aircraft's flight path, altering course as necessary to avoid the area behind and below the generating aircraft.

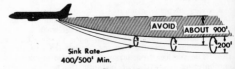

Figure 6—5

(4) When the vortices of large aircraft sink close to the ground (within about 200 feet), they tend to move laterally over the ground at a speed of about 5 knots.

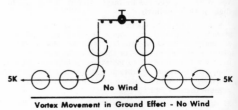

Vortex Movement in Ground Effect - No Wind

Figure 6—6

(5) A crosswind will decrease the lateral movement of the upwind vortex and increase the movement of the downwind vortex. Thus a light wind of 3 to 7 knots could result in the upwind vortex remaining in the touchdown zone for a period of time and hasten the drift of the downwind vortex toward another runway. Similarly, a tailwind condition can move the vortices of the preceding aircraft forward into the touchdown zone. THE LIGHT QUARTERING TAILWIND REQUIRES MAXIMUM CAUTION. Pilots should be alert to large aircraft upwind from their approach and takeoff flight paths.

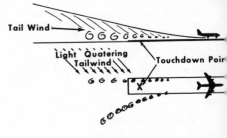

Figure 6—7

OPERATIONS PROBLEM AREAS

a. A wake encounter is not necessarily hazardous. It can be one or more jolts with varying severity depending upon the direction of the encounter, distance from the generating aircraft, and point of vortex encounter. The probability of induced roll increases when the encountering aircraft's heading is generally aligned with the vortex trail or flight path of the generating aircraft.

WAKE TURBULENCE

b. AVOID THE AREA BELOW AND BEHIND THE GENERATING AIRCRAFT, ESPECIALLY AT LOW ALTITUDE WHERE EVEN A MOMENTARY WAKE ENCOUNTER COULD BE HAZARDOUS.

c. Pilots should be particularly alert in calm wind conditions and situations where the vortices could:

(1) Remain in the touchdown area.

(2) Drift from aircraft operating on a nearby runway.

(3) Sink into takeoff or landing path from a crossing runway.

(4) Sink into the traffic patterns from other airport operations.

(5) Sink into the flight path of VFR flights operating at the hemispheric altitude 500 feet below.

d. Pilots of all aircraft should visualize the location of the vortex trail behind large aircraft and use proper vortex avoidance procedures to achieve safe operation. It is equally important that pilots of large aircraft plan or adjust their flight paths to minimize vortex exposure to other aircraft.

VORTEX AVOIDANCE PROCEDURES

a. *GENERAL.* Under certain conditions, airport traffic controllers apply procedures for separating aircraft from heavy jet aircraft. The controllers will also provide VFR aircraft, with whom they are in communication and which in the tower's opinion may be adversely affected by wake turbulence from a large aircraft, the position, altitude and direction of flight of the large aircraft followed by the phrase "CAUTION—WAKE TURBULENCE." WHETHER OR NOT A WARNING HAS BEEN GIVEN, HOWEVER, THE PILOT IS EXPECTED TO ADJUST HIS OPERATIONS AND FLIGHT PATH AS NECESSARY TO PRECLUDE SERIOUS WAKE ENCOUNTERS.

b. The following vortex avoidance procedures are recommended for the various situations:

(1) Landing behind a large aircraft—same runway: Stay at or above the large aircraft's final approach flight path—note his touchdown point—land beyond it.

(2) Landing behind a large aircraft—when parallel runway is closer than 2,500 feet: Consider possible drift to your runway. Stay at or above the large aircraft's final approach flight path—note his touchdown point.

(3) Landing behind a large aircraft—crossing runway: Cross above the large aircraft's flight path.

(4) Landing behind a departing large aircraft—same runway: Note large aircraft's rotation point—land well prior to rotation point.

(5) Landing behind a departing large aircraft—crossing runway: Note large aircraft's rotation point—if past the intersection—continue the approach—land prior to the intersection. If large aircraft rotates prior to the intersection, avoid flight below the large aircraft's flight path. Abandon the approach unless a landing is assured well before reaching the intersection.

(6) Departing behind a large aircraft: Note large aircraft's rotation point—rotate prior to large aircraft's rotation point—continue climb above and stay upwind of the large aircraft's climb path until turning clear of

his wake. Avoid subsequent headings which will cross below and behind a large aircraft. Be alert for any critical takeoff situation which could lead to a vortex encounter.

(7) Intersection takeoffs—same runway: Be alert to adjacent large aircraft operations particularly upwind of your runway. If intersection takeoff clearance is received, avoid subsequent heading which will cross below a large aircraft's path.

(8) Departing or landing after a large aircraft executing a low approach, missed approach or touch-and-go landing: Because vortices settle and move laterally near the ground, the vortex hazard may exist along the runway and in your flight path after a large aircraft has executed a low approach, missed approach or a touch-and-go landing, particularly in light quartering wind conditions. You should assure that an interval of at least 2 minutes has elapsed before your takeoff or landing.

(9) Enroute VFR—(thousand-foot altitude plus 500 feet). Avoid flight below and behind a large aircraft's path. If a large aircraft is observed above on the same track (meeting or overtaking) adjust your position laterally, preferably upwind.

HELICOPTERS

A hovering helicopter generates a downwash from its main rotor(s) similar to the prop blast of a conventional aircraft. However, in forward flight, this energy is transformed into a pair of trailing vortices similar to wing-tip vortices of fixed wing aircraft. Pilots of small aircraft should avoid the vortices as well as the downwash.

PILOT RESPONSIBILITY

a. Government and industry groups are making concerted efforts to minimize or eliminate the hazards of trailing vortices. However, the flight disciplines necessary to assure vortex avoidance during VFR operations must be exercised by the pilot. Vortex visualization and avoidance procedures should be exercised by the pilot using the same degree of concern as in collision avoidance.

b. Wake turbulence may be encountered by aircraft in flight as well as when operating on the airport movement area.

c. Pilots are reminded that in operations conducted behind all aircraft, acceptance from ATC of:

(1) Traffic information, or

(2) Instructions to follow an aircraft, or

(3) The acceptance of a visual approach clearance, is an acknowledgment that the pilot will ensure safe takeoff and landing intervals and accepts the responsibility of providing his own wake turbulence separation.

d. For operations conducted behind heavy aircraft, ATC will specify the word 'heavy' when this information is known. Pilots of heavy aircraft should always use the word "heavy" in radio communications.

WAKE TURBULENCE

AIR TRAFFIC WAKE TURBULENCE SEPARATIONS

a. Air traffic controllers are required to apply specific separation intervals for aircraft operating behind a heavy jet because of the possible effects of wake turbulence.

b. The following separation is applied to aircraft operating directly behind a heavy jet at the same altitude or directly behind and less than 1,000 feet below:

(1) Heavy jet behind another heavy jet—4 miles.

(2) Small/Large aircraft behind a heavy jet—5 miles.

In addition, controllers provide a 6-mile separation for small aircraft landing behind a heavy jet and a 4-mile separation for small aircraft landing behind a large aircraft. This extra mile of separation is required at the time the preceding aircraft is over the landing threshold

c. Aircraft departing behind heavy jets are provided two minutes or the appropriate 4 or 5 mile radar separation. Controllers may disregard the separation if the pilot of a departing aircraft initiates a request to deviate from the separation requirement and indicates acceptance of responsibility for maneuvering his aircraft so as to avoid the possible wake turbulence hazard. However, occasions will arise when the controller must still hold the aircraft in order to provide separation required for other than wake turbulence purposes.

AIRSPEED INDICATOR MARKINGS

Light airplanes must be equipped with airspeed indicators that conform to this standard color-coded marking system:

Normal operating range—green arc.
Flap operating range—white arc.
Caution range—yellow arc.
Never-exceed speed—red radial line.
Maximum structural cruising speed—upper limit of green arc.
Power-off stalling speed, wing flaps and gear in landing position—lower limit of white arc.
Maximum flaps extended speed—upper limit of white arc.
Power-off stalling speed, wing flaps and gear retracted—lower limit of green arc.

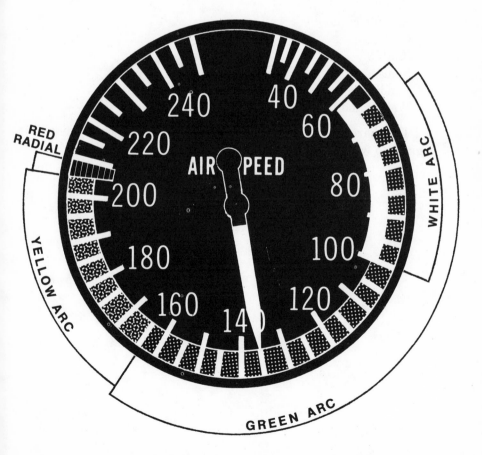

AIRCRAFT/ENGINE PERFORMANCE AND OPERATION

The next 13 pages consist of the aircraft and engine performance and operating data from a typical airplane Owner's Manual, in this case that of the popular Cessna Model 172. Owners' Manuals are prepared by the manufacturer as a guide to help you get maximum utility from your aircraft commensurate with the greatest safety.

Included here are operating directions and performance data for the following stages of flight:

Before takeoff.
Takeoff.
Wing flap settings.
Performance charts.
Crosswind takeoffs.
Enroute climb.
Cruise.
Stalls.
Spins.
Landings.
Weight and balance procedures.

The charts and graphs here are all similar to the ones you will be given to work with in the FAA written test.

BEFORE TAKE-OFF.

WARM-UP.

If the engine accelerates smoothly, the airplane is ready for take-off. Since the engine is closely cowled for efficient in-flight engine cooling, precautions should be taken to avoid overheating during prolonged engine operation on the ground. Also, long periods of idling may cause fouled spark plugs.

MAGNETO CHECK.

The magneto check should be made at 1700 RPM as follows: Move ignition switch first to "R" position, and note RPM. Next move switch back to "BOTH" to clear the other set of plugs. Then move switch to the "L" position, note RPM and return the switch to the "BOTH" position. RPM drop should not exceed 125 RPM on either magneto or show greater than 50 RPM differential between magnetos. If there is a doubt concerning operation of the ignition system, RPM checks at higher engine speeds will usually confirm whether a deficiency exists.

An absence of RPM drop may be an indication of faulty grounding of one side of the ignition system or should be cause for suspicion that the magneto timing is set in advance of the setting specified.

ALTERNATOR CHECK.

Prior to flights where verification of proper alternator and voltage regulator operation is essential (such as night or instrument flights), a positive verification can be made by loading the electrical system momentarily (3 to 5 seconds) with the optional landing light (if so equipped), or by operating the wing flaps during the engine runup (1700 RPM). The ammeter will remain within a needle width of zero if the alternator and voltage regulator are operating properly.

TAKE-OFF.

POWER CHECK.

It is important to check full-throttle engine operation early in the take-off run. Any signs of rough engine operation or sluggish engine acceleration is good cause for discontinuing the take-off. If this occurs, you are justified in making a thorough full-throttle, static runup before another take-off is attempted. The engine should run smoothly and turn approximately 2260 to 2360 RPM with carburetor heat off.

NOTE

Carburetor heat should not be used during take-off
unless it is absolutely necessary for obtaining smooth
engine acceleration.

Full-throttle runups over loose gravel are especially harmful to propeller tips. When take-offs must be made over a gravel surface, it is
very important that the throttle be advanced slowly. This allows the airplane to start rolling before high RPM is developed, and the gravel will
be blown back of the propeller rather than pulled into it. When unavoid-
able small dents appear in the propeller blades, they should be immediately corrected as described in Section V under propeller care.

Prior to take-off from fields above 3000 feet elevation, the mixture
should be leaned to give maximum RPM in a full-throttle, static runup.

WING FLAP SETTINGS.

Normal and obstacle clearance take-offs are performed with wing
flaps up. The use of 10° flaps will shorten the ground run approximately
10%, but this advantage is lost in the climb to a 50-foot obstacle. Therefore, the use of 10° flaps is reserved for minimum ground runs or for
take-off from soft or rough fields. If 10° of flaps are used for minimum
ground runs, it is preferable to leave them extended rather than retract
them in the climb to the obstacle. In this case, use an obstacle clearance
speed of 65 MPH. As soon as the obstacle is cleared, the flaps may be
retracted as the airplane accelerates to the normal flaps-up climb speed
of 80 to 90 MPH.

During a high altitude take-off in hot weather where climb would be
marginal with 10° flaps, it is recommended that the flaps not be used for
take-off. Flap settings greater than 10° are not recommended at any
time for take-off.

PERFORMANCE CHARTS.

Consult the Take-Off Data chart in Section VI for take-off distances
under various gross weight, altitude, headwind, temperature, and runway surface conditions.

CROSSWIND TAKE-OFFS.

Take-offs into strong crosswinds normally are performed with the
minimum flap setting necessary for the field length to minimize the
drift angle immediately after take-off. The airplane is accelerated to
a speed slightly higher than normal, then pulled off abruptly to prevent
possible settling back to the runway while drifting. When clear of the
ground, make a coordinated turn into the wind to correct for drift.

TAKE-OFF DATA

TAKE-OFF DISTANCE FROM HARD SURFACE RUNWAY WITH FLAPS UP

GROSS WEIGHT POUNDS	IAS AT 50' MPH	HEAD WIND KNOTS	AT SEA LEVEL & 59°		AT 2500 FT. & 50°F		AT 5000 FT. & 41°F		AT 7500 FT. & 32°F	
			GROUND RUN	TOTAL TO CLEAR 50 FT OBS	GROUND RUN	TOTAL TO CLEAR 50 FT OBS	GROUND RUN	TOTAL TO CLEAR 50 FT OBS	GROUND RUN	TOTAL TO CLEAR 50 FT OBS
2300	68	0	865	1525	1040	1910	1255	2480	1565	3855
		10	615	1170	750	1485	920	1955	1160	3110
		20	405	850	505	1100	630	1480	810	2425
2000	63	0	630	1095	755	1325	905	1625	1120	2155
		10	435	820	530	1005	645	1250	810	1685
		20	275	580	340	720	425	910	595	1255
1700	58	0	435	780	520	920	625	1095	765	1370
		10	290	570	355	680	430	820	535	1040
		20	175	385	215	470	270	575	345	745

NOTES:
1. Increase distance 10% for each 25°F above standard temperature for particular altitude.
2. For operation on a dry, grass runway, increase distances (both "ground run" and "total to clear 50 ft. obstacle") by 7% of the "total to clear 50 ft. obstacle" figure.

MAXIMUM RATE-OF-CLIMB DATA

GROSS WEIGHT POUNDS	AT SEA LEVEL & 59°F			AT 5000 FT. & 41°F			AT 10,000 FT. & 23°F			AT 15,000 FT. & 5°F		
	IAS MPH	RATE OF CLIMB FT/MIN	GAL. OF FUEL USED	IAS MPH	RATE OF CLIMB FT/MIN	FROM S.L. FUEL USED	IAS MPH	RATE OF CLIMB FT/MIN	FROM S.L. FUEL USED	IAS MPH	RATE OF CLIMB FT/MIN	FROM S.L. FUEL USED
2300	82	645	1.0	81	435	2.6	79	230	4.8	78	22	11.5
2000	79	840	1.0	78	610	2.2	76	380	3.6	75	155	6.3
1700	77	1085	1.0	76	825	1.9	73	570	2.9	72	315	4.4

NOTES:
1. Flaps up, full throttle, mixture leaned for smooth operation above 3000 ft.
2. Fuel used includes warm up and take-off allowance.
3. For hot weather, decrease rate of climb 20 ft./min. for each 10°F above standard day temperature for particular altitude.

ENROUTE CLIMB.

CLIMB DATA.

For detailed data, refer to the Maximum Rate-Of-Climb Data chart in Section VI.

CLIMB SPEEDS.

Normal climbs are performed at 80 to 90 MPH with flaps up and full throttle for best engine cooling. The mixture should be full rich below 3000 feet and may be leaned above 3000 feet for smoother engine operation. The maximum rate-of-climb speeds range from 82 MPH at sea level to 79 MPH at 10,000 feet. If an enroute obstruction dictates the use of a steep climb angle, climb at 68 MPH with flaps retracted.

NOTE

Steep climbs at low speeds should be of short duration
to improve engine cooling.

CRUISE.

Normal cruising is done between 65% and 75% power. The power settings required to obtain these powers at various altitudes and outside air temperatures can be determined by using your Cessna Power Computer or the OPERATIONAL DATA, Section VI.

Cruising can be done more efficiently at high altitudes because of lower air density and therefore higher true airspeeds for the same power. This is illustrated in the table below, which shows performance at 75% power at various altitudes. All figures are based on lean mixture, 38 gallons of fuel (no reserve), zero wind, standard atmospheric conditions, and 2300 pounds gross weight.

To achieve the lean mixture fuel consumption figures shown in Section VI, the mixture should be leaned as follows: pull mixture control out until engine RPM peaks and begins to fall off, then enrichen slightly back to peak RPM.

Carburetor ice, as evidenced by an unexplained drop in RPM, can be removed by application of full carburetor heat. Upon regaining the original RPM (with heat off), use the minimum amount of heat (by trial and error) to prevent ice from forming. Since the heated air causes a richer mixture, readjust the mixture setting when carburetor heat is to be used continuously in cruise flight.

The use of full carburetor heat is recommended during flight in heavy rain to avoid the possibility of engine stoppage due to excessive water ingestion or carburetor ice.   The mixture setting should be readjusted for smoothest operation.

In extremely heavy rain, the use of partial carburetor heat (control approximately 2/3 out), and part throttle (closed at least one inch), may be necessary to retain adequate power. Power changes should be made cautiously followed by prompt adjustment of the mixture for smoothest operation.

MAXIMUM CRUISE SPEED PERFORMANCE
75% POWER

ALTITUDE	RPM	TRUE AIRSPEED	RANGE
SEA LEVEL	2490	123	575
5000 ft.	2600	128	600
9000 ft.	FULL THROTTLE	132	620

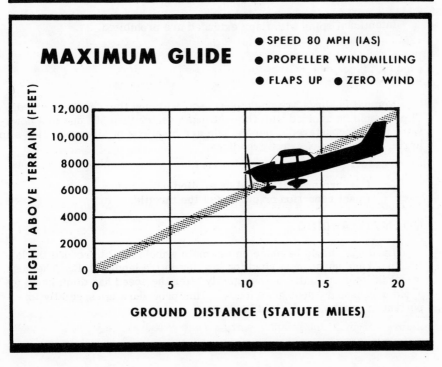

STALLS.

The stall characteristics are conventional and aural warning is provided by a stall warning horn which sounds between 5-and 10 MPH above the stall in all configurations.

Power-off stall speeds at maximum gross weight and aft c. g. position are presented on page 6-2 as calibrated airspeeds since indicated airspeeds are unreliable near the stall.

SPINS.

Intentional spins are prohibited in this airplane, except in the Utility Category. To recover from a spin, use the following technique.

(1) Retard throttle to idle position.
(2) Apply full rudder opposite to the direction of rotation.
(3) After one-fourth turn, move the control wheel forward of neutral in a brisk motion.
(4) As rotation stops, neutralize rudder, and make a smooth recovery from the resulting dive.

Intentional spins with flaps extended are prohibited.

LANDINGS.

Normal landings are made power-off with any flap setting desired. Slips should be avoided with flap settings greater than 30° due to a downward pitch encountered under certain combinations of airspeed, side slip angle, and center of gravity loadings.

NOTE

Carburetor heat should be applied prior to any significant reduction or closing of the throttle.

NORMAL LANDING.

Landings should be made on the main wheels first to reduce the landing speed and subsequent need for braking in the landing roll. The nose wheel is lowered to the runway gently after the speed has diminished to avoid unnecessary nose gear loads. This procedure is especially important in rough or soft field landings.

LANDING DATA

LANDING DISTANCE ON HARD SURFACE RUNWAY
NO WIND – 40° FLAPS – POWER OFF

GROSS WEIGHT LBS.	APPROACH IAS MPH	@ S.L. & 59° F		@ 2500 ft. & 50° F		@ 5000 ft. & 41° F		@ 7500 ft. & 32° F	
		GROUND ROLL	TOTAL TO CLEAR 50' OBS.	GROUND ROLL	TOTAL TO CLEAR 50' OBS.	GROUND ROLL	TOTAL TO CLEAR 50' OBS.	GROUND ROLL	TOTAL TO CLEAR 50' OBS.
2300	69	520	1250	560	1310	605	1385	650	1455

NOTES: 1. Reduce landing distance 10% for each 5 knot headwind.
2. For operation on a dry, grass runway, increase distances (both "ground roll" and "total to clear 50 ft. obstacle") by 20% of the "total to clear 50 ft. obstacle" figure.

SHORT FIELD LANDING.

For short field landings, make a power-off approach at approximately 69 MPH indicated airspeed with 40° of flaps. Touchdown should be made on the main wheels first. Immediately after touchdown, lower the nose gear to the ground and apply heavy braking as required. For maximum brake effectiveness after all three wheels are on the ground, retract the flaps, hold full nose up elevator and apply maximum possible brake pressure without sliding the tires.

CROSSWIND LANDING.

When landing in a strong crosswind, use the minimum flap setting required for the field length. If flap settings greater than 20° are used in side-slips with full rudder deflection, some elevator oscillation may be felt at normal approach speeds. However, this does not affect control of the aircraft. Although the crab or combination method of drift correction may be used, the wing-low method gives the best control. After touchdown, hold a straight course with the steerable nose wheel and occasional braking if necessary.

The maximum allowable crosswind velocity is dependent upon pilot capability rather than airplane limitations. With average pilot technique, direct crosswinds of 15 MPH can be handled with safety.

BALKED LANDING (GO-AROUND).

In a balked landing (go-around) climb, reduce the wing flap setting to 20° immediately after full power is applied. If obstacles must be cleared during the go-around climb, leave the wing flaps in the 10° to 20° range until the obstacles are cleared. After clearing any obstacles the flaps may be retracted as the airplane accelerates to the normal flaps-up climb speed of 80 to 90 MPH.

AIRSPEED CORRECTION TABLE

		40	50	60	70	80	90	100	110	120	130	140
	IAS	40	50	60	70	80	90	100	110	120	130	140
FLAPS UP	CAS	55	58	65	72	82	91	101	110	120	129	139
FLAPS DOWN	CAS	48	54	63	72	82	93	105	•	•	•	•

STALL SPEEDS – MPH CAS

	CONDITION	ANGLE OF BANK			
		0°	20°	40°	60°
2300 LBS. GROSS WEIGHT	FLAPS UP	57	59	65	81
	FLAPS 10°	52	54	59	74
	FLAPS 40°	49	51	56	69

POWER OFF — AFT CG

WEIGHT AND BALANCE.

The following information will enable you to operate your **Cessna** within the prescribed weight and center of gravity limitations. To figure the weight and balance for your particular airplane, use the Sample Problem, Loading Graph, and Center of Gravity Moment Envelope as follows:

Take the "Licensed Empty Weight" and "Moment" from the Weight and Balance Data sheet (or changes noted on FAA Form 337) carried in your airplane, and write them down in the column titled "YOUR AIRPLANE" on the Sample Loading Problem.

NOTE   The Weight and Balance Data sheet is included in the aircraft file. In addition to the licensed empty weight and moment noted on this sheet, the c.g. arm (fuselage station) is shown. The c.g. arm figure need not be used on the Sample Loading Problem. The moment shown on the sheet must be divided by 1000 and this value used as the moment/1000 on the loading problem.

Use the Loading Graph to determine the moment/1000 for each additional item to be carried, then list these on the loading problem.

NOTE   Loading Graph information is based on seats positioned for average occupants and baggage loaded in the center of the baggage area. For other than average loading situations, the Sample Loading Problem lists fuselage stations for these items to indicate their forward and aft c.g. range limitation (seat travel or baggage area limitation). Additional moment calculations, based on the actual weight and c.g. arm (fuselage station) of the item being loaded, must be made if the position of the load is different from that shown on the Loading Graph.

Total the weights and moments/1000 and plot these values on the Center of Gravity Moment Envelope to determine whether the point falls within the envelope, and if the loading is acceptable.

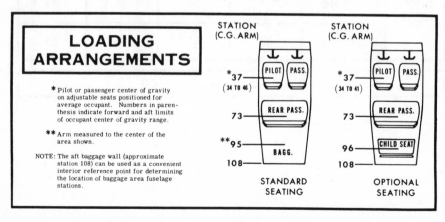

SAMPLE LOADING PROBLEM

	SAMPLE AIRPLANE		YOUR AIRPLANE	
	Weight (lbs.)	Moment (lb.-ins. /1000)	Weight (lbs.)	Moment (lb.-ins. /1000)
1. Licensed Empty Weight (Sample Airplane)	1364	51.7		
2. Oil (8 qts. - Full oil may be assumed for all flights)	15	-0.2	15	-0.2
3. Fuel (Standard - 38 Gal at 6#/Gal)	228	10.9		
Fuel (Long Range - 48 Gal at 6#/Gal)				
4. Pilot and Front Passenger (Station 34 to 46)	340	12.6		
5. Rear Passengers	340	24.8		
6. Baggage (or Passenger on Child's Seat) (Station 82 to 108)	13	1.2		
7. TOTAL WEIGHT AND MOMENT	2300	101.0		
8. Locate this point (2300 at 101.0) on the center of gravity moment envelope, and since this point falls within the envelope, the loading is acceptable.				

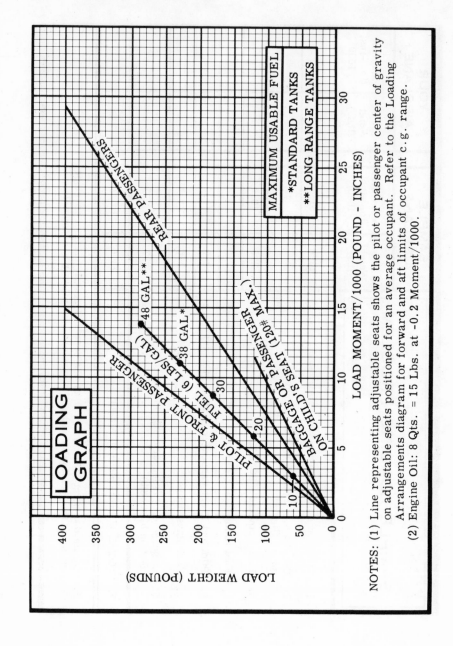

NOTES: (1) Line representing adjustable seats shows the pilot or passenger center of gravity on adjustable seats positioned for an average occupant. Refer to the Loading Arrangements diagram for forward and aft limits of occupant c.g. range.

(2) Engine Oil: 8 Qts. = 15 Lbs. at -0.2 Moment/1000.

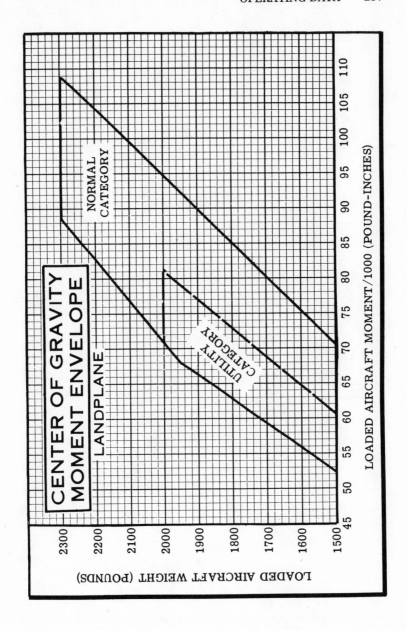

INDEX